"You just don't know what people have encountered in life until you walk in their shoes. Cheryl's raw memoir gives you a walk in the shoes of an abortion-minded woman both before and after crisis."

~Abby Johnson, author of *Unplanned* and founder of And Then There Were None

"Abortion affects all of us whether we know it or not. *ReTested* provides much-needed insight into the pro-choice mindset and the pressures women face before having their choices dictated to them. A compelling memoir that demonstrates how suffering neglect often causes women to dehumanize their own children in the abortion decision. But more, in *ReTested* there is hope and redemption and grace."

~Kim Ketola, broadcaster, writer, speaker, and the author of *Cradle My Heart: Finding God's Love After Abortion*

ReTested

*The Story of a
Post-Abortive
Woman Called to*
Change the Conversation

*Mosaic - Virginia,
Chapter 14 is for you!
I love you!*

Cheryl

CHERYL KRICHBAUM

AUTHOR ACADEMY elite

Printed in the United States of America

Published by Author Academy Elite
P.O. Box 43, Powell, OH 43035
AuthorAcademyElite.com

Library of Congress Control Number: 2018966589

Paperback ISBN: 978-1-64085-510-6
Hardcover ISBN: 978-1-64085-511-3
E-book ISBN: 978-1-64085-512-0

To protect the privacy of the many people who are part of my story, some details and most names have been changed. In addition, any internet addresses (websites, blogs, etc.) in this book are offered as resources and are not intended in any way to be or imply an endorsement by Author Academy Elite, nor does Author Academy Elite vouch for the content of these sites for the life of this book.

for

Joy Marie

d. June 18, 1987

&

Russ

My hero. Thank you for never giving up on me. A&F

TABLE OF CONTENTS

INTRODUCTION

It breaks my heart that my pro-life stance automatically associates me with the Republican party.

Simultaneously, it breaks my heart that politicians in the Democratic party vote pro-choice or get bullied out of their elected positions. Why should I contact my legislator if he or she has already decided to vote pro-choice no matter what his or her constituents say? Our political system is supposed to represent its people, not money-making companies like abortion clinics and pharmaceutical companies.

Ever since we've seen the pre-born on ultrasound machines in the 1970s, we have known scientifically that they are alive. Science shows that they are alive. Our laws acknowledge the value of pre-born eagles and pre-born sea turtles but not the value of pre-born humans. Our thinking is backwards. Our political system is broken.

But even when we overturn Roe v Wade and every other pro-choice law in each of the states, abortion will continue. It'll go underground. We'll have a new illegal drug trade. There are countries all over the world where abortion is illegal yet abortion continues. Don't expect the United States to be any different.

If we want to end abortion, we must change hearts. This starts with The Church. We have a lot to repent for (2 Chronicles 7:14a). We have a lot of disciples to make (Matthew 28:19). We have a lot of teaching to do (Matthew 28:20). All three are necessary if we expect God to hear from heaven, forgive our sin, and heal our land (2 Chronicles 7:14b).

> *"and My people who are called by My name humble themselves and pray and seek My face and turn from their wicked ways, then I will hear from heaven, will forgive their sin and will heal their land."*
> *(2 Chronicles 7:14 NASB)*

> *"Go therefore and make disciples of all nations, baptizing them in the name of the Father and of the Son and of the Holy Spirit, teaching them to observe all that I have commanded you. And behold, I am with you always, to the end of the age."*
> *(Matthew 28:19-20 ESV)*

SURVIVING

SURVIVING

1
FEELING NEGLECTED

Nancy paced back and forth—three feet this way, three feet that way. She was talking to someone, but no one was there. Her words were unintelligible, but she seemed to enjoy her conversation. About every other turn—three feet this way, three feet that way—she'd laugh.

Then she saw me watching her from the kitchen door and her face sank for a moment. Only a moment. She went back to pacing, talking to no one, listening, and laughing.

If I weren't so disturbed by her behavior, I'd be happy that she was happy. Her delusions were better than reality. Whatever conversation she was having was better than being left by her husband, better than being a single mother of a toddler, better than living with her parents and their worry, better than living in the same house as her little sister whose life she envied. I am the little sister.

Nancy, my big sister—the one I used to look up to, the one with whom I used to share a room, the one who used to have all the wise answers to my annoying little-sister questions—was insane.

I know we don't use that word any more, but it seems perfectly accurate. Her behavior was something out of a movie, a stereotype for people in an insane asylum.

Nancy was 24, slim, about five-foot-four—just a little shorter than my five-foot-six inches. Her arms were always bent, and her hands always seemed stressed. Her shoulder-length brown hair was only curly because she got her hair permed.

I always thought it ironic that Nancy wanted curly hair. She has perfectly straight, 1970s hair. I always wanted that. Her hair was easy. It always went where it was supposed to go.

Mine was wavy at the time of this story. My hair never went where I wanted it to go. I would get one side to look good and then the other side would look different—typically good but odd because it wasn't the same as the first side. And it wouldn't stay there, even with hair spray. Nancy always wanted my curly hair. I always wanted her straight hair.

I was 16 when Nancy moved back into our house, a three-bedroom lower-level apartment in our duplex, which was a big old farmhouse in small-town Minnesota. My world was now shaken.

I was the youngest. When I was done with third grade, Nancy graduated from high school and moved out to go to college just 15 minutes away. When I was done with fifth grade, Paul, my big brother, graduated from high school and moved to Boston to go to college. All through my sixth through ninth grade years, I felt like an only child. I enjoyed having my parents all to myself.

My parents and I would laugh during dinner. We enjoyed our two dogs. We split up the chores. We coordinated calendars to make sure everyone got to their rehearsals and concerts and genealogy meetings on time since we had only one car. We were just busy enough to enjoy life but not be overly stressed.

At Christmastime in the middle of my tenth-grade year, Nancy moved back into my parents' house with her six-month-old baby boy. Her husband had left her. He left her because he couldn't handle her mental illness, whatever it was.

We didn't know what was wrong. The doctors didn't know, either. They diagnosed her with one mental illness after another, requiring different medications over the next few years and finally landed on the diagnosis "paranoid schizophrenia"—sometime after I graduated from high school. It took years to get the correct diagnosis.

The American Psychiatric Association's *Diagnostic and Statistical Manual version 5*[1] (DSM-5®) says that schizophrenia includes delusions, hallucinations, disorganized thinking, and grossly disorganized or abnormal motor behavior (p. 87-88). Yes, that is what we saw in Nancy's behavior.

I don't want to capitalize the word *schizophrenia*. I don't want to give it that much importance. I hate schizophrenia. But it was important. It is important. Because schizophrenia does not affect just my sister. It affects my whole family.

My last few years of high school were supposed to be just my parents, the dogs, and me—years of being in the pep band, being in musicals, writing for the school newspaper, and applying for all the best colleges. I still did all that, but I did it with a dark cloud over my head because I dreaded going home after each activity.

I graduated at the top of my class. I was a nerd who played alto saxophone, who sang in the choir, and who was editor of the high school newspaper. I wasn't overly popular, but I had a good group of friends. We were the musicians—choir, band, orchestra kids who performed in the school musicals.

My whole family is musical. Dad was a school choir teacher, church choir director, singer, and composer. Mom had been a church organist and sang. Nancy played flute and sang. My brother, Paul, played trombone and sang. That's just my immediate family. Mom and Dad both have musical aunts and cousins as well.

I was an awkward teenage girl, but I was kind of cute. I didn't think I was cute at the time; really I just looked like every other teen girl in the '80s, trying to fit in with my big, blondish hair, jeans that were tight at the ankles, and big glasses. Well, there was one difference between me and other teens: my left eye didn't look right. I was born with my left eyelid nearly closed.

I had three surgeries when I was five and six years old to open the lid. At this point in the story, my lid was still a little low and looked swollen because there was scar tissue trapped in the lid from the surgeries. Often, concerned moms would ask me if my eye was okay. I didn't like people noticing my eyes, but I learned to answer their questions frankly and ignore negative reactions.

JUST NORMAL FAMILY STUFF

Until my sister moved back into the house, life had been normal for the most part.

There was some upheaval when my sister, Nancy, eloped and then had a wedding ceremony six months later during a snowstorm. Imagine a little white church in a small Midwestern town with a couple feet of snow on the ground. It was just like in the movies.

Dad was calm. Mom was stressed and angry that they eloped and that they thought the wedding ceremony was just going to happen without them doing any planning. But we got through the wedding stress and moved on with life.

There was more upheaval when Paul had to move back to Minnesota because he had flunked out of Boston University. How my brother flunked out, I don't know. He's literally the smartest person I have ever met.

According to my parents, Paul refused to do his homework. I bet he knew everything, though, and aced all the tests. If I had to guess, I'd say that my brother thought that homework was a waste of time because he already knew everything on the test— and he probably did.

Paul then chose to go to college at the University of Minnesota an hour-and-a-half away from our house. He settled in there and seemed to be happy.

We got through that stress and moved on with life.

Other than those two happenings, things were normal, I guess. We were just doing what we were supposed to do. My parents worked. I went to school. We went to church.

THEN IT ALL BEGAN

However, after Nancy had the baby (my super cute nephew, Drew), she didn't handle life well.

I don't know all the particulars. I just remember that after Drew was born in May, Nancy and I planned Mom and Dad's 25th wedding anniversary party for Labor Day weekend. I wasn't quite 16 at the time, and I did a lot of the planning. Or at least *I* thought I did, but Dad probably did most of the work for what was supposed to be a surprise for him and for Mom.

A few weeks before the anniversary party, my brother Paul decided at the last minute to get married. We knew he was in a serious relationship, but we were surprised to find out about his engagement just two months before their wedding. Nancy didn't go to the wedding because she was in the psych ward at the local hospital.

Mom was caring for Drew, so Dad, Mom, Drew, and I went to the wedding, which was in the backyard of Paul's in-laws in the Twin Cities.

I guess Paul's wedding was in the backyard because it was not religious. My sister-in-law was Jewish but because my brother did not convert, his in-laws said they must have a small wedding. I liked my new sister-in-law. She was quiet but nice.

On the day of Mom and Dad's anniversary party, Nancy got a pass from the hospital so that she could be at the party. After the party, she went back into the hospital for at least a few more days.

About three months later, maybe around the time of the formal dinner to celebrate Paul's marriage, Nancy's husband left her.

That was just before the Christmas shopping season. We didn't have much money in general—I mean, my dad was a teacher—but we were doing better than previous years because Mom was working.

Nancy wanted a food processor so that she could make baby food. Food processors were relatively new, at least that was the first time that I had ever heard of a Cuisinart.® A good Cuisinart costs $100-130 today and probably cost about that same amount

30 years ago, but that would be like spending $225 today. That was more money than all the gifts given to any one person on a typical Christmas morning in our home. Because food processors were expensive, this would be Nancy's one big gift.

Dad did all sorts of research to figure out which food processor to get for Nancy. Dad, Mom, and I were shopping together. Mom had plenty of suggestions, of course, since she had been cooking so many more years than Dad and me.

Mom finally realized she was jealous. "We're giving Nancy a food processor, and I don't even have one." As a result, Dad bought her one, too, and he was smart enough to get Mom the better one. Mom was really surprised on Christmas morning.

What did I get? Care Bears® were the big seller that year, but I wasn't the Care-Bear type. I probably would've enjoyed a Walkman® and cassette tapes or new clothes, though.

But I got a desk organizer with my nickname engraved on it. My mom ordered it when she saw it in a catalog. It was about 6x3 inches with small note paper (a precursor to PostIt® Notes), a couple of small drawers, a tape dispenser, and a holder for pens.

I also got a toy truck. It was a joke—a reference to when my dad had given me a toy truck years before so that I could move my Barbies® from our previous home, a trailer (aka mobile home) where we used to live five years before, to the duplex where we lived at the time of this story.

"It's a Transformer,®" Dad laughed. Transformers were still fairly new. This was long before the movie franchise, which started in 2007. The Transformers toys debuted in 1984, a year before this Christmas. But my truck was not a Transformer. It was a knock off. You had to take pieces off of it and then snap them back on in a different place to transform this dump truck into a robot.

I didn't think it was funny. I was disappointed in only receiving a desk set and a toy truck, and I was hurt that I didn't get anything that I wanted when Nancy and Mom got what they wanted. I didn't say anything, though, because I didn't want to hurt Mom and Dad's feelings.

During Christmas break from school, I was sitting on the couch watching a sitcom on our nine-inch black-and-white TV, which had rabbit ears for an antenna. I had found something interesting, evidently, on one of only five channels. It was probably channel 9. I still remember that channel 2 was PBS, channel 4 was CBS, channel 5 was ABC, and channel 11 was NBC. I'm not sure what channel 9 was, but it had all the good sitcoms.

It seemed like Nancy was watching me. Whenever I looked her way, she would look me straight in the eye. Every time. It was weird. I was tired of Nancy being there all the time. Wasn't Christmas over?

"Nancy, when are you going back to your place?"

Mom broke in. She must've been walking through the living room at just that moment. "She's not going home. She's moving in here."

Nancy looked away, embarrassed. I didn't feel sorry for her. I didn't understand at the time how challenging it was to be a single mother. I was just angry that she was still in *my* house.

My heart sank. I wasn't getting my house back. No one had told me that Nancy and her baby were moving in. No one had asked for my opinion.

I went to my room.

Now my house was no longer fun. No longer routine. It was full of stress, a crying baby, an insane sister, and parents who didn't have time for me anymore.

HOW THE KING AND I NIGHT CHANGED ME

A couple months later, I had a minor role in the school musical, *The King and I*. I was one of the wives. If you know the show, then you know it takes place in Asia, so my pale white self was made up to have darker skin.

My grandma was coming into town to see me perform in the Friday night show. My parents always sat in the balcony, and I figured that I could pick them out of the crowd by seeing the light that reflected off their eyeglasses, but I couldn't find them.

I couldn't find them after the show, either. A friend of mine who was in the pit orchestra lived nearby. This was long before cell phones, so I went to her house to call home.

Mom answered the phone. I asked, "What's going on? Why weren't you at the show?"

"Your dad took Nancy to the hospital." She went on to explain that she and Dad took the opportunity of my grandma's arrival to force Nancy to go to the psych ward because Grandma could watch the baby while they made Nancy get in the car.

What my mom described was not a pretty scene. "Force" is the correct word. Nancy didn't go willingly.

I didn't think about how grateful I should've been that I wasn't home to see that happen. All I could think was it was supposed to be my night. I felt robbed. I had never been more disappointed.

The lie I believed before that night was that I had to perform well to be loved. That night I performed well, and it didn't make any difference because my parents weren't there to see me perform. The new lie I believed was that I wasn't important and that I wasn't worthy of anyone's time or attention.

> *The lie I believed before that night was that I had to perform well to be loved. The new lie I believed was that I wasn't important and that I wasn't worthy of anyone's time or attention.*

I was crying on the phone. I was still wearing makeup from the show, so my face was a mess with that dark make up dripping all over my hands as I tried to wipe away the tears.

The next night, Mom, Dad, and Grandma were at the show. They praised me for my performance as the alto in the "Uncle Tom's Cabin" trio, which is part of *The King and I*, but I didn't care. I might have appreciated their praise the night before but not then. I had already put up a wall around my heart and nothing was getting through it.

Nancy must not have been in the hospital long because things quickly returned to the way they were before the show. There were arguments every morning before I left for school between Mom and Nancy. Usually, Nancy would not do something for the baby that she should've done. When Mom would do it, Nancy would get mad at her for interfering.

I wonder if this happens in many three-generation homes because the grandma and mother have different perspectives on how to raise the children. But this was more. It wasn't so much that they had differing opinions on what to do. It was that my sister wasn't doing essential things for my baby nephew.

Each morning, I increasingly went to the bus stop earlier and earlier.

Dinner was no longer full of laughter. Instead, there was more arguing between Nancy and Mom over Drew.

One night when Drew was a toddler, my dad asked me about school. I was surprised that he asked because no one had asked me about myself over the last year, yet I started telling him about my day. Just then, Drew did something he shouldn't have. Nancy wasn't paying attention, so Mom corrected him. Nancy got upset with Mom for doing what she should have done herself, and there was a heated exchange. We never did get back to my story about school.

That's what life was like for me. I didn't want to be home. It was not a fun place to be. It wasn't even a boring place to be. It was riddled with arguing and a babbling sister who talked to the air.

For Nancy, schizophrenia presented itself as if she had an imaginary friend. She was often talking to him in gibberish, quiet for a time while she listened to whatever he was saying, and then laughing.

Disturbing, you say? Yeah, that's an understatement.

SCHIZOPHRENIA DEFINED BY THE AMERICAN PSYCHIATRIC ASSOCIATION

When someone uses the word schizophrenic, they usually mean that there's an inconsistency between two things. Dictionary.com provides the following example: The movie "wavers from comedy to thriller to docudrama—a totally schizophrenic plot." That sounds more like split personalities to me.

As a result, I react every time I hear someone using *schizophrenic* in that way. I've even corrected pastors. They used the word correctly per the dictionary, but I react emotionally every time. I am adamant: schizophrenia and multiple personality disorder are not the same.

The American Psychiatric Association has a new name for multiple personalities: *Dissociative Identity Disorder*. The first diagnostic criterion in the DSM-5® defines Dissociative Identity Disorder this way:

Disruption of identity characterized by two or more distinct personality states, which may be described in some cultures as an experience of possession. The disruption in identity involves marked discontinuity in sense of self and sense of agency, accompanied by related alterations in affect, behavior, consciousness, memory, perception, cognition, and/or sensory-motor functioning. (p. 292)

In contrast, schizophrenia includes delusions, hallucinations, disorganized thinking, and grossly disorganized or abnormal motor behavior (DSM-5, p. 87-88). Not distinct personalities but delusions and hallucinations. This describes my sister's behaviors very well.

2

MY ABORTION "CHOICE"

About six months after *The King and I*, I met a guy. His mom and my dad were in the same community theater production of a Gilbert and Sullivan musical. I don't remember which one. "The Mikado," maybe? I know it wasn't "The Pirates of Penzance." We first saw each other after the Thursday performance while we waited for our parents. I knew who he was, but he didn't know who I was.

Arnold was five-and-a-half years older than me. He graduated from high school a year after my brother. Arnold, his older brother, Jed, and my brother, Paul, hung out with the same group of musicians.

Arnold played alto saxophone in the band, percussion in the orchestra, and sang in the choir. Paul played trombone in band and orchestra and sang in the choir.

I remembered that Arnold and Jed, along with many more of their group of musical friends, were at Paul's graduation party. I was only 11 years old at the time, but I remember Arnold and

Jed being there because they were teasing my grandma. It's a story that my mom enjoyed telling for years.

They were standing near the punch bowl, and my grandma, trying to make conversation, asked, "Are you here for the party?"

They chuckled politely and responded with a kind-hearted wise crack: "Well, we were just walking by and wanted to see what was going on."

"Oh," Grandma said, a little worried. She quietly made her way to my mom to see if she knew those two guys. Mom got a good chuckle out of that. "Oh, yes, I know these two."

Our families knew each other from a regional choir. Dad stood next to Arnold's dad in the baritone section, and Arnold's mom sang soprano.

But that day, after the Thursday Gilbert and Sullivan performance, we were waiting for our parents in the hallway behind the stage near the history classrooms of our high school. There was one official dressing room there and then classrooms were used as dressing rooms, too. There were desks in the hallway to make more space in the classrooms for the cast.

Arnold and his friend were leaning up against the little yellow lockers. Arnold was paying attention to me but talking with his friend. He didn't say anything to me, at least not that night. His friend noticed him noticing me, but they just chatted and joked with each other. I sat at a desk awkwardly, waiting for my dad. Eventually, Arnold's mom was ready to go. She knew who I was and said goodbye to me as they left.

After the Saturday night performance, I had to tag along with my parents to the cast party. We only had one car, and it would've added another 30 minutes to the trip if they were to take me home, so I went with them.

Arnold was there. I can't remember why. Arnold was 22 and in college. I was 16 (almost 17) and about to start my junior year in high school. Arnold, a male classmate of mine who was in the pit orchestra, and I stood around and talked all evening. I didn't have anything else to do.

It seemed like both guys were interested in me. It was really awkward. I didn't like my classmate as anything more than a friend, and I knew Arnold was too old for me. As a general rule, guys didn't seem interested in me. I was not particularly cute. I had been wearing glasses since I was five years old. My left eyelid didn't look right, so I wasn't just an awkward teenager: I was an awkward teenager with glasses and weird eyes. Their attention to me was unexpected, and I really had no idea how to act.

Some days later, Arnold called. He figured out who I was and looked up the number. We were easy to find in the phone book.

We talked for a long time—on the one-and-only phone in the house. Anyone else remember the dial phones with the really long cords? Ours was mustard yellow, and our phone number was 558-2864, no area code needed. I remember how it felt like the 8s took for*ever* to dial.

I kept expecting Arnold to ask me out on a date, but he didn't. When I said my goodbyes, he pointed out that I had not asked him out.

What?

Arnold said he had made a New Year's resolution to not ask anyone out; therefore, it was my responsibility to ask *him* out. So, I did.

And with that, we started dating.

In retrospect, I bet my dad wishes he had taken the extra 30 minutes to drive me home before going to the cast party.

FRIENDS & LOVERS

"Friends and Lovers" recorded by Gloria Loring and Carl Anderson[2] was at the top of the music charts in 1986. It's line "nothing would change if we made love" illustrates that the whole song is about friends considering having sex and how they could be both friends and lovers.

Arnold said, "I keep thinking that song is about us."

That hit me the wrong way—well, differently than what he intended, anyway. He thought that was special, that we would have our own song.

But in my heart, I knew that song meant friendship, not love. Today they'd call it "friends with benefits." I wasn't dating him for friendship. Dating was supposed to be more than that.

I didn't say anything. I didn't know how to put words to my feelings.

I kept dating Arnold. He was nice. He was smart. He was funny. And we had music, camping, hiking, and canoeing in common. After a few months, he said he was in love with me.

A few months after that, I told him that I was in love with him. I'm not sure if I really was in love with him at that point. I had asked him how he knew that he was in love with me because I was trying to figure out whether I was in love with him. I know I was in love with him later in our relationship, but I'm not sure if I was that first year, to be honest.

Another Christmas was fast approaching, and my family had just moved out of the small-town duplex and into a single-family home in the city just blocks from my high school. I didn't know what to give Arnold as a gift. I didn't have any money of my own because I wasn't working. So, I gave him my virginity.

We made it a special night, but I can't say that sex felt good. Now that I'm much older—30-something years older—I can say that sex as a teen wasn't good. I've heard that sex for women is better when you are older, and I'll attest to that.

Hanging out with Arnold was much better than being at home. I would be home for dinner at the new house because I was expected to be. Our family always had dinner together before our evening activities. After dinner, I would leave for Arnold's. I did more homework in his apartment than I did at home. And, yes, I really was doing homework. (I was a nerd, remember?)

My parents complained about me never being home. My response? "Why should I be? No one ever talks to me anyway."

I proved myself right by staying home one night to study for a test. I didn't go to my bedroom to study. I chose the kitchen table—nice and central to all the activity.

After dinner, Mom and Dad went downstairs to the family room. They never even asked what I was studying.

CHURCH HURT

Do churches ever talk about mental illnesses?

As I mentioned earlier, my dad was the choir director at church. I don't remember what volunteer work my mom did at that time other than sing in the choir, but suffice it to say the three of us were very involved in the church.

There were probably 200 people at service on any given Sunday. The choir always sang. We were always there for every event, including potluck Thanksgiving.

Confirmation class was done, so now my Wednesday evening activity was the youth group. My peers and I were disgruntled with youth group. I don't remember why, but I do remember taking a survey to get some details on what the group wanted to change.

The pastor not only wasn't happy with me for surveying the group, but he took offense to the results and let me know. He was not gentle. I don't think a pastor today would ever talk like that to a 17-year-old. At least I hope not.

My dad in his role as the choir director was also in conflict with the pastor. I don't know nor need to know the whys. I just know that church was stressful.

I remember asking my mom if the pastor knew what we were going through at home. I didn't understand why we had so many conflicts with the pastor if he knew the stress we were under. Mom said he knew. I asked her recently if she and Dad ever went to the pastor for counseling, and she said, "No."

Church felt like work. It was a job that we had to do every Wednesday night for choir rehearsal and youth group and every Sunday morning for Sunday school and church service.

The church I go to today isn't like that. If there were a family in similar circumstances, we would have people praying over them and our pastor would meet with them regularly to provide godly counsel. I hope that is true in other churches as well.

Mom and I were so frustrated that we convinced Dad to leave the church. I could tell that he didn't want to go. He loves to sing to the Lord and direct choir. But he reluctantly agreed to quit.

The choir had a gathering at someone's house to say thank you and goodbye to my dad. I remember one of the men asking me to convince my dad to stay, and I quickly told him that we convinced him to quit. Poor guy didn't know what to say.

Mom went to another church. I don't remember what my dad did. I know he wanted to be at the church that we had just left. Eventually he did go back after the pastor moved on to another church.

As for me, I was done with church.

SEX & ABORTION

Sex was a stupid decision. It really was. What happens when you have sex? You get pregnant or get sexually transmitted infections (STIs, previously called STDs—sexually transmitted diseases) or both. I got both.

My period was late. I went to the local non-Christian family planning center to get a pregnancy test because it was free. I don't remember if there were home pregnancy tests back then, but I didn't have any of my own money, and even if I did, I didn't want the possibility of that test being wrong. I didn't have to use my parents' insurance or make a doctor's appointment, all of which would've required a talk with my parents. I didn't want them to know about my worry.

> *Premarital sex was a stupid decision. It really was. What happens when you have sex? You get pregnant or get STIs. I got both.*

The local family planning center was not religiously affiliated, but it also did not offer abortions. There weren't any abortion clinics in my city. For an abortion, you had to drive 90 minutes to the Twin Cities.

I was pregnant. One of the women who worked there asked me if I knew what I wanted to do. I was embarrassed and really didn't know what to say. I don't think I even knew how I felt. I wasn't good at feelings.

I never put a word to how I felt about anything. I never acknowledged that my feelings were okay or normal. As a general rule, I hid my feelings from other people because then I'd have to defend them, and I didn't want to have that conversation. I didn't know how to have that conversation. As a result, I hid my feelings, even from myself.

I didn't know what I wanted to do. Well, I knew I wasn't going to raise a child, but I didn't know whether I was going to have an abortion or put the baby up for adoption. The woman gave me information about all the options.

Arnold had gone with me to the clinic. Unfortunately, a friend who knew that I was worried was also there, and she had brought a friend—someone I knew. They were all out in the lobby when I came out, chatting.

I didn't want to tell Arnold until we were alone, but my friend asked. I just shook my head. She and her friend understood. So did Arnold.

We went back to my house because we knew no one was there, so we could talk freely. I asked Arnold what he thought we should do. He said, "Whatever you want." He wasn't willing to tell me what to do with my body. As a feminist,[3] I appreciated that. In one way, I loved him for that. In another way, I felt lost because I wasn't getting any help in making this decision.

I asked Arnold if we should get married and raise the baby. "Absolutely not." I honestly don't remember his exact words, but that was the message. He had no interest in getting married nor in raising a child. He wouldn't stop me from raising the child, but he wasn't going to marry me. My feelings were hurt by his response, but I quickly buried my feelings and moved forward in solving the problem. Today I know that interaction just cemented in me that I am not worthy of love. Arnold did not love me enough to start a family together. Sadly, I knew that if I did want to raise the baby, I'd be doing so on my own. Why did I stay with him?

I had no interest in raising a baby, honestly. There was already "too much baby" in my house. (Drew was a typical terrible two-year-old at this point.)

I didn't give adoption much thought because, frankly, I didn't want the embarrassment of pregnancy as I walked through the halls of high school. I didn't want to see the judgmental eyes. I didn't want to see the disappointment in my teachers' eyes. I just wanted the whole problem to go away, and that's what abortion seemed to provide.

I also didn't want the pain of giving birth. My mom certainly didn't make the birthing process sound like fun. I think each of us three kids provided progressively more challenging labor for my mom. As a newborn, I got out of the hospital a few days before my mom did. Nancy was in labor for a couple *days* before the doctor did a C-section to deliver Drew.

If they were giving birth today, my mom probably would've had three C-sections and my sister probably would not have had to be in labor for days. So, no, giving birth is not easy in my family. Knowing that, I had no incentive to go through with the pregnancy at all.

I don't remember what else Arnold and I talked about. I just remember that I looked up abortion clinics in the Twin Cities, found one that was not Planned Parenthood (because I didn't want to encounter protesters) and that had a female doctor. I made an appointment for June 25.

I had to be at the clinic for a long time because I had to get there a couple hours beforehand. With the 90-minute drive there and 90-minute drive back, I knew it would be an all-day thing. How was I going to hide that from my parents?

So, I told Arnold that I had to tell my parents. And if we were going to tell my parents, then we should tell his parents because our parents knew each other and saw each other just about every week. He said, "Okay."

My parents thought we were going to tell them we wanted to get married, so they were more than just a little shocked at our news. When I said I was going to have an abortion, my mom said, "Well, I don't know what else to do." I don't remember my dad saying much.

When we told Arnold's parents, his mom immediately got up and gave the two of us a hug. I don't remember his dad saying anything. I heard later that his dad didn't get much sleep that night. I bet my dad didn't, either.

My mom didn't understand why I was waiting until the 25th, but I had strategically chosen that date because we had two three-hour trips planned to my cousins' place for a party one weekend and a family reunion the following weekend. I thought recovering after the family events would be better than in between. I didn't explain all that to my mom, but I wish I had.

At my mother's behest, I moved the appointment up by one week, in between the two family events. At the first family get together, I could go swimming. At the second one, I could not because that was one of the post-operative restrictions. I couldn't give my cousins the real reason I wasn't swimming. I think they assumed that I had my period but didn't understand why I wasn't willing to use tampons.

Mom and I met Arnold at his mom's house. We were all driving the 90 minutes together in his car. He was late, which was against his character. He was late because he stopped to get me a rose. It was beautiful.

Both of our moms went to the Twin Cities with us that day, Thursday, June 18, 1987. Drew was 25 months old, and I was aborting his cousin, although I didn't think of it like that at the time.

I was only allowed to have one person sit with me in the clinic. I chose Arnold, so the moms waited for us in the lobby. It was a long day, like outpatient surgery is today.

I had to sign in with my birthdate. No HIPAA laws existed back then, so I quickly scanned the sign-in sheet; I was the youngest.

The waiting room was very somber. Arnold and one other guy were the only men. A few of the women were accompanied by their mothers, but most of the women were there alone. The room was packed. I think Arnold and I got the last two chairs, which were not together. It was cold and eerily quiet.

The room slowly cleared out as women went inside for their "procedures." Eventually, I was able to move so that I was sitting next to Arnold. I don't know that we said much of anything to each other, but at least I wasn't sitting alone in a crowd. That's what it was like. I was alone in a room full of women. After a while, my name was called to go back for *my* "procedure."

The room looked like any patient room at a doctor's office. The table was like any table that would be used for a woman's Pap smear, except that I had never had a woman's checkup at this point in my life.

The nurse was very caring and reassuring, and I was reassuring her back that I was okay. I know that sounds strange that I was reassuring her, but I didn't want to be a bother to anyone. More so, I had to be okay with the procedure in order to go through with it, so I acted like I was okay.

I was okay right up until my baby was gone. I could feel my face fall. I wasn't okay any more. Whatever joy I had was sucked away5 right at that moment, and I have been fighting to get it back ever since.

The doctor came in hurriedly. She went right down to business until she saw my eyes. Then she came up near my shoulders to point out that my right eye was drooping. I said that actually my right eye was acting normally but my left eyelid was staying open because of the surgeries I had when I was little. As soon as she understood, she cut me off and went down to business. She was like a machine, cranking out abortions.

The doctor performed a vacuum procedure. I was okay right up until my baby was gone. I remember when she left me because I could feel my face fall. I wasn't okay any more. I tried not to let my feelings show because I had that wall around my heart—nothing got in, and I wouldn't let anything out—but I'm sure the nurse noticed. Whatever joy I had was gone completely right at that moment, and I have been fighting to get it back ever since.[4]

The doctor said I was six weeks pregnant. That means that I got pregnant about a week before junior prom, but I bet our parents thought I got pregnant the night of prom. At six weeks, my baby had her own blood cells. Her heart was beating. The foundation of her entire nervous system was established. Her vascular system had regular blood flow. Her ear and nasal development had begun. Her eyes had started to develop, and she had 40 pairs of muscles. Even her brain waves were detectable. Of course, I didn't know all that at the time. Nevertheless, my baby was dead, and I was responsible.

Thankfully my abortion was a textbook procedure—little bleeding. That was not the case for every woman in the recovery room. There was one woman who wasn't doing well, and others were whispering to her that she had to tell the nurses. "Don't let them intimidate you into not saying anything." I'm not sure if she ever told the nurses.

Several weeks later, I had to go back for a follow-up exam to make sure everything was okay. The weather was awful that day. There may have been a tornado warning because I remember a male security officer for the building talking to the doctor in the waiting room about being prepared to get everyone in the basement. She replied, "We can't stop what we're doing here."

The doctor was just as hurried as the day of my abortion, but everything was behind schedule. Arnold and I sat in the waiting room for a long time. When I was finally called back for my exam, the nurse acknowledged that I had been there almost as long as a "regular" patient. I knew she meant a woman who was there for an abortion.

The doctor did the Pap smear and whatever else she had planned. I'm sure it was a complete pelvic exam, although I don't remember the particulars. I just remember that after I got dressed, the doctor came back in, still in a hurry, to put me on the pill. I must have looked surprised because she said, "You don't want this to happen again." She showed me how the dial worked, threw away one of the sugar pills, and told me to be on a 27-day cycle instead of 28 days because that would be more effective in preventing pregnancy. I have no idea if that is true or not, but I took her word and the "free" one-month supply of pills. I was left with the impression that she was not looking for repeat business.

Pregnancy was not all I got with sex. I also got an STI. Arnold was not a virgin before we were together, and his previous girl-friend was not a virgin before she was with him. Seems that HPV got passed from her to him to me.

Both Arnold and I got medicine for the HPV from the abortion doctor. Arnold was not happy about that because she wasn't his doctor, so she didn't know if he had any allergies or medical conditions. But I doubt she knew if I did, either. I asked him to take the medicine anyway. I think he did, but I'm honestly not sure whether he did or not.

The injustice of it all nagged at me. Not only did it take two of us to get pregnant, but *he* gave *me* the STI. Yet *I'm* the only one who had a medical "procedure," and *I'm* expected to be the one who takes medicine to get rid of the STI. Perhaps he didn't love me as much as I thought he did. I wish I had realized that then.

WHO'S THE SMART ONE?

Someone else I knew in school was pregnant at about the same time I was. I heard that her high school counselor said she had to go to the alternative school. Historically, the alternative school was created for girls like us who were pregnant out of wedlock. In the 1980s, however, we knew it as the school where delinquents were sent whether male or female. It didn't matter that this pregnant student was at the top of our class. It was clear she wasn't welcome in our high school any more.

As a result, she took advantage of the dual-enrollment option and finished her high school credits while simultaneously getting college credit from the local university. She went on to get both her bachelor's degree and her master's degree. She completed both of her degrees before I finished my bachelor's degree, and my master's degree is unfinished. She was smarter than me—academically and pragmatically.

After the abortion, my dad wanted me to see a counselor, so he made an appointment for me. The counselor talked to me on the phone first. I gave him a run-down of everything that had happened recently, and he made a reflective comment about feeling the loss from abortion on top of all that. But I didn't feel like I had lost anything. (What I didn't know is that my feelings were numbed. I didn't even realize I had no more joy.)

The counselor didn't get it. I made the rational choice. I didn't have to deal with all the disapproving people, I didn't have to deal with all the physical discomfort and pain of pregnancy and birth, and I didn't have to figure out how to put a baby up for adoption.

I did have to deal with my parents, I did have to deal with my boyfriend's parents, I still had to deal with my sister's schizophrenia and my annoying nephew, and I did have to keep my secret. It was too much.

Seeing the counselor was not helpful at all. He didn't help me work through what I was feeling. I think I saw the counselor three times. My dad was not happy that I stopped going, but I think he later realized he needed to see the counselor more than I did.

MY NEW BEST FRIEND

Sometime that summer, Arnold and I started hanging out with people from his work, including his brother, Jed. Arnold and Jed worked at an old-style drug store with a cafe, card and gift shop, and a photography shop.

Arnold and Jed worked in the photography shop (a rival to Ritz Photography, long before digital). Lynn worked in the cafe. She, Diane from the pharmacy, Jed, and Arnold started hanging out. I was invited, too. Lynn's brother Fred would join us every now and then, as well.

We played frisbee golf at the park along the river, watched movies, etc. Eventually, it was just Lynn, Jed, Arnold, and me. Arnold was the only one who knew about the abortion, and that was just fine by me.

That fall, my senior year in high school, *Star Trek: The Next Generation* premiered. Arnold was a Trekker. He wanted every episode recorded on VHS tape but without commercials. To do that, he had to be sitting right in front of the TV with his remote, ready to press PAUSE at just the right moment. He was really good at it, too. He never cut off a scene, and he rarely got even a second of the commercial. Saturday nights became a thing. The four of us would eat at Arnold's and watch *Star Trek*.

Lynn and I became good friends. So did Lynn and Jed. Right under our noses, Lynn and Jed fell in love. In December, they took us out to a fancy meal and told us they were engaged. Arnold wasn't surprised, but I had totally missed all the clues.

Arnold had just gotten back from a week with his grandmother. While visiting her, he also visited his aunt and told her that he wouldn't be surprised if Lynn and Jed got married, but he never said a word to me about his perceptions.

What really surprised me, though, was that Lynn asked me to be her maid of honor. I didn't even know what a maid of honor did other than sign the marriage license.

I was a pretty crappy maid of honor. Arnold and I threw Lynn and Jed a gettin' hitched party rather than a bachelor's party and a bridal shower, but I didn't make sure all of Lynn's friends were invited. I didn't know them. I should've asked her for a list. I really had no clue about protocols. I should've asked my mom what I should do, but I never did.

THE HIGH SCHOOL NEWSPAPER

Did I mention that I was the editor of my high school newspaper? Beware of a woman with a pen, even if she is a teenager.

I became the editor-in-chief of my school newspaper at the end of my junior year, at about the time that I got pregnant. The previous editor-in-chief was working a lot and not in the school building very much, so she let her editorship go early.

About a month after the abortion, another editor and I were at newspaper camp. Yes, there was a newspaper camp, and I was just nerdy enough to go.

The other editor and I roomed together. I told her that I had an idea to have each issue of the newspaper follow a theme. She liked the idea, and we brainstormed several themes.

We ended up publishing newspapers about the history of the school, teenage sexuality and pregnancy, drugs and alcohol abuse, and school spirit, to name a few.

Yes, teenage sexuality and pregnancy. What was I thinking!?!

I know exactly what I was thinking. I was thinking that if we had a whole newspaper about this taboo subject, perhaps my classmates would not go through what I went through.

I told the other editor about my pregnancy and abortion. She wasn't judgmental. She and I talked about how we could get both pro-life and pro-choice groups to talk to us. We lived in a very Catholic city, and we didn't know if any pro-life group would talk to us. We also didn't know how to talk to them because we were both pro-choice.

Our advisor liked our idea of each issue having a theme and didn't seem to have any problem with the teenage pregnancy and sexuality topic. However, she was a college student, not a faculty member of our school. Sometimes I wonder how much I messed up her career.

We published our first issue a month earlier than previous years. I remember that I had to work late on my birthday to get the issue to the printer on time.

This was before the school had a computer and software for producing the newspaper. We had to send the articles to the printer specifying the column width. Then we'd get everything back and paste it all together with our photos and artwork—yes, paste it with glue on pica paper—before sending it back to the printer for publication. It was tedious compared to today, but I really enjoyed the design challenge.

The second issue was on teenage sexuality and pregnancy. It was published November 20, 1987. I didn't even have to find my copy of that newspaper to tell you the date because I don't think that I could ever forget it—kind of like the date of my abortion.

My plan was to have two pregnancy stories on the front page, mine and a story of a teen who had kept her baby. The other teen agreed to the idea, but I never made the time to interview her. Maybe I didn't have the guts. Maybe I didn't want to hear why she chose to go through with her pregnancy. Maybe I didn't want to expose myself to rethinking my decision.

The reporters on our newspaper staff were mostly younger than me. Everyone was gung-ho about the idea. We came up with a list of organizations to interview, including the local family planning center (pro-choice) and Birthline (pro-life).

The family planning center talked to us. None of the pro-life organizations would talk to us.

Our biggest mistake was not printing a statement saying that we asked for interviews at all these pro-life organizations but were turned down. As a result, the newspaper was full of pro-choice articles... in a Catholic city.

My biggest mistake was writing a letter to the editor of the city newspaper. There had been an ongoing discussion about abortion in the letter-to-the-editor section. I don't know why. It's not like it was an election year. It was 1987, and Ronald Reagan was President for another year-and-a-half.

There was one pro-life woman who was writing all sorts of letters to the editor, and she really made me mad. She was president of a pro-life organization that had sent out a teen survey about sexuality the year before. I remember getting and filling out the survey and adding all sorts of comments to tell them exactly what I thought of their survey. I thought they were asking all the wrong questions because they were out-of-touch with teens. And that's exactly what I told her when I wrote my letter to the editor. "If you really want to know what teens think, read our next issue. It will be published November 20th."

My advisor couldn't believe I wrote that—without telling her.

Yeah, that was stupid. I don't think I told anyone. I just did it. My guess is that deep down, I knew I shouldn't tell the readers of the city newspaper about our upcoming issue of the school newspaper, but I wanted to be heard. I wanted teens to be heard. It seemed like adults were talking about us, not with us.

Because of my letter to the editor, the whole city was a-buzz about the upcoming issue of the high school newspaper, which was sure to be full of teen sex.

Generally, when students at our school got in trouble, they went to see the assistant principal who was assigned to that grade level. If you were sitting in the office on the black chairs, everyone knew you were in trouble. A year before, I had to sit on the black chairs before seeing the assistant principal who oversaw the newspaper. Someone I had babysat many years before was also sitting on the black chairs that day. He asked what I did wrong. I said, "Nothing. The Assistant Principal just wants to talk to me about the newspaper." But I did get in trouble because the newspaper had quoted a student who said, "I was pissed off." Evidently publishing "pissed off" as a direct quote was not acceptable. Okay, got it.

This time, I didn't have to see the assistant principal about the newspaper's issue on teenage sexuality and pregnancy. I had to see the principal. *The* principal. His office was in a totally different wing of the school.

I had the nicest meeting with the principal. Don't get me wrong. I clearly was in trouble, but he was kind. He made it clear that I was not to write to the city paper any more with reference to the school.

The school handled the situation with mercy. Even though it cost them extra money, they made sure that everyone who wanted a copy of the school newspaper got it. However, they made the newspaper staff take all the phone calls and mail out the newspapers. That was us. That was me.

Also, the pro-life woman who had been writing letters to the city newspaper and her organization filed a complaint with the school district. I'm sure that the school expected it. I didn't. But then I didn't think ahead.

In their letter of complaint, the organization criticized the number of articles concerning teen sexuality in one issue, how the articles were overwhelmingly pro-choice, how our articles assumed contraception as the way to prevent STIs and pregnancy without mention of abstinence, and our grammar.

As a newspaper staff, we had to sit with our advisor and respond to each point in the letter of complaint. One of the staff members, who happened to be a couple years younger than me, let me know how mad he was at me because we were all in so much trouble. I let him vent. He wasn't wrong. I can't remember exactly how I handled it. I can't remember if I apologized. I have a feeling that I took responsibility. At least I hope I did.

I recently re-read that issue of the school newspaper. Our grammar was not that bad. We had one dangling modifier and a few other mistakes that were not as noticeable. The complaint letter made it seem like we were illiterate. Ironically, I had the grammar-intensive part of my English classes after we published that issue. Most of my classmates had that level of grammar their junior year, but I had taken an elective news-writing class that pushed back my taking of the grammar class until my last semester, which was a few months after the organization's complaint letter.

We defended the number of news articles on sex by explaining that we were publishing issues on themes that year. However, we hadn't established the pattern before we wrote this controversial issue.

We were frustrated that we didn't have pro-life articles in the issue because we had asked pro-life organizations for interviews, and they all said no.

We also noted that we did list organizations that support pregnant teens, both pro-life and pro-choice. None of these offered abortions—no organizations in our city offered abortions.

The pro-life woman and her organization were accusatory, only pointing out what they wanted to point out. They took out a full-page ad in the city newspaper with headlines from our newspaper in it, encouraging people to request a copy and read it for themselves.

One reporter in the city newspaper took this on as her project. She investigated the woman who made me mad. She interviewed me. She wrote two articles in the newspaper. By name, I was famous.

I didn't know that I was famous. I didn't think about my feelings. I was just trying to hold my head above water while under so much stress. Remember that not only was I responding to the school and the city about the newspaper, I was still living in the same house as my mentally ill sister and my toddler nephew.

The Letters to the Editor section of the city newspaper were full of letters both supporting our news staff and supporting the woman and her organization. The city was split.

At the end of the school year, I found out that my economics teacher talked about me all the time. He didn't talk about me during my class, of course, but evidently he talked about me in all his other classes. That was really weird to find out. I wasn't sure how to feel about that.

The guy who printed the newspaper never seemed to like us much—until this whole controversy happened. Then he was extremely nice and easy to work with. I guess he was pro-choice.

No One Knew But Everyone Knew

Who did I tell that I had had an abortion? Arnold, my parents, his parents, the friend who was at the family planning center and I'm sure her friend was told or figured things out, and the other editor. That's eight people.

But everyone knew that the front-page article was about me. Well, all my classmates knew. At least that's my assessment. My best guess is that the "friend" who figured things out spread the rumor. Rumors are not always untrue.

My friend Lynn didn't know. Jed didn't know. They were my escape. Arnold, Lynn, Jed, and I would spend time together, and

I never heard a thing about all the controversy that I caused in the city.

Arnold supported me through all of that. He never shunned me. He even agreed to be interviewed by the other editor for that front-page article.

My mom also agreed to be interviewed by the other editor. I don't remember my parents saying much to me about the whole fiasco, and they never chastised me for writing to the city newspaper.

I have all the newspaper articles and letters to the editor. Several of them have my mom's handwriting on them. Seems that she was quietly proud of me for standing up for my beliefs.

I do remember that my dad was proud of me. He told me that he had run into my principal. The principal told my dad that students and their parents were talking about teen sex because of the whole controversy and that he thought it was a good thing.

I remember my response very clearly: "Good. That's exactly what I wanted."

I didn't realize that's what I wanted until I said those words. Mission accomplished.

THAT DAY IN JANUARY

When we had moved into the city, we lived three blocks from my high school. One of the benefits of living so close was that I could go home for lunch.

It was January 1988. I can't remember why I walked the three blocks home in the cold of a Minnesota winter for lunch that day. And I don't remember what I had for lunch or whether I saw Nancy.

I just remember where I was on the walk when I was suddenly struck with the idea that that was the day my daughter would've been born.

I didn't know scientifically that my baby was a girl; I was only about six weeks along when I had the abortion, so there was no way to know for sure. It was a gut feeling. Even today, I am certain she was a girl. I have no explanation for that feeling, and I won't know for certain this side of heaven.

As I was returning to school, I started to cry, and I couldn't stop.

I was supposed to be in World History class after lunch, but all I could do was cry. I was embarrassed. I didn't know where to go. I didn't want to talk to anyone, but I also didn't want to get in trouble for skipping class. I walked around the building to the door closest to the nurse's office and went there.

As I came in, my favorite teacher was about to walk out. Evidently, she had just walked a sick student down to the nurse's office. She looked at me and asked me what was wrong, but I couldn't stop crying long enough to explain. And what would I say? I didn't want anyone to hear me say that I had had an abortion.

My teacher said she had the hour open, so we went to the room where we worked on the newspaper. I knew no one was there that hour, providing us time to talk without interruption.

I told her I had gotten pregnant last spring, had had an abortion last summer, and just felt like today was the day that my baby would've been born. My teacher was kind to me. I don't remember what she said. I just remember that I was struck by her kindness even though I had done two shameful things—got pregnant[5] and had an abortion.

Of course, being the nerd that I was, I was concerned about getting in trouble for not being in history class. She said she'd talk to my teacher. She did, and I did not get in trouble for missing class.

I never told my parents about that. It never even occurred to me until just now that perhaps I should have.

THE TUNA

Later that spring, I went home for lunch again. I'm guessing it was May because the weather was much nicer.

Arnold was done with college at this point but hadn't yet found a job in his field. He was still working at the camera shop.

He was going to be working the evening shift, so we decided to meet for lunch at my house.

I was going to make tuna salad sandwiches so when I got there, I went to the pantry and grabbed a can of tuna from the stack. I noticed that it wasn't Mom's usual brand but didn't think much of it.

I got the tuna and Mom's homemade relish mixed together when Nancy walked to the doorway between the kitchen and the dining room and said, "You stole my tuna!"

"What?"

"You stole my tuna!"

Then she giggled in that weird way when she would "talk" to her imaginary friend.

"I just took a can out of the pantry."

"That's mine! You stole it!"

"There's plenty more."

Nancy stopped paying attention to me and paced in the dining room. I heard her giggling with her imaginary friend. Then she suddenly snapped back to consciousness, and the smile fell from her face. "It's my tuna!"

"They are inexpensive. I'm sure Mom will buy you plenty more on Saturday when you two go shopping."

Nancy continued to be mad at me. She also continued pacing in the dining room, having a nonsensical conversation with her imaginary friend and giggling.

When I saw that Arnold had pulled into the driveway, I went out to meet him and told him not to come inside because Nancy was mad at me. I finished making the tuna salad sandwiches, and we ate them at the picnic table in the backyard.

At the end of my 30-minute lunch break, Arnold left and I started crying, bawling. I went into the kitchen to call my mom because I was late, and I didn't want to get in trouble with the staff who patrolled the school grounds—we called them *bouncers*. (Nerd, remember. I was a rule follower, and I didn't want to get in trouble for not following the rules.)

Mom called the school to give them some explanation for why I was going to be late. Arnold drove me the three blocks to school.

Once again, I walked in crying. Once again, I was supposed to be in World History class. I pulled myself together long enough to get into my seat. I was fine until someone talked to me.

Poor guy. This class had both sophomores and seniors in it. I was a senior. He was a sophomore, a really nice guy. I don't know what he said to me, but I'm sure it was nice. I just couldn't handle talking to anyone. If the teacher had just come into the class and started teaching, I could've hidden my tears long enough to get control over my emotions.

But I started to cry and got up to leave. My teacher (a really nice guy, by the way) usually stood outside his classroom door talking to another teacher between classes. I was going to talk to him as I left, but he wasn't there.

I went to the nurse's office again. At least this time my reason for crying wasn't shameful. It was just really hard to explain.

Once again, I ran into my favorite teacher. She said I had to go back and tell my history teacher where I was because that's what the two of them had agreed to after the last time I missed his class for crying.

As a result, this rule follower went back up to the classroom. Class had started. My teacher was sitting on one of the desks, which was his usual place at the start of the class. All I could get out was, "I can't stay in class today." He nodded his head, and I left.

I was embarrassed to be crying in front of my classmates, especially another musician who happened to be my history teacher's daughter. Evidently enough of my classmates knew that Arnold and I planned to live together after graduation because she said she figured I was crying because my parents were mad about that.

"No. I was crying because of my sister." She had no clue what I was talking about. I guess no one knew. Had I told anyone? I know that my friend whose phone I used after *The King and I* knew because our parents were friends, attended the church that we had left, and were even in Dad's church choir. But did anyone else know that my sister had a mental illness? I guess not.

If my classmates didn't know about all the challenges going on in my home, then I'm sure I didn't know about all the challenges going on in their homes.

Once again, my favorite teacher was kind and understanding and helped me to stop crying.

MY FAVORITE TEACHER

At the end of the school year, we had an award ceremony specifically for seniors. There were a number of awards. Some of them came with scholarships. I got two.

My favorite teacher presented me with one of the awards, which is given to a senior who has given outstanding service to the high school. I was given the award in recognition for my leadership in the newspaper, in an anti-drinking-and-driving program, in two bands, in choir, and in Honor Society.

After the ceremony, my teacher told me that in previous years it was hard to choose who would receive the award because each student would get only one or at most two nominations from teachers and staff. This year, three faculty members nominated me—that is, the most nominations for a single student received to that point. One of them was my band director, who I didn't even think liked me. One of them was my economics teacher, who wrote: "For her grace under pressure."

A few weeks later, I graduated 16th in my class of 400 students and moved out of the house and in with Arnold, 90 minutes away in the Twin Cities.

3
LOVELESS MARRIAGE

When I graduated from high school, I couldn't wait to get out of Dodge. I left home two days after the graduation ceremony. Arnold and I moved into an apartment in the Twin Cities. He got a summer job doing construction work while continuing to look for a job related to his major. I worked full time at McDonald's.

I planned to be in the apartment just for the summer because I promised my parents I would live in the dorms on the college campus, but I hated living in the dorms. I had three roommates. I couldn't get any sleep, and I had to get up early most mornings to work. I was not the typical college student. I wasn't interested in parties. I just wanted to do my schoolwork and get paid for my job. Arnold missed me, so I moved back into the apartment after the first semester.

That first fall in the Twin Cities, Arnold got the "real job" he wanted. He called his dad first. He somberly told me late that night after I got home from work. I was super excited for him, but he didn't act excited. He had more of an entitled attitude.

I was hurt that Arnold didn't tell me first. He said he felt perfectly justified in telling his dad first because his dad paid for his education. His dad's job as a professor meant that he got his classes "free" as a benefit of the job. Okay, but I didn't understand why he wasn't excited to tell me about the job.

Arnold liked the job. He started off as a traveling demonstrator of the company's software. When he left town, he almost always gave me his traveling agenda, but I remember one time when he forgot. I was really upset. What if there were an emergency? (Remember, no cell phones, yet.) He didn't think it was a big deal.

After a while, Arnold became a trainer and got a lot of compliments from his coworker students. He was proud of himself for being a good trainer without having any education in how to train. "Why would I need training? It just makes sense to teach it that way."

A year later, I was no longer in school. I didn't have the money to go back, and I didn't have an incentive because I didn't know what I wanted to do for a career. I didn't want to incur education debt without a career plan. I knew I liked to write, but I didn't know what careers were available other than novel writing and scriptwriting, neither of which seemed practical, so I worked full-time as a McDonald's Assistant Manager while I figured out what my career should be.

After a year of his "real job," Arnold wanted to buy a house. At age 19, I was content with an apartment, but this wasn't about us. It was about him. He wanted to buy himself a house. He didn't talk about buying a house with me. He only talked about buying himself a house.

I didn't think about how I felt about that.

I started searching for a house that was on a bus route to my job, that was in a neighborhood he could afford, and that was at least an "okay" commute to his job in a suburb.

One weekend when Jed and Lynn were visiting, we went to several open houses and found one house we really liked, even though it didn't have much of a curb appeal. We almost drove off without going inside. It had a big family room on the main floor that we immediately called "the game room." Arnold walked to the sliding doors and said, "It just needs a deck. I can build that."

According to a financing estimate, Arnold couldn't afford that house. He couldn't afford any of the houses that we looked at, according to the estimate. Arnold, however, knew he could make the payments. He was very particular about his finances. After Jed and Lynn had left, I was looking at the estimate while Arnold was watching TV. Hmm. I wonder what would happen if I added my income, however meager? The addition of my income bumped up the loan eligibility by quite a bit. According to the numbers, we could easily buy that house together. I could see from his expression that caught Arnold's attention, but he didn't say anything.

That night, we had an argument. Evidently, Arnold, his parents, Jed, and Lynn were invited to his uncle's home out east for Christmas. Arnold didn't tell me that—Lynn did. I was mad that Arnold didn't tell me. He was mad that Lynn *did* tell me. Lynn was my best friend. We're women. Of course, she talked to me about it because she assumed I already knew.

I was crying. For me, this was telling of how Arnold felt about us. I should've left the room, but he didn't give me time. He pulled me out of the chair and hugged me and said, "Let's buy that house as our engagement present to each other."

"What? Are you asking me to marry you?"

"MmmHmm."

"Make love to me."

"But *Star Trek* will be on soon."

Yes, recording *Star Trek* without commercials was his priority. He did have sex with me, but he also made it back into the living room in time to record *Star Trek: The Next Generation* without commercials.

I didn't like how I felt about how he proposed, but I never put words to my feelings, and I didn't let myself think about it.

We bought the house and moved in just before he and his family went out east to his uncle's home for Christmas. After we got engaged, I was invited to go along, but I didn't have the money to spend on the trip, and he didn't offer to pay.

I didn't let myself think about how I felt about that, either.

My parents were not excited about us buying a house together until they heard we were engaged. When we told Arnold's parents, his mom wanted to hear the story of how he proposed. "No," I said. I didn't tell anyone how he proposed.

Two years after we bought the house, we got married.

A few months after we were married, Arnold had his golden birthday. That's the day that your age matches the date.

I invited Arnold's best friend and his wife to go out to dinner with us at a fancy restaurant. When we got back to the house, we had a houseful of guests. Surprise! Everyone brought gag gifts, and we had a great time.

The following summer, I had surgery. The result of my annual Pap Smear was abnormal tissue. That led to more testing and eventually surgery. During the outpatient procedure, the doctor used a laser to take out a cone-shaped segment of tissue from my cervix to remove pre-cancerous cells.

I don't remember the doctors saying anything about human papillomavirus (HPV), but in hindsight I'm sure that's what I had that resulted in nearly having cervical cancer. It had been five years since I had had the abortion. Did I have HPV that whole time? When I thought about the possible cause of the precancerous cells many years later, I was mad at Arnold all over again. Had he ever taken that medication to treat the HPV?

Not long after that was my golden birthday. Arnold wanted a truck. He found the one he wanted. We decided that both of our names should be on the truck title. Maybe we decided that because we were married now everything should be in both of our names. When it came time to sign the paperwork, Arnold said my name should be first since it was my birthday.

Somehow, I got a truck for my birthday. I didn't want a truck. And I didn't get a truck, really—I didn't drive it; he did. I didn't want to drive it; he did. Yet I got all the junk mail associated with it. Yay me.

I also got a flannel shirt for my birthday because he didn't like me stealing his. His shirt was comfortable, and I thought I looked good in it. He never wore that shirt any more, but evidently he didn't like me wearing it. I wasn't happy about receiving the truck or the new shirt as birthday gifts. I was hurt. But I didn't define my feelings, and I never told him I was hurt.

About that same time, I went back to school because I found out about a degree program that I could get excited about—technical communication. I could play with computer programs and then write the instruction manuals that get sent out to the buyers. That sounded like writing I would enjoy.

The degree was officially called Scientific and Technical Communication from the Department of Rhetoric.[6] Yes, rhetoric, classical rhetoric, not "that's just *rhetoric*," but what-is-the-best-way-to-write-your-essay-or-speech-to-convince-your-audience *rhetoric*. Once in the degree program, I took a corporate scriptwriting class. Oh, I definitely enjoyed that class!

Right after that, I took a multimedia class. We scripted and "programmed" a multimedia presentation. Hmm. What would this be like today? Today, I think that you could use Adobe Flash animation software. But in 1994, we used Macromedia Director and Adobe Premiere and learned how to use the software without training. It played back from a Zip disk—no burn-able CDs, no World Wide Web.

I fell in love with multimedia. Not long after that, students in our program and I were learning how to write HTML and therefore to create our own Web pages. We couldn't do multimedia on the web, yet, but it was exciting to write something and then immediately get it online for anyone to see (that is, anyone with Internet access—we still had dial-up modems back then).

I was soon working on campus, first in the student computer lab and then in the Digital Media Center. In the Digital Media Center, we helped professors get portions of their classes online. That was a big deal in 1996.

When I finished my bachelor's degree, I thought we were going to move to Anchorage shortly thereafter because Arnold wanted to partner with his friend as a computer consultant. His friend had moved there and was doing well with his own computer consulting company. They often talked about being business partners, and Arnold loved the outdoors, which are bountiful in Alaska.

I did a bunch of research about living in Alaska. Arnold wanted to live out in the middle of nowhere. I did not. I agreed to moving to Anchorage, but I wasn't moving to any other town. I prefer city life over small towns. Anchorage, the largest city in Alaska, is smaller than the Twin Cities, but at least it is warmer in the winter and cooler in the summer. That sounded nice. I did not want to live in the cold tundra. Minnesota was cold enough.

Once I finished my degree, Arnold finally verbalized that we weren't going to move. His friend had partnered with someone else, so there was no pending partnership with Arnold.

Since we weren't moving, I started my master's degree in Rhetoric and Scientific and Technical Communication, still from the Department of Rhetoric, while working full-time at the Digital Media Center. I thought I would go on to get my PhD. We had no plans to have kids, and I loved to learn. Deep down inside, though, I wanted to feel worthy, and I thought I would feel worthy if I had a PhD.

My sister-in-law Lynn had kids. She was (and still is) a really good mom. I didn't even feel comfortable around kids. I saw that she was successful as a mother, something that I would never be because I would never have kids. Instead, I found my worth in a degree.

Arnold had no interest in having kids of his own, and neither did I. We liked being DINKS (Double Income No Kids). We took pride in it.

Most of our time together was spent in front of the TV watching James Bond movies or *Star Trek* even though we owned a canoe, a tent, and sleeping bags. On Saturdays, Arnold would put in his VHS tapes that he had recorded of *Star Trek: The Next Generation* and just let them play all day long. We would pop back into the game room to see the scenes we wanted to revisit. Otherwise, we would listen to the episodes while we were doing whatever we were doing around the house.

I got tired of sitting around the house all the time, so after my bachelor's degree, when I had real income, I would pay for us to go out for dinner. Afterwards, we would stop at the video store (remember Suncoast Motion Pictures in the malls?) to buy a new movie. Eventually, we rented from Blockbuster or Hollywood Video instead.

Even though we owned a canoe and lived in the land of 10,000 lakes (which is more like 15,256 according to Arnold's t-shirt) and almost as many rivers, we rarely went canoeing or camping. We only went camping and canoeing on Memorial Day weekend with my parents and Drew. Sometimes my brother Paul and his wife would go, too.

Paul, his wife, Arnold, and I used to double date. Usually, they would come over to watch *Star Trek* and have dinner. We went to more than one *Star Trek* convention together. There we saw Nichelle Nichols (the original Uhura) and Michael Dorn (Lt. Worf). We even went to a play that, although it had nothing to do with *Star Trek*, had Jonathan Frakes (Commander Riker) and Brent Spiner (Lt. Commander Data) as cast members.

MY PARENTS RAISED MY NEPHEW

Nancy was still living with Mom and Dad, and therefore so was Drew. Nancy wasn't getting any better, and the county was resistant to hospitalizing her. They finally told my parents that they couldn't hospitalize Nancy because she was living in their house. The laws make it difficult to hospitalize an adult with mental illness because historically Americans would put family members in psychiatric hospitals whether they had a mental illness or not. Sometimes people would commit their family members because they couldn't afford to take care of them or because they didn't like them or because spouses didn't want the stigma of divorce.

This meant that the only way for my sister to get the help she needed was for my parents to tell her she had to leave their house and then for someone else to recognize that she was a danger to herself or others. She wasn't a danger to others. She just wasn't capable of taking care of herself.

My parents chose Labor Day weekend. They sent Drew to stay with Paul and his wife and then talked to Nancy. She left. Dad followed her around all weekend to make sure she was okay.

Nancy ended up at a Salvation Army soup kitchen at which she had once volunteered. The man running the kitchen that night recognized her schizophrenia and called the police. The police took her to the hospital. The hospital sent her to a state psychiatric hospital. It was there that she finally got on medicine that helped her. Eventually, she transitioned to her own apartment across the county line from my parents. That was a good choice because that county had a lot more money for psychiatric care than the one in which my parents lived.

My parents got custody of Drew. This seemed to take the pressure off of Nancy. She got a really good social worker and settled into her new way of life.

At her social worker's suggestion, Nancy decided to get a Psychiatric Living Will, which was a new thing at the time. Typically, people with mental illness are in denial that they have the illness. So when they are thinking clearly, they sign the Psychiatric Living Will to acknowledge they have the illness and to give consent to be medicated even if they refuse at the time of hospitalization.

At first, the social worker thought Nancy should have someone be the doctor's contact to get permission to medicate her. She originally asked Grandma to be that person, but Grandma declined, saying, "You need someone younger. We don't know how much longer I'll live."

Nancy decided to ask Paul and me. Paul and I drove the 90 minutes to Mom and Dad's house and met with Nancy, her social worker, and Mom. It must have been the middle of the week because Dad wasn't there. At the time, he worked a long way from home and was only home on the weekends.

That night, we asked a lot of questions about the document. I was blown away by Paul's ability to remember what information was on which page. Mom had always said he had a photographic memory, but that night was the first time I had experienced it myself.

Paul and I agreed to be the doctor's contacts. A few weeks later, the recommendation changed that we should simply be witnesses so that the doctor could administer the medication even if he couldn't get in contact with us.

Today, the document is called a Psychiatric Advance Directive.

Before we left that night, I had one more question. This one was specifically for Nancy and had nothing to do with the document. I had heard from Mom that Nancy said Dad had abused her. So, I asked Nancy if that was true.

"Yes."

"When did Dad abuse you?"

"It was in the trailer," she said. We lived in a mobile home until shortly after Nancy graduated from high school. "I wanted to go out with my friends. Dad said, 'No,' and slapped me across the face."

"Were there any other incidents?" I asked.

"No."

I didn't tell Nancy that I didn't believe her, but I didn't and I don't. When we lived in the trailer, we had one car. The likelihood that Mom, Paul, and I would be out of the house with the car while Dad was home alone—even if Nancy had been dropped off by her friends—were slim to none.

Dad and Nancy had a good relationship until schizophrenia. After schizophrenia, Nancy actively avoided Dad. That's still true today.

Mom and Dad raised Drew. Well, mostly Mom raised Drew. Dad was working three-and-a-half hours away. He had an apartment near work and drove home for the weekends. Several years later, he changed jobs and worked one-and-a-half hours away. He bought a triplex there, lived in one of the apartments, rented out the other two, and was home on the weekends.

Mom was working full-time, raising her grandson, and managing Nancy's finances. But it was more than that. Nancy would be over at Mom and Dad's house a lot. She didn't do anything to help with her son or the house, but she would talk and talk while she paced. She made perfect sense, and she was talking to Mom, not to her imaginary friend, but it was exhausting for my mom.

Drew was not an easy child to raise, especially when he was in high school, but today he is 30-something, married, and the worship leader at his church.

PAUL'S DIVORCE

Paul's wife divorced him. Remember that she was Jewish? I only mention that because Paul chose to convert to Judaism after the divorce. I never got a straight answer from him as to why he waited to convert. I always thought it would've made more sense to convert to Judaism while married to a Jew. Wouldn't that make sense?

I went with Paul to my parents to tell them about his conversion to Judaism. My mom, who is a preacher's kid, did not like hearing this at all, but it seemed to hit my dad hardest because Paul's conversion meant that he wouldn't sing Christian music with my dad any more. My dad loved singing duets with Paul, but so much classical music is Christian. Just about everything that my dad composed was Christian. There were no more duets.

MY DIVORCE

I had been married eight years when it became abundantly clear that something wasn't right. I started having nightmares that Arnold wanted a divorce. It didn't make sense because when we talked about divorce before we married, he was adamant that divorce was never an option. It wasn't for me, either. We both felt strongly that marriage was forever.

Yet it seemed like Arnold had no love for me. I can't remember what we argued about that night, but I remember telling him that I was having nightmares that he wanted to divorce me. I got emotional and went into another room.

You see, I usually didn't get emotional. The last time I was emotional was the night we got engaged, but that is honestly the last time I remember getting emotional until this night—10 years later. This time, I did leave the room.

Arnold followed me and sat down next to me. It was his way of telling me that divorce was exactly what he wanted. Even as we talked over the next couple weeks, Arnold didn't say the word *divorce* until I pointed out to him that he hadn't said it. So, then he said the word: "Divorce. There. I said it."

Arnold agreed to counseling, so we went weekly. In one counseling session—or maybe it was afterwards because we would talk for hours after we met with the counselor—I found out that Arnold proposed to me in order to get me to stop crying. In my head I thought, *and to get the house. He proposed that night to get me to stop crying and to get the house that he wanted.*

I felt used.

My brother Paul went with me to tell my parents that Arnold was divorcing me. Arnold was responsible for telling Jed and Lynn because Jed is his brother, and because Arnold always gets upset with me when I tell Lynn things. I don't know the particulars, but Lynn later told me that Arnold sent them an email with the news and that she and Jed were really upset to hear the unpleasant news that way.

Arnold's mom wanted to understand why we were getting a divorce. She would propose reasons via email, and I would "Reply All" saying, "No, that's not it." I wouldn't tell her why. Telling her was Arnold's responsibility, not mine. He was the reason we were getting a divorce, not me. I probed and probed to find out why. The only reason he said that made any sense was, "I don't love you, and I'm not sure that I ever did."

I remember Lynn telling me years later that she was teaching her kids how to know if they were in love. One of the ways, she said, was that person is the first person you want to talk to when something good happens in your life.

Arnold, however, wasn't excited to tell me about his first job. He wasn't excited to buy a house with me (until I was providing the income that allowed him to get a loan). He wasn't excited to take me out on dates (I paid for them). He wasn't excited to celebrate my birthday (the truck was just one example). The only flower he ever gave me was on the day of my abortion. There was even one anniversary that we were going to be apart, and he had no interest in celebrating on another day—we were either going to celebrate on our anniversary or not at all.

Did he love me? I didn't feel loved. Why didn't I ever think about this before we got married? Why wouldn't I let myself contemplate all those things until he wanted a divorce?

"If you didn't love me, then why did you marry me?" I asked.

"To take care of you. I had gotten you pregnant. I felt bad. And you didn't want to live with your parents. I like helping people," he said.

In my head I added, *And you got sex.* Yes, I felt used.

I moved out.

Usually the person who wants the divorce moves out, but I didn't want that house. I never wanted that house. I just wanted to be married to Arnold.

Arnold suggested that I move in with my brother because, in Arnold's estimation, I couldn't afford to live on my own on my salary from the university—or so he thought. I was offended once again.

I did the math and figured out that I could easily afford an apartment, so I moved out and lived on my own for the first time in my life—at age 30.

Arnold had the divorce paperwork written up by a paralegal, not a lawyer. He would get the house. He had paid for it, so that made sense. My girlfriends were livid and talked me into hiring a lawyer.

After some convincing, I did hire a female lawyer. The lawyer told me that, according to Minnesota law, I had a right to half of our assets. My job was to figure out what half was, and she told me how to do that. I hated the process. I hated negotiating with Arnold. I hated going back-and-forth with him on what our assets were and advocating for myself to get the half to which I was legally entitled.

I was living in my "divorce apartment." It was winter, and I have never been a Minnesotan who likes winter. Minnesota winters are long. This winter, I was depressed.

I got a call from my parents telling me that my brother, Paul, had not been heard from in about a month, so my parents drove the 90 minutes to his house and knocked on his door.

Paul shuffled to the door and answered. Evidently, he had turned off the phone's ringer for Shabbat (the Jewish Sabbath) and forgot to turn it back on. Something was wrong with the car and now with all the snow, it was plowed in, or maybe Minneapolis towed it away because they did not like cars left on the street when they are plowing. Paul's legs were hurting, so he couldn't walk to the grocery store. He had eaten everything he had in the house, and Dad and Mom said he was really thin. Why didn't he think to call someone?

My parents convinced Paul to go to the hospital to get help for his legs. He agreed. It didn't take long for the hospital to admit him to the psych ward. It was clear to the medical professionals that he was a danger to himself since he wasn't doing whatever was necessary to eat.

My parents had now put both my sister and my brother in the hospital. I was *not* going to be next.

It was like someone slapped me out of my stupor. I was suddenly tired of being depressed and now determined to stand up for myself with Arnold. I started walking around Como Lake, which was not far from my St. Paul apartment, in my big winter boots even though I hated being in the snow. The angrier I was at Arnold, the faster I walked.

Arnold was not happy about splitting the value of the house. He looked for every way he could think of to reduce the value. Most notably, he wanted to deduct the roof repairs, which were started and messed up by the roofer long before we separated. He finally gave in on that. However, he wouldn't include my student debt as part of the calculations. He didn't have any student debt, of course, because his dad's job as a professor paid for his education. He reasoned that he was poor all through college whereas he took care of me while I was in college.

Fine. Whatever. I was still going to be financially okay even if I accepted the student loans as my own rather than ours. At this point, I just wanted to be done with the negotiating.

My lawyer wrote up the paperwork. I was okay with everything except it said *I* was petitioning for divorce. I asked her to change the paperwork to the way his paralegal had written it, saying *he* was petitioning for divorce because this was his idea, not mine. She explained that she couldn't change it. Because my lawyer was the one who wrote it up, the paperwork had to say I was petitioning for divorce. I even had to appear in court as the petitioner. He did not have to go to court at all. I was livid.

Once again, I did all the work while he sat *Feeling* back and waited for the results. That's what *Insecure* happened with finding the house. That's what *Neurotic and* happened with moving to Alaska. That's even *Emotional* what happened with the disagreement he had with the roofer.

I was angry during the divorce. I was stressed during the divorce. When people asked me, "How are you?" I'd respond, "FINE," which really meant Feeling Insecure, Neurotic, and Emotional. It was my own code word. If you knew me, you knew that FINE meant that I was not okay.

4
GETTING MY PAST OUT OF MY FUTURE

Not long after my divorce was final, a friend told me about a class she took called the Landmark Forum. I don't remember what she told me about it, but it piqued my interest. I went to an information meeting, used my own life as an example to work through with the group, and decided I needed to take the class.

How do I explain the Forum? Well, I have always told people that it's about getting your past out of your future. That's what it was for me.

It was an intense three days of figuring out what it was I was angry about. Not that I *thought* I was angry when I went into the class. I still didn't let myself think much about how I felt.

But I was angry. I realized I had put up a wall around my heart, and I wouldn't let feelings in.

I thought I was mad at Arnold (and I was). I thought I was mad at Nancy (and I was). I even thought I was mad at Drew because he took all the attention away from me when he was a toddler living in "my" house.

Then I realized I was also mad at my parents. I was able to pinpoint the moment I stopped letting feelings in. It was the night my parents didn't show up for *The King and I.*

Part of the Forum required homework. We were to call someone and tell them how we felt in a kind way and to add that we wanted a different kind of future. I called my dad. I told him about the class and that I realized I was hurt by him choosing Nancy over me the night they were supposed to be at *The King and I* (some 14 years earlier).

I knew my parents had done the best they knew how, yet I was hurt.

My dad took the call very well and loved me well. I don't know what that call did for my dad, but for me it was freeing. I had forgiven him.

After the class, I had a similar phone call with my mom. She had a harder time with what I had to say, but she was kind. Again, I don't know what that call did for my mom, but for me it was freeing. I had forgiven her.

My sister was pretty stable at this time. She was quirky, but her schizophrenia was not obvious. As a result, I had a conversation with her, too. I didn't talk to her about her illness or about her interrupting my life by moving into my parents' home, but I did talk to her about a particular nickname she had for me, "Shortstuff," and how I didn't want her to call me that any more. I thought the nickname was belittling. She said, "okay" and she hasn't called me by that nickname since.

I asked Nancy if she had anything she wanted to say to me. She said she didn't like it when I followed her around when I was little (for example, when I was 4 and she was 12) or how I liked things she liked (for example, jazz music). I laughed and said that everything she did was interesting, and she had good taste. She seemed surprised at my response; maybe she seemed a little more self-confident, too. She laughed. I apologized for annoying her when I was little. Since then, we've been able to laugh together.

I took another class from Landmark, which I'll tell you about later. My dad did the Landmark Forum, and so did my nephew, who was 15 years old at this time.

FORGIVING ARNOLD

Even after Landmark, I would have conversations in my head with Arnold. I would replay scenes in my head and change what I said to what I should have said and said it with confidence—in my head.

Then it hit me. I was just getting more upset as I replayed these scenes. I didn't feel better by venting. Venting just put me in a bad mood. But how do I stop?

Then the next thought hit me. *I could forgive Arnold.* The silence in my head was deafening. I didn't know what to do with that thought. Well, I guess I could forgive him. So, I did.

The next time I started to replay scenes in my head, I stopped myself and forgave him. And I did it again. And again. Until one day Arnold no longer popped into my head.

It was wonderful! It was freeing!

Arnold didn't know, of course, that I was upset with him. It's not like I ever called him up and told him I was still mad about this thing or the other. He didn't know I forgave him, either.

It was that day I realized forgiveness is less about the other person and more about me. When I am unforgiving, I am miserable. The other person isn't miserable much because he doesn't even know! When I forgive, I let go and I feel better.

The only way Arnold will ever know I had those conversations in my head is if he reads this book. Poor guy. Can you imagine reading all those things about yourself never knowing the other person felt that way? If Arnold ever writes his memoir about our relationship, I am quite certain

How ironic is that? The two of us who never wanted kids now both have kids. Interesting how people change, isn't it? Him and me both.

I will not be happy about what he says about me. I'm sure I owe him all sorts of apologies.

Arnold is a different person today. He is married and has two kids. How ironic is that? The two of us who never wanted kids now both have kids.

Last summer, I went to Uganda and had the opportunity to speak to teens about the sexual purity and abortion. I knew that once I got back, I was going to blog about these same topics and that my own abortion would become public knowledge. I told Arnold I was going to be speaking publicly and blogging about my abortion because he needed to know before a mutual friend told him. He surprised me with a truly kind response.

Arnold now plays in the worship band at a church. Playing in a band doesn't surprise me. That the band is a worship band does! Seems that Arnold found healing.

Interesting how people change, isn't it? Him and me both.

EVERYTHING BUT LYNN

Although I got the pain from my first marriage out of my future, I kept my best friend Lynn. Lynn made it clear that the divorce did not include her, and we became even better friends. We have adopted each other as sisters of the heart, and we look enough alike that people think we are blood related.

See if you can follow this: Arnold and Jed are brothers. Jed is married to Lynn. Lynn is the sister-of-my-heart, so Jed is still my brother-in-law, and Jed and Lynn's five children, which she bore while Arnold and I were together, are still my niece and nephews.

HUH, THAT'S DIFFERENT

It was the summer of 2000, and I was divorced. I wanted to date, but I didn't want to get married. I put an ad in the singles section of a community newspaper saying that I love rollercoasters. I was hoping to date guys who liked to go do things.

I got a call from a guy named Joe. He was really nice. Divorced. Had a real job with Northwest Airlines. I think we went out twice—once to meet and then once more. He was a nice guy, but there was no mutual romantic interest at all.

Turns out that we had both joined a group called Single Volunteers of the Twin Cities. It's a clever concept. The leaders find volunteer work and then create a sign-up for the same number of men as women. For example, there was a non-profit called Books for Africa. They needed 10 people to box books for a couple hours on a Saturday morning. Five women and five men would sign up to box books. This was a great way to get to know people who have interests similar to yours. Afterwards, the group would usually go out to a restaurant, again providing an opportunity to talk without the pressure of a date.[7]

The Single Volunteers were volunteering at the Anoka Ramsey Regional Airport's hangar dance on my 31st birthday. I didn't want to volunteer on my birthday, but it was a fundraiser, and we were encouraged to go to the dance. I did like the idea of dancing on my birthday, so I made plans to go. By myself.

I figured Joe would be there. I mean, I knew he was into airplanes, but I wasn't going to the dance to see him. I just had plans to be polite.

Joe and his friend Russ were at the dance. Russ was nice. They were both nice to me.

I danced some, but I really didn't talk to many people. I felt like an awkward teenager again.

I was deciding when to make my exit when Joe said he, Russ, and some others were going to get a bite to eat. Joe had invited another woman and so had Russ, so there should have been five of us, but the woman who Russ invited didn't show. There were four of us.

Russ and Joe were telling stories on each other. Evidently, they went to college together, roomed together for a while, and now were both working for Northwest Airlines.

After a while, Russ asked me about myself, so I explained that I was about to change jobs from the University of Minnesota to a dot.com consulting company and that I was about to move out of my apartment and into a condo. Oh, yes, and my master's degree. I was still working on my master's degree.

I was sitting across the table from Russ—and winking at him the whole time. I had had four surgeries by now on my left eyelid so that it wouldn't droop so much. As a result, that eyelid stays open and my right eyelid blinks like normal. But what others see is me *winking* at them. Sometimes people think that I'm being insincere, but sometimes people think I'm flirting with them. This is particularly confusing for women, who are trying to figure out if I'm a lesbian. Although I don't remember my ophthalmologists giving my condition a name, it may be that I was born with a more severe form of ptosis than actor Forest Whitaker.

Russ seemed irritated at Joe whenever he interrupted the conversation. It was charming. Russ wanted to know about me! And, of course, he thought I was flirting with him.

At one point, Joe said I needed a drink to loosen up. He was right. I was pretty quiet because I felt awkward, but I was wound pretty tightly in general. I was never good at conversations with people I didn't know well. I told Joe the drink had to be hot because I was cold sitting under the air conditioning. Arnold didn't drink, so I didn't drink. I was 31 and had no knowledge of what to order from the bar. Russ didn't have any suggestions for a hot drink. Joe suggested Baileys in hot coffee, but I don't like coffee. Yeah, I know I'm the only person in America who doesn't like coffee.[8]

Joe ordered vodka in hot chocolate. The waitress said the drinks were two for one, so I had two vodka hot chocolates sitting in front of me. I grew up in a house where you didn't leave any food unfinished. Having two vodka hot chocolates when I had little experience with alcohol was a bad idea. Stupid, actually.

Joe was right, though—I loosened up and talked more. Thankfully, I didn't say anything embarrassing.

At the end of the night, I couldn't drive. Thankfully, I lived only blocks away. I was content to walk home, but Russ wouldn't have it. He drove me to my apartment in my car, and Joe followed. Once I was safely through the secured door, Russ and Joe left.

Gentlemen. They were gentlemen.

The following weekend, I went to the Landmark Forum and got my past out of my future. While there, a young man got up, scared, and said he had no place to sleep that night. Well, I remembered that when we were done with class. I had to make sure he had a place to go. His name was Malik, and he was a 19-year-old African American man. There was one other person who was able to help him. Malik asked if we were both okay with whomever he chose. We said yes. I should've said no. I was living by myself. I had no idea if "this kid" was a thief or honest. But I said yes, and he chose to go home with me. I later figured out that he expected me to be like a mom, making meals for him and taking care of him. Ha! That's funny. I barely make food for myself.

When Malik walked into my apartment, the first thing he saw was a picture of Dr. Martin Luther King, Jr. on top of my TV. I could tell he was surprised. Maybe it was later that day or the next morning I said, "I bet you were surprised to see Dr. King's photo."

"Yeah," he said.

"I really admire Dr. King."

I don't think we ever talked about race again after that.

Russ called me and asked me out on a date. We went out for the first time on Friday after Landmark.

We had met on my birthday. The following weekend, I did the Landmark Forum. The Friday after that I went on my first date with Russ—October 6, 2000.

Russ was kind. He was interested in everything I had to say. He came from a big family—he's the oldest of seven. He thought his family was full of drama. (He does have five sisters, after all.) All I could think was, "Oh, you have no idea what family drama is."

I told him that I'm the youngest of three. I can't remember what I told him about my sister or my brother. At this point, Paul was divorced, still working in a restaurant, still going to school working towards his bachelor's degree (he would've been 37 years old at that point), and still super smart.

Russ asked me out every weekend, and I always said yes. He was smart. He had a fantastic smile, and his blue eyes lit up when he smiled. He was always a gentleman, which was actually challenging for me. I was not accustomed to (and even often hostile toward) men holding the door open for me. I was quite capable of doing that by myself, thank you. But the new me after the Landmark Forum was trying hard to let people love me. And love me, he did.

Russ fell hard and fast. That scared the crap out of me.

But when I decided to move out of my "divorce apartment" (because that's what it was to me—a reminder of my divorce) and buy a condo, I couldn't wait to show it to Russ. He liked it right up until I had my cousin sponge-paint it yellow. When I bought all new furniture, I couldn't wait to show Russ.

Hmm. Maybe. Just maybe I was in love.

But I couldn't be in love. I had just gotten a divorce. In my thinking, you don't jump from one relationship to another. That just shows how emotional you are, how unstable you are, and how you just have to have a man to take care of you. I was none of those things. I was a feminist. I didn't need a man to take care of me.

I tried to get Russ to break up with me. I told him that my sister has schizophrenia. I told him that my parents were raising my nephew, who was 15 years old. Nothing scared him away.

But I knew what would scare him away. He was a Christian. He was conservative. I was neither. Not only was I politically on the left, but I was a pro-choice feminazi.[9] Okay, so not in the militant sense that Rush Limbaugh raved about, but certainly more adamant about "women can do anything" than the dictionary definition of *feminist*.

Russ lit up every time he saw a baby. His eyes would light up then he would play with the baby. I would not. I reacted as if babies knew intuitively that I had aborted one of them, so I avoided babies.

As a result, I told Russ that I had had an abortion. I knew he would break up with me now.

He said, "That's in the past. It's over. Done."

Um, what? I was shocked. I didn't know what to do with that. He loved me despite my big sin. How could a holier-than-thou, pro-life Christian love me knowing that I had had an abortion?

And was it done? Over?

I knew that I had killed my baby—even if I wouldn't have admitted it at the time—and it seemed like every baby I had ever met knew that about me, too.

I knew that I had killed my baby—even if I wouldn't have admitted it at the time—and it seemed like every baby I had ever met knew that about me, too.

If Russ wasn't going to break up with me, then I'd have to break up with him. I knew our relationship wouldn't work. He loved babies and kids. They freaked me out. He was conservative. I was liberal. He was a Christian. I had left The Church. So, I broke up with Russ.

Then I took the Advanced Course from Landmark. While in the Advanced Course, I realized I was mad at God. I also realized that although I had let go of my past so that I could have a different future, and I was afraid to step into my future.

One of the activities that we did in the Advanced Course was to go out into the community and ask people to do things for us. For example, we could ask a restaurant manager to turn the thermostat up because we were cold. The idea was to get used to people telling us, "No." We were a bunch of Minnesotans, not New Yorkers. This was an uncomfortable exercise.

The catch, though, was that if we asked someone to do something, we had to follow through with the request. We couldn't say, "Oh, I was just kidding." Someone in my class asked me to meet her early the next morning to go for a walk around Como

Lake before we went to class. I am not a morning person, but I found this woman, Debra, interesting and wanted to talk to her more, so I said, "Yes."

When we went back to class, everyone was reporting how people always said, "Yes." Even my newfound friend Debra said everyone said, "Yes" to her requests, including me. The instructor looked at me and said, "You know you do have to show up and go for that walk, right?"

I said, "Yes," and I did show up for that walk. I was even on time. (I was never on time for anything.) On that walk, I told Debra I needed to have a conversation with someone from the church that I attended when I was in high school because I was still angry and hurt, but I didn't know who to talk to. Maybe I should talk to the pastor, but I had no idea how to find him.

Debra said, "Do you think, maybe, you're actually mad at God?" That made sense, but having a conversation with God seemed like a cop out. It's not like I could call God and get a real response from Him.

Debra suggested she pretend to be God, and I could have the conversation with her. "Why not?" I thought. So, I put my hand to my head like I was holding a phone, and I called God/Debra.

In that conversation, God/Debra said, "Don't you know that I saw everything you did and everything you went through?"[10]

That was a revelation to me. Never before had I given any thought to God knowing[11] I was mad that Nancy moved into "my" house, to Him knowing I had premarital sex, to Him knowing I had an abortion, to Him knowing I lived with my boyfriend before the wedding, to Him knowing I was unhappily married, to Him knowing I was divorced.

Well, duh, I did grow up in church, so I did hear God is omniscient.[12]

Interestingly, I didn't feel condemned by God. I felt surprised that He cared.[13]

I wasn't quite sure what to do with this revelation.

In the meantime, I realized I was in fact in love with Russ. The class talked about stepping into our future. I realized I had gotten my past out of my future, but I didn't have a clue what that future was. I didn't like not knowing.

Then it hit me that I had broken up with Russ because the idea of having a future in which a man actually loved me was scary. Even though that's what everyone wants—to be loved—I was afraid to be loved. I admitted to one of my Landmark[14] class-mates I was in love with Russ. Because when you tell someone, it becomes real. Now I had to tell Russ.

When I asked Russ if we could meet that night, he was happy to oblige. I admitted I was in love with him. You could say he was happy to hear that. I think his exact words were, "Well, it's about time you figured that out" as he smiled, and his blue eyes lit up.

I also told him, though, that if we were going to get serious, then he had to know everything about me up front. I took Russ on a tour of my life, taking him to the trailer park where we lived when my sister graduated from high school, showing him the duplex and then the house in the city, and finally introducing him to my parents and nephew.

I asked Russ about his family. He started telling me about all sorts of people, but I couldn't keep track of who was whom. We were at Perkins restaurant, which had paper place mats. I flipped over the place mat and started drawing a genealogy chart. Russ is the oldest of seven and has many cousins on both sides of his family. With the chart, I could see who was related to whom. Russ looked at me wide-eyed. "What?" I asked.

"I can't believe you just drew a chart," he said.

"My mom's a genealogist," I said. "This genealogy chart is the only way I could think of to keep track of who Aunt Joanie is and how she's related to you." He chuckled.

Sometime that fall, Russ told me that if I wasn't a Christian, then he wouldn't marry me. "Fine by me!" I responded. Even though I was letting him love me, I had no interest in getting married. I had just gotten divorced, after all. I have always looked down on people who jump from one relationship to another, and I was not going to be one of those people. Besides, I had no interest in being a Christian.

Russ invited me to his small group. I didn't know what that was. I now know that it is a group of Christians who (generally) attend the same church and get together weekly or bi-weekly to study the bible and pray together.

Well, I was not going to join a group of people who already knew each other, especially since I knew nothing about what they were studying and had no idea how to pray.

At Christmastime, I flew with Russ to Chicago to meet his parents and several of his sisters.

By New Year's, I had had enough of Malek staying in my condo. He never stole anything from me, but he used my laptop to access porn. Considering that I used my laptop for my contract work, I was pretty upset. What if something had popped up on my screen while I was working with a client? Malek also ran up my phone bill by calling 900 numbers. Of course, he didn't pay me back. I finally got the guts to send him on his way.

Russ was supportive of my helping out Malek until he figured out that Malek was taking advantage of me. Russ helped me figure out how to talk to Malek and ask him to leave, but he didn't interfere. He just supported and encouraged me as I talked to Malek on my own.

I started going to church with Russ. I have no idea how that happened. I guess I wanted to see what his church was like.

It was nothing like what I had experienced growing up. His church met in a school auditorium. They invited people to come up after the service to pray over whatever was on their hearts. They sang songs that sounded like pop music—there were no hymnals, no organ, no choir.

I remember that winter I had been curious about something written in the church bulletin. On the information card, it asked if I had a personal relationship with Christ. I grew up in church, but I didn't know what a "personal relationship with Christ" would be. What did that mean?

A Family Life marriage conference came to Minneapolis. Russ probably found out about it from church. It had a track for "pre-marrieds," and he asked me if we should go. I said, "Yes." I have no idea why I said that. It just came out of my mouth.

At the conference, they invited all of us to have a personal relationship with Christ. They had two prayers written out in one of the handouts. I read through them, and I had complete peace about both of them.

The leaders invited us to pray those prayers. Afterwards, they said if we had prayed those prayers or something like them for the first time, then we should sign our names under them. I could see Russ peeking at my handout. Yes, I signed. Here are the prayers:

Lord Jesus, I need You. Thank You for dying on the cross for my sins. I acknowledge that I am a sinner and that I am separated from You. I receive You as my Savior and Lord. Thank You for forgiving my sins and giving me eternal life. Take control of my life. Make me the kind of person You want me to be.

Dear Father, I confess that I have been in control of my own life, and as a result, I have sinned against You. I invite You to have unhindered access to all of my life. Fill me with the Holy Spirit as I now allow You complete control of my life. As an expression of my faith, I now thank You for directing my life and filling me with the Holy Spirit. In Jesus' name, amen. [15]

At our lunch break, Russ led me through the Minneapolis skyways until we found a jewelry store—to shop for an engagement ring.

Later in the conference, there was a session for pre-marrieds in which the men went in one room and the women went in another. In the women's session, the speaker talked about biblical submission. Okay, now submission is one of the reasons this particular feminazi—that's me—was anti-Christian. But I didn't go into the session hostile. I was curious as to what the speaker had to say. I wasn't offended. Can you believe that? At the end of the session, Russ found me crying. I wanted to live this biblical lifestyle, but I didn't know how to do that. Russ comforted me and prayed.

Later, I read books on biblical submission. One was particularly helpful: *Creative Counterpart* by Linda Dillow.[16] She described the husband-wife relationship as similar to running a corporation. There can be only one CEO and the rest of the corporation follows the CEO's leadership. Well, I could identify with that. I've worked for a university and for corporations. I can tell the difference in what gets done when things are decided by committee (whether at the university or at a corporation) rather than by a team leader. Yes, we all contribute to the leader's decision, but the leader has the final say. When I've worked on projects with leaders who make decisions, projects get done. When I've worked on projects who have a committee with no designated leader or with two people fighting for the leadership role, the projects take forever to get done and are not fun to work on. After I understood biblical submission, I was resolved to make Russ the CEO, and I would take a title of COO—Chief Operating Officer.

THE PROPOSAL

Russ proposed to me on Easter Sunday. We drove the 90 minutes to my parents' house for dinner. Drew sat to my right. Russ sat to my left. Drew was wearing cargo pants. I accidentally hit the pocket near his left knee and noticed that something hard and box-shaped was in his pocket. I asked him what it was. He said, "Don't go there, Cheryl." I bugged him about it for a little while and then let it go.

At the end of dinner, I excused myself. My stomach wasn't feeling very well. While I was gone, Russ asked my parents for their blessing. When I returned, I was standing behind him. He wanted me to sit down, but I didn't want to sit because my stomach was still upset. After trying to convince me again, he said, "Okay, then I'll do it like this." He got down on one knee and asked me to marry him.

I was surprised! I knew he was going to propose, but I never expected him to ask me in front of my family. I think I said something like, "Of course I'll say, 'Yes!'"

Russ reached his hand out to Drew and said, "Drew!?!" Drew handed him the box that had been in his pocket, and Russ pulled out the ring.

"You!" I pointed at Drew, who laughed and laughed!

MY RUSS

Russ is a hard worker. At the time we got married, he was a shift manager in airline maintenance. He worked second shift, which was about 3-11 pm. Before he would go to work, he would do yard work or house maintenance projects. He was always making sure the house was in tip-top shape.

Russ owned the cutest house on the block. It was a 1940s one-and-a-half story foursquare with stucco exterior and beautiful hardwood floors on the interior. He and the neighbors across the street, who were groundskeepers for golf courses, had the two best lawns on the block.

Russ didn't buy the house because it was the cutest. He bought the house because it had a dry, flat basement for his workshop because he is a woodworker who wanted space for all the tools he owned. And he owned many! If you were to ask him if you could borrow a clamp, he would say, "What size do you need?" He works with tools at work, and he works with tools at home.

Russ is also a news hound and a voracious reader. He reads everything. He always knows what's going on in the world. He also knows everything about every airplane. He and his friend Joe look at every airplane or helicopter flying overhead to see what kind it is. Russ usually identifies it by sound and then verifies by sight.

Russ also knows everyone. He remembers everyone's name (I rarely know someone's name). He's a genuine networker without a hint of cheesiness. He's also a good judge of character. Whereas I am always assuming the best, Russ quickly assesses whether someone is genuine.

FOLLOWING RATHER THAN LEADING

Following, rather than leading, did not come naturally to me. It was a challenge even in the simple things. For example, Russ and I would be holding hands and walking in downtown Minneapolis, enjoying the outdoor concerts or walking to Brit's Pub. Russ would guide me by moving our hands in the direction he thought we should go. At the same time, I would guide him by moving our hands in the direction that *I* thought we should go. I had to learn to trust that his decision would work out fine. It didn't have to be my way, and my way was not the right way but a different way. We talked about following him rather than leading—we even joked about it. Slowly, I learned to let go of control.

CHANGING MY LAST NAME

When Arnold and I married, I didn't change my last name. I tried to convince him that we should both change our last names, but he wouldn't even consider it. He said, "You can do whatever you want, but I'm not changing my name." That was the end of that.

With Russ, I was still a bit of a feminazi. I wasn't going to change my name just because that's what everyone else did. As a result, the name I was given at birth was mine for 31 years.

Russ assumed that I was going to change my name when we married. I was not happy. He was not happy. He felt like I was emasculating him. I didn't even know what that meant, so I looked it up in the big unabridged dictionary that was on his built-in book shelf. Basically, it means that I was depriving him of strength, that he was feeling effeminate. But I was offended, too, that my name wasn't good enough.

After about a month of not talking about it, I decided to take his name. We were walking around Lake Harriet when the topic came up again. I said something about the marriage license and getting my name changed. Russ said, "But we haven't decided about that, yet."

I got in front of him to look him in the eye and said, "Yes, we have." We both smiled, and he kissed me.

> *Cheryl Krichbaum is not just my married name. It's my Christian name.*

Today, I consider Cheryl Krichbaum to not just be my married name but my Christian name because I became a true believer in Christ the same year that Russ and I married. The Lord gave me a new name when I chose Him.

FINDING FORGIVENESS FOR MYSELF

Russ has several nieces and nephews, but it struck me that two nieces were the same age as my daughter would have been. One of those nieces is adopted. I couldn't help but think that my daughter could have been adopted by a nice couple like Russ' brother and sister-in-law.

Remorseful. I felt remorseful. It's as if the Lord softly said to me: "Come now, let us reason together" (Isaiah 1:18a NASB), an invitation to discuss my decision to abort.

Nine months after we were married, we went to a couples' retreat-like conference through our church. They told us ahead of time that there would be baptisms, but I didn't think much of it. However, when the night came, I felt compelled to tell my story. I leaned over and asked Russ in a whisper, "Okay with you if I talk about my abortion?"

"If that's what you feel compelled to do, then do it!"

I went up on the stage. Another couple from our small group was up there, too. I don't know all the details of their story, but they shared how they had sinned against each other for years. Even though they were each broken by what the other had done, they wanted to stay together. Someone told them about our church, and they started going. Gradually, their relationship became better and better.

The first time I had heard their story at a small group meeting, I cried the whole time because I realized that unlike the two of them, Arnold had no interest in staying with me even though I wanted to stay with him. That was heartbreaking. It was the final nail in the coffin of our dead marriage. Even though I bawled my eyes out at hearing their testimony, I knew that I was completely free. My love for Arnold was completely gone. I was Russ' forever.

After the couple told their story to the 200 men and women in the hotel conference hall, I told mine. I explained how I didn't want to be in my parents' home, that I got pregnant, that I had an abortion. I explained how Russ had been Christ-like in my life, showing me love despite my big sin. Then the following words came out of my mouth:

"But now I know that I am washed white as snow."

"Come now, let us reason together. Though your sins are as scarlet, they will be as white as snow."
(Isaiah 1:18)

I knew in my gut that those words were in the Bible somewhere, but I don't remember reading them.

"White as snow." God had forgiven me. I felt vulnerable. Exposed. Naked. But clean! I was shaking.

After we all told our stories, we changed clothes and got into the pool. I was baptized by Russ and the wife of our small group leader—a full dunk.

Afterwards, one of the pastors, Pastor Brendon, came up to me and gave me a hug.

There were many pastors there. Pastor Brendon was the only one to give me a hug. Of the 200 people there, he was the only person who said anything to me—except Russ, of course, who was as happy as can be at how brave I was to confess my sins and to choose baptism.

Although I was more aware of my feelings since choosing Russ and Christ, I still didn't think too much about how people reacted or didn't react to my story. I think it bothered me more in later years upon reflection. I expected them to be more excited about a lost soul choosing Christ. Now I know that they didn't know how to respond to me. They had no intention of hurting me at all, but I felt judged nonetheless. Perhaps that's when I first felt like I was wearing a Scarlet Letter A for abortion.

Today I know that "washed white as snow" is in the Bible in more than one place. King David, after sinning with Bathsheba and having her husband killed to cover his sin, said:

"Purify me with hyssop, and I shall be clean; wash me, and I shall be whiter than snow." (Psalms 51:7 NASB)

Through the prophet Isaiah, God says:

"Wash yourselves, make yourselves clean; remove the evil of your deeds from My sight. Cease to do evil... Come now, let us reason together. *Though your sins are as scarlet, they will be as white as snow; though they are red like crimson, they will be like wool." (Isaiah 1:16, 18 NASB*[17]*, emphasis mine)*

These verses and my testimony are now captured in a worship song—not that it was written about me, but it certainly feels like my theme song: "Glorious Day" by Passion featuring Kristian Stanfill.[18]

STRIVING

5

STRIVING TO FIX HIS CIRCUMSTANCES

R uss and I were married three weeks before the 9/11 tragedy of 2001. He worked for an airline. I worked for a failing dot.com consulting company. I owned a condo in a downtown high rise, and I put it up for sale on 9/12. Great timing.

A couple weeks after 9/11, I got laid off. The airline did lay off people, but thankfully Russ wasn't one of them. However, we didn't sell my condo until the following spring. At least I was unemployed for only about six weeks.

That first year of marriage was not challenging because we had to learn to live together but because of external things going on in our lives, like my parents separating, my nephew running away, and my brother losing his house to foreclosure and becoming homeless, all in addition to my unemployment and our two mortgages.

My brother Paul and I were not friends growing up. I was the irritating little sister, six years younger and seven years behind in school because of my fall birthday. Paul was my mysterious big brother. Nancy (two years older than Paul and eight years older than me) acted like our second mom, and that was irritating to both Paul and me. But after we were both married (back when I was married to Arnold), Paul and I enjoyed spending time together.

I remember that before he converted to Judaism, we were cooking together. Paul loved to cook. We decided to make Swiss Steak, which is a slow cooker meal that Mom used to make on Sundays. She would put it in the slow cooker before we went to church and it would be ready when we got home.

The recipe says that we should pound the meat. Paul and I had never pounded meat before, so we didn't know why, what it should look like when it's done, or for how long we should pound it. So, I called Mom.

"Hello?" She answered.

"How long do we pound it for?" I asked. Paul was laughing in the background. I hadn't said, "Hello." I didn't tell her who was calling (and that was long before caller ID). She knew exactly who was calling and just laughed. Mom and I still enjoy telling that story.

As adults, Paul and I became good friends. When I worked at the university, he would find me and sit by my desk to talk.

Of course, it helped that my desk was in the library. He was quite the nerd. He didn't have his bachelor's degree, but he knew Hebrew, Aramaic, and Mandarin and was doing PhD-level work in computational linguistics.

When Russ and I were engaged, Paul's house went through foreclosure. He got some cash out of the deal and decided to travel. He packed up all his books in his car and started driving.

I guess his car broke down in another state, and he had to put his books into a storage unit. Somehow, and I don't remember the particulars, he made it back to Minneapolis. He thought he had missed our wedding. I remember when he called me, he said, "Hello, Mrs. Krichbaum." Well, the joke was on him because the wedding was a couple weeks away, and he had no excuse for not being there.

Paul found an apartment, but he never found a job. I'm not sure if he ever looked for a job.

One day, Paul stopped by our house to visit and told me people were talking about him wherever he went. He described how he was in downtown Minneapolis near the courthouse, and a man was on his phone reporting to someone where Paul was. Another time, he was on the bus, and the police were following him. Yet another time, he was at a café, and the same cars were driving by over and over. He even wrote down their license plate numbers.

I told Paul that I was concerned about him. I didn't say that none of it sounded real, but it didn't sound real. He said, "I'm concerned, too." He meant he was concerned about his safety. I meant I was concerned about his mental state, but I didn't know how to express that without upsetting him.

Paul's money ran out, and he stopped paying the rent. Sometime in the spring after Russ and I married, Paul was evicted.

Mom and Dad had split up by this time. Dad was living with his girlfriend. Mom was raising Drew, who was 17 years old. Nancy had her own apartment and, all-in-all, seemed to be doing well.

Russ and I like going to movies. We like romantic comedies and action flicks. One Saturday night, he asked me what movie I wanted to see. I suggested "A Beautiful Mind."[19] It looked like a good action movie.

"A Beautiful Mind" is not an action movie. "A Beautiful Mind" is a story about John Forbes Nash, Jr., a mathematical genius who won a Nobel Prize. He also had schizophrenia.

As soon as Nash's diagnosis was revealed, I started crying. Russ asked me if I wanted to leave. I said, "No, I have to see how this ends." I cried through the rest of the movie.

That was the first time I thought about what schizophrenia might be like for Nancy. I was glad she didn't receive electric shock treatment like Nash had. The scariest thing to me, though, was that Nash didn't remind me so much of Nancy—he reminded me of Paul.

It shortly became clear to me that Paul had a mental illness, and I was guessing it was schizophrenia. He said people in the hallway were talking about him. He said the police were following him. He said people on cell phones around him were reporting his whereabouts to the police.

Paul had arranged with family friends to live with them for a while. That was a bad idea. I knew he would stay there indefinitely. The friend had young children, and I didn't want them to see what mental illness looked like. I also didn't want the friend to be in the position of having to ask Paul to leave. As a result, I called the friend and explained the situation and compelled him to call Paul to say they couldn't have him stay with them after all.

Why didn't Paul live with me? Or with one of my parents? Because we all knew from our experience with Nancy that Paul would not get the help he needed if he lived with family. Remember the law does not allow family to commit adult family members. A person has to be a danger to himself or others—and that has to be noticed by someone other than the family.

Some 12 years earlier, my parents gently told Nancy she had to move out. It broke their hearts. She wouldn't go to the hospital on her own, though, because she didn't think she was mentally ill. My dad followed her around all weekend until someone else recognized that she was not taking care of herself.

The same was now true for Paul. He didn't think he had a mental illness. It broke my heart to leave Paul in the parking lot of his apartment with only his backpack and his bike. I have no idea where he slept that night.

I have replayed Paul's eviction day over and over in my head. There are things I wish I had done differently, and I hope Paul will forgive me someday. But I knew Paul could not live with anyone in the family because no one was ready to go through the pain of asking him to leave if that were necessary to get him the help he needed.

I had intermittent contact with Paul's rabbi. He was upset with me for not providing Paul housing. I tried to explain, but he didn't understand.

I cried. How do you explain that loving someone sometimes means not giving them a handout?

My dad and I took turns meeting Paul for lunch once per week. By doing so, we knew that he was fed, we would know where he was staying, we could encourage him to get help, we could give him some cash, and we could buy him the practical things he needed.

Why didn't my mom meet Paul for lunch? Because she was already stressed with raising Drew, helping Nancy, taking care of Grandma, and emotionally dealing with her divorce.

Mom and Dad used a "divide-and-conquer" strategy without even realizing they were doing so. Mom got Drew, Nancy, and Grandma. Dad got Paul. Everyone had their hands full.

Russ and I had been married for a year when I started taking a class offered by the National Alliance for the Mentally Ill (NAMI).[20] Today the class is called NAMI Family Basics. The class was taught by a couple who had an adult child with a mental illness, and everyone in the class had a family member with a mental illness.

We learned about a long list of mental illnesses. We learned how to communicate with our family members. We learned what our rights were in light of HIPPAA. What I remember most is that although the doctors couldn't tell us much, if anything, we could tell them everything. It was through that class I became more and more convinced Paul had schizophrenia.

Dad had an idea to convince Paul to see a doctor. Dad could buy rental property in which Paul could live on the condition that he got help. Paul said no. He thought we were manipulating him.

Paul's refusal just made me all the more worried. My beloved brother was homeless, had a mental illness, and refused to be treated. Here I was tested once again by a sibling with schizophrenia.

The last time I was confronted with schizophrenia—when my sister was first sick some fifteen or so years earlier—I left the church. When I left the church, I made all sorts of bad decisions, like premarital sex, abortion, living with my boyfriend, and marrying the wrong guy—all done in the wrong order, too.

Was I going to leave the church this time? No. I wanted help. I wanted help from my church. I was not going to feel abandoned by church again. I wasn't going to go through this storm anonymously. As a result, I went to church for help.

With all that Russ and I were going through in our first couple years of marriage, we were up front after service praying with the prayer team every Sunday. *Every* Sunday.

After praying one Sunday, Pastor Brendon told me to go to my small group leaders for support. They were a nice couple with several kids. She was friendly and made time for me even though her kids were active all around us.

I also called the church office to ask if they could recommend a Christian counselor because I was having a hard time with everything that was going on in our family. They did, and I started receiving counseling.

I felt responsible for Paul. I was striving to fix the situation. If only I could convince him to get help. The counselor pointed out that I was the youngest, not the oldest. "Yeah, but I act like the oldest, and the oldest has a mental illness herself." He also pointed out that this responsibility was largely my parents'. "Yeah, but they are stressed with divorce, caring for others, and their jobs, and they live 90 minutes away."

I asked the counselor about whether Paul would get violent. It was nagging at me. The counselor asked me where I got the idea that he might be violent. Then I realized I had gotten the idea from *Law & Order*. I watched all the *Law & Order* series, but the one that had schizophrenics on the show all the time was *Law & Order: Criminal Intent*. I swear someone on that writing team had someone in their life with schizophrenia because schizophrenia was in the storyline all the time. I stopped watching *Criminal Intent*.

Later, I watched *Criminal Minds*. I love crime shows, and this one was intriguing. What I didn't like about the show was all the gore. I would close my eyes during the gore, but once the storyline included more and more schizophrenia, I stopped watching it altogether. I was not going to let someone else's fiction affect my view of my siblings.

I searched the Bible for verses about worrying because I was worrying *a lot*. I read the verses over and over. I added these verses to my email signature so that I would see them all the time. I would read them when I went to bed, and they would help me get to sleep. Here they are:

"Do not be worried about your life," Jesus said in Matthew 6:25. In verse 27, He adds, *"And who of you by being worried can add a single hour to his life?" (NASB)*

In Philippians 4:6, the Apostle Paul says, *"Be anxious for nothing, but in everything by prayer and supplication with thanksgiving let your requests be made known to God." (NASB)*

The Apostle Peter said, *"Cast all your anxiety on Him because He cares for you." (1 Peter 5:7 NIV)*

One night, I finally understood what God was telling me. I read the whole section in Matthew 6 about worrying from verse 25 to 34 and got stuck on verse 33. I read it over and over. Jesus said:

"But seek first His kingdom and His righteousness, and all these things will be added to you." (Matthew 6:33 NASB)

"But seek first His kingdom and His righteousness." What does it mean to seek first His kingdom and His righteousness? What is His kingdom and how do I seek it? How do I seek His righteousness here on earth? These were all questions I was asking myself.

Then it hit me. If I put God first in my life, I will worry less. As a result, I worked on trusting God more and worrying less.

One Sunday after service, we were again praying with Pastor Brendon. I was still worried, even though I was less so. I didn't know what I should do for my brother Paul. Pastor Brendon pointed out that when Paul is in heaven and has to account for his life, he cannot say, "My sister did this," or "My sister didn't do that." He will be accountable for his own life.[21]

Whoa. I hadn't thought of it like that before.

Paul was an adult. He was accountable for his own life. He could choose to get help. He chose not to. I felt like a burden had been lifted off my shoulders.

I was pregnant with our first boy, Daniel, but I continued to have lunch with Paul every week. Dad would still join us every other week, sometimes every week. I never canceled. I made time, even though I was working, even though I was getting the house ready for the baby, even though I was tired from pregnancy.

A couple weeks before my due date, Paul told me that he wasn't going to meet me for lunch anymore because of the baby. He didn't want to get in the way of what I needed to do for the baby. I know that sounds considerate, but I just cried. Wasn't that my decision to make? Don't you think that I would feel better if I knew you were okay?

I was a mess.

Dad and his fiancée, Bea, brought Paul to the hospital to visit me after Daniel was born. Paul brought me a gift. Now, I was sure my future stepmom took him shopping and paid for the gift, but it was sweet, and Paul seemed proud that he could give me something. I don't remember everything that was in that box, but I do remember the wooden letter blocks. Paul is such an intellectual, such a forever learner, and he chose those blocks so that my boy would learn. I'm keeping them forever.

After that, Paul didn't meet me for lunch. It was his choice. I would've taken baby Daniel and met him, but Paul said no. Dad met Paul for lunch about every other week until Paul stopped showing up. Then we lost contact with him completely. We didn't know where he was or whether he was okay.

When Daniel was about 10 months old, I took him downtown to the farmer's market on the Nicollet Mall. Every Thursday, the Minneapolis farmer's market would be on the outdoor mall through lunchtime. I loved the farmer's market. I got to be in the city (not far from my condo, which now belonged to someone else but remained near-and-dear to my downtown-loving heart), and I got to shop for Minnesota-grown fruits and vegetables.

I was pushing the stroller while shopping for strawberries. California has nothing on Minnesota-grown strawberries. Bigger is *not* better when it comes to strawberries. I was going to make strawberries and cream for my friend that night. My friends and I were having a little baby shower for her at my place.

As I walked the mall, I saw up ahead that there was a group praying on the corner. They were wearing aprons that said something about sidewalk prayers. I was going to cross over to the other side to avoid them, but I felt compelled to go toward them instead.

I poured out tears to a man and a woman about my brother. While I was talking to him, she was keeping Daniel entertained. After I talked forever, the man said, "What do you want?"

Huh. What did I want? I was so wrapped up in my story that I didn't think about what I wanted God to do.

I asked small: "I just want to know that Paul is okay." With that, he prayed. The woman told me afterward that she was praying for Daniel the whole time—which was so sweet. I was done crying, and I went off to buy my strawberries.

That evening, my girlfriends were all at the house helping me put the finishing touches on dinner and get it to the patio. Russ hadn't left, yet (he would take Daniel out on Thursdays for "Dude's Night" so that I could hang out with my girlfriends).

The phone rang.

It was my former sister-in-law—Paul's ex-wife. She called to tell me she had just gotten a call from her friend who also knows Paul. The woman had seen him in Minnehaha Park, and "he's okay."

I started crying and thanked her for the call.

Russ was immediately concerned that something was wrong. I couldn't get any words out. I finally mumbled that it was about Paul and that he was okay. Russ was relieved.

Prayer answered. Thank You, God! But I should've asked bigger.

The next time I saw Paul was at Thanksgiving. Somehow, he contacted Mom and was staying with her and Drew for a few days. Russ, our toddler Daniel, and I joined them for dinner. Paul didn't talk to me the whole time.

Daniel was walking by now, and he was super cute. Not to brag too much, but he rivaled the Gerber baby.

Paul ignored my cute boy.

After dinner, we left and drove the 90 minutes home. I found out later that my mom was mad at Paul for ignoring me. She pressed him to explain why he wouldn't talk to me. He said I had wronged him, and he was mad. Mom responded by saying I hadn't wronged him the way he claimed and made him call me.

As we walked in the door of our house, we heard the phone ringing. I answered. It was Paul: "Did you say that I raped someone?"

I was shocked by his question but not indignant. "No, of course not," I responded kindly.

Paul hung up the phone.

I was bewildered but didn't have time to ponder the conversation because we needed to get our tired toddler off to bed. The phone rang again. It was Paul. "Did you call the police and tell them that I raped someone?"

"No, of course not. I would never say something like that. You didn't, and I didn't." I still was not indignant. I was sad that he would think such a thing of me.

Paul hung up the phone. From that point on, Paul cut me off from his life.

I heard from Mom later that my Dad and stepmom, Bea, had come over to her house with the police that night to try to get Paul into the hospital. The police said they couldn't do anything. Paul wasn't a danger to anyone, and he wasn't a danger to himself, at least not while in my mom's home. Those are the criteria.

No one heard from Paul after that. Once again, there were many months that we did not know where he was or whether he was okay. At least with my sister, we always knew where she was and that she had food, shelter, and clothing.

After many months, I got a phone call from a psychiatric intern at a Minneapolis hospital. Paul had been admitted. How did the intern happen to call me? Paul and I didn't even have the same last name any more. But evidently, Paul had given the hospital the name of his rabbi, and the rabbi had given the hospital my name.

Thanks to the NAMI class, I knew that I could tell the doctors everything, and so I did. I told that intern story after story about Paul's behaviors. I told her that my dad had kept a list of dates of when things happened and that I would gladly send it to her. Every question she asked, I answered. I didn't hold back anything. I'm sure I even told her that our sister has schizophrenia.

The intern was out of questions, so I said, "I know there are things that you cannot tell me, but I'm going to ask anyway. If you can't answer them, I understand." This was Minnesota. If you aren't upfront with people, they get uncomfortable quickly, and it can ruin relationships. I wanted this intern to be willing to call me again.

I asked, "Why was Paul admitted to the hospital?" She couldn't tell me. "Is he physically okay?" She couldn't tell me. "What happens next?" She couldn't tell me.

I told my parents everything about the phone call. No one made it to the hospital in time to see Paul. We found out later that he was transferred to a state hospital in a suburb and had been diagnosed with schizophrenia.

Eventually, the state got Paul an apartment in St. Paul, which is in a different county than Minneapolis. He was on medication and had regular check-ins with a social worker.

In my opinion, the medicine didn't help much. Paul didn't want to do things. He stopped cooking. He didn't go to the library. He would spend time with Dad or Mom if they asked, but he seemed to go out of obligation. I only saw him at family events to which my parents brought him. He never talked to me. We had been good friends before schizophrenia. I was hurt.

Paul still had hallucinations. He would "hear" things said in the hallway outside of his apartment. He even sent me an email once asking if Mom had died—he "heard" that she had died and was checking the facts. At least he was checking the facts.

At least he wasn't homeless. He had food, shelter, clothing, and we knew where he was.

Psalm 46:10 in popular translations says, "Be still and know that I am God," but the NASB says, "Cease striving and know that I am God."

When I think back to the years of Paul's homelessness and diagnosis, I can see that I had strived to fix his situation. Psalm 46:10 in popular translations says, "Be still and know that I am God," but the New American Standard Bible (NASB) says, "*Cease striving* and know that I am God" (emphasis mine). The word *cease* is the Hebrew word *raphah*, the definition of which includes *relax* and *let go*. Hmm. Perhaps *cease striving* is just another way to say *trust in the Lord*.

6
CAREER IDENTITY CRISIS

My Daniel was the last of three babies born to couples in our small group. Before Daniel was born, I held each of the other two babies, but I felt uneasy. It wasn't that I was worried whether I was holding them the right way. It was that I didn't feel worthy to hold babies.

When Daniel was born, I remember the nurses having me up at 6 am and giving him to me. I am not a morning person, so I wasn't ready to be awake to say nothing of having the responsibility of a baby. Additionally, I hadn't had much sleep because the heart monitor kept me awake by making noise every five minutes all night long. I had a heart monitor because Daniel was born at 9 pm via C-section—after a full day of induced labor. But as moms, we all know to "get used to it" because you don't get much sleep when you have a newborn.

Feeling uneasy about being alone with my baby, I called Russ to ask him when he was going to be at the hospital. He said, "I didn't expect you to be up so early. I was going to let you sleep."

"The nurses wouldn't let me sleep," I said.

Russ hurried over. Later in the day, he was talking on the phone with his brother. He was trying to pay attention to his conversation, but he was distracted by Daniel and me. I was holding my baby and playing with him. Russ was distracted because he was seeing us bond. It's a sweet memory that I treasure. I was no longer afraid of babies.

I had quit my consulting job as a web-based training expert and project manager a few days before Daniel was born. Now I was not only a new mom but a stay-at-home mom. I never would've guessed that this would be my life.

I knew that staying home was what I was supposed to do. It was a gut feeling. I do not want to tell you that I think all women should stay home. That's not my position nor is it my business to tell other families what to do. I just know that that's what I was supposed to do at that time.

Being a stay-at-home mom was hard for me for a number of reasons, one of which was making dinner. Russ had moved from night shift to day shift while I was pregnant. Now that we had a baby, I had to feed Daniel and prepare dinner for the two of us. I had no idea how to plan meals and cook them so that they were done on time. Or perhaps it would be more accurate to say that *I didn't remember how*. I hadn't done that since high school, over 15 years before. I didn't cook for Arnold because he would eat as soon as he got home from work, which was usually one-and-a-half hours before I got home. He didn't want to wait for dinner, so we rarely ate together. But Russ and I wanted to eat together, and he was very patient and kind, probably even oblivious to how much I disliked cooking dinner. Making dinner for Russ and me and feeding Daniel at the same time stressed me out. To be honest, until recently it still stressed me out.

I didn't like being at the dinner table, either. I couldn't wait for dinner to be over. At breakfast and lunch, I would feed Daniel in the kitchen then set him down to play in his room while I quickly ate my food alone. When he was a preschooler, I would give him educational TV time while he ate so that we didn't have to sit at the table at all for lunch. I know now that this was a reaction to sitting at my parents' dinner table when Drew was a toddler, listening to him whine and to my sister getting angry with my mom for parenting him.

I didn't know how to take care of a baby or how to parent. I had read *What to Expect When You're Expecting* when I was pregnant so after Daniel was born, I read *What to Expect the First Year* and *What to Expect the Second Year*, too.[22]

I remember having a lot of things to do in order to be a good mother to Daniel, but all those things were tedious and boring. I called myself "busy bored" because I was busy, but I was also bored. How anyone enjoys cleaning or doing laundry is beyond me. Cooking meals is satisfying when everyone likes what I cook, but it takes more time to cook than to eat, so it's a lot of time to prepare, which I do not enjoy, for a much shorter time of enjoying the food, assuming that it turns out. Then I had to clean the kitchen and do the dishes. Before Daniel was born, Russ would do the dishes. After Daniel was born, Russ would bathe Daniel while I did the dishes so that they had father-son time together. (They had way more fun together anyway. Russ would be soaked by the end of bath time. On the other hand, I'm a task master, so I just get the boy clean and out of the tub. Russ played.)

Feminism that includes *not* doing household chores is so much more appealing than staying home or doing chores. Arnold liked tearing apart rooms and remodeling, whereas I would rather make a bunch of money so that I can pay someone else to do that. Once I had Daniel, I sometimes wished that I worked so that I could pay someone else to cook, clean, and do laundry, but I knew that I was supposed to stay home with Daniel to learn how to mother.

As a result of being "busy bored," I started praying all the time. I didn't have time to sit down to pray by myself, so I would pray while doing my boring chores. I would also pray with Daniel when it was nap time. Every night, we'd read three books, the last of which was a bible story, and then we'd pray. I wouldn't remember to pray when I was cooking dinner because I was stressed, but I should have. As I think back, it's interesting to me that I had learned not to worry about my brother by putting God first, seeking first His kingdom, but I didn't apply that same practice to "small things" like making dinner.

I do remember praying as I did the boring laundry and as I was getting Daniel to sleep. I would pray that the Holy Spirit would fill Daniel's room like a fog. After a while of doing that, I would pray that the whole house would be filled with the Holy Spirit like a fog. Eventually, I prayed that our house would glow with God's glory like Moses' face would glow after he spent time with God on Mount Sinai. I felt a great deal of peace when I prayed like that. In retrospect, I wish I had prayed like that at dinnertime.

THE CHRISTMAS TEA

Before Daniel's second Christmas, I was one of four women at church who were planning the program for the women's Christmas Tea. We talked about what the theme should be, but no one had ideas. As a result, we were tasked with praying and returning with ideas.

I re-read the Christmas story in Luke chapters 1 and 2 and was struck by the word *treasure* used twice in chapter 2.

But Mary treasured *up all these things and pondered them in her heart. (Luke 2:19 NIV[23] emphasis mine)*

Then he (Jesus) went down to Nazareth with them and was obedient to them. But his mother treasured *all these things in her heart. (Luke 2:51 NIV emphasis mine)*

Somehow, I connected Mary treasuring memories with my abortion. I had a deep reverence for Mary, a teenager pregnant out of wedlock, for being brave whereas I had not been.

None of the other women had any ideas for the theme. Two out of the other three liked my idea and tasked me with presenting. We called the theme "Treasures of the Heart."

I didn't know what I was doing. I had given many presentations in the professional world, but this was personal. I struggled to put together the message, but the women were patient and encouraging. Well, two out of three of them were.

The one who wasn't encouraging fought me on everything I drafted. I didn't try to defend myself. I just took it all in. All I could think is that these were the words that the Lord had impressed on my heart. I was simply writing what He told me.

Honestly, I didn't want to present about my abortion, but the other women were saying that if this is what was pouring out of my typing, then this is what I needed to say. The other women liked my drafts and helped me to make the presentation more complete.

I guess everything came to a head at one point because the women's ministry director joined our meeting to hear what I had drafted. She liked it and gave me good advice on making it better.

There were four of us on the Christmas Tea committee. Three of us had had abortions. *Three of us!* One of the women who had an abortion was the woman who was fighting everything I had to say. The other one was encouraging me but wasn't willing to speak up and tell the other two that she had also aborted.

When the upset woman finally come to peace with my presentation, she said she realized it wasn't her story; it was mine. From then on, everything went smoothly.

Two people spoke at the Christmas Tea: Martha, who is Pastor Brendon's wife, and me. After the Christmas Tea, Martha and I stood in the lobby so that we could talk to people as they made their way to the door. Most of the women stopped to talk to Martha. One of them asked her about mental illnesses. I had talked about my sister's schizophrenia in my presentation because schizophrenia is a large part of my testimony. Martha said, "You'll have to ask Cheryl." The woman then came over and talked to me. She was the only person who stopped to talk to me. Everyone else walked past me and out the door. The silence was deafening. I felt like I got the Christian cold shoulder.

I knew the women's ministry leadership loved me and supported me. I knew Martha and Pastor Brendon loved me and supported me. But the silence and avoidance from the 200 attendees resulted in my feeling as if I were wearing a scarlet letter A for abortion.

> *The silence and avoidance from Christians resulted in my scarlet letter A for abortion.*

Today I realize that they didn't know what to say. When I tell people my story now, they still don't know what to say. After the Christmas tea, though, I thought it odd that I was forgiven by God but still felt judged by Christians. I wore my scarlet letter A, but I hid it under my coat.

MY BABY GIRL'S NAME

After presenting at the Christmas Tea, I wanted to name my baby girl, the baby I had aborted. I couldn't decide between Mary Elizabeth or Elizabeth Marie. Both were wonderful names to honor Mary and Elizabeth, who were brave and steadfast in the Lord (read Luke 1 and 2).

SICK WITH SOMETHING

At Christmas, we visited Russ' parents in Chicago. We drove because we needed our vehicle to bring home all of Daniel's presents from his generous aunts and uncles. As we approached his parents' house, Russ joked, "Now, no visits to the ER on this trip."

The summer before, Daniel had been stung by a bee at Russ' parents' house, and we took him to the emergency room. One of the previous Thanksgivings, his dad had gone to the ER. When I was pregnant with Daniel, I fainted in church, so Russ took me to the ER. Therefore, no ER visits was a good goal.

On Christmas day, I was having gastrointestinal (GI) troubles and noticed a lump in my abdomen. It hurt when I put pressure on it. I didn't want to ruin our visit by going to the emergency room, so I didn't say anything until we got home a day or two later. Russ was a bit exasperated with me for not saying anything.

I went to the doctor the day after we arrived home. She couldn't figure out what the lump was but knew from my blood test that I had an infection, so she put me on antibiotics.

Now my GI troubles were flip-flopped. Day after day, I was absolutely exhausted, so not only would I nap while Daniel was napping, but I'd put him in his "saucer" with a video and nap while he watched the video.

I was like that for months. I didn't leave the house much, except for doctor's appointments. The doctor did many disgusting tests. I'll spare you the details.

I asked the doctor what I could do about my GI symptoms. Her only suggestion was to take Imodium.® I took Imodium and got out of the house more often. We lived about 20 minutes from the Mall of America, so I would take Daniel over there to walk. (Winters are cold in Minnesota, so walking in the Mall was both warm and entertaining.) Daniel loved watching the big rides, one in particular: the Timberland Twister.[24] We would go underneath that ride and watch it go by. I walked very slowly while pushing the stroller because walking at my normal pace was painful. It wasn't much of an outing, but at least I wasn't stuck in the house.

During that time, we switched churches simply because there was a new church starting right in our neighborhood. We liked the opportunities to serve right where we were living in the city rather than in the suburbs. I remember missing many Sundays in those first few months of attending because I was sick. I was sick of being sick. I remember crying out to God saying, "I don't know how to glorify You when I'm sick because I am just miserable all the time." Then I started feeling better.

The doctor's tests eliminated all sorts of results but did not provide any answers. In June, even though I was feeling better, I had the last test—a colonoscopy. It showed nothing. The nurse thought I would be pleased with that result, but I just cried. I had been sick for six months and still had no answers. My GI symptoms went away with no explanation.

BACK TO WORK

Sometime after that, benefits changed, and healthcare expenses went up. I went back to work to help pay the bills. I returned to the consulting company for whom I had worked before Daniel was born at about 30 hours per week. Daniel was in daycare and preschool not far from our house. My hours worked out well with his schedule.

ANOTHER BABY

I always tell people that Russ talked me into the first boy and that I talked him into the second boy. Daniel was a bit more challenging than just having the "terrible threes." Russ thought that the terrible threes were enough of a parenting challenge. I thought Daniel needed a sibling. Russ thought that being an only child sounded appealing (he is the oldest of seven!), but I did not like that idea at all. I enjoyed having a relationship with my brother before mental illness overshadowed his life, I wished I had a normal relationship with my sister, and I wanted Daniel to enjoy having a sibling, too. In God's providence, we got pregnant with Joshua, who was born just a few months before Daniel turned four. Russ and Joshua became fast friends.

I was hoping that we would have a girl because then everything would be in balance—one boy and one girl. I thought about names and remembered how much I liked the names Mary Elizabeth and Elizabeth Marie, but I had already chosen those names for my daughter. I was torn, but it all became moot once we found out that we were having another boy.

Once I became pregnant, I needed the work to pay for the upcoming hospital expenses. I found a position with a different consulting company working for Northwest Airlines—Russ' employer. I really enjoyed that job. I was a project manager working with a team to create web-based training. Half of my job was to work with technical operations (Tech Ops), which was where Russ worked. I never worked with Russ, but it was fun to work with his co-workers.

I worked until the day before Joshua was born. He came by scheduled C-section. My manager had offered me a permanent position as an employee after maternity leave, but since I'd be working for the same company as my husband and therefore already had all their benefits, the permanent position was actually less money than I was making as a contractor. Besides, Russ and I both knew that I should be a stay-at-home mom once again.

Joshua was as sweet as his brother. Daniel adored him.

Russ was still sure that he was done having babies. I was not so sure I was done. Russ asked me about tubal ligation (getting my tubes tied), but I wasn't interested in having any more "female procedures," especially since he was the one who was sure we were done having children, not me. Russ eventually had a vasectomy. He later found out that the wife of one of his coworkers had her tubal ligation done at the same time as her C-section. Russ asked why I hadn't done that. I said, "Because you were the one who was sure about not having more children, not me. Besides, why should I put my body through even more? It was your turn."

After Joshua was born, I quickly figured out that I had post-partum depression. The doctor put me on an anti-depressant that wasn't supposed to affect my breast milk. It helped some.

I didn't sleep much those days because Joshua didn't sleep much. He was spitting up more than the usual baby so much so that he couldn't sleep for more than a couple hours at a time. Nor did I. His doctor checked for reflux but said it wasn't bad enough for that diagnosis.

I didn't pray as much when Joshua was a baby as I had when Daniel was a baby. I was focused on getting Daniel out the door to preschool and trying to get Joshua to sleep. If I had it to do over again, I would have had worship music playing all the time and sang and prayed to God as I was busy taking care of everyone.

When Joshua was a few months old, I learned about leaky gut syndrome (also called intestinal permeability) and realized this was probably why I was so sick two years before. Basically, my gut was leaking things into my blood stream that it shouldn't. The result for me was an unexplainable infection and many GI troubles.

I decided to get tested for food sensitivities, which are reactions to food that may take a day or two to notice (whereas food allergies result in an anaphylactic reaction, which may require medicine or an ER visit). At the time, doctors did not recognize leaky gut syndrome and only diagnosed celiac disease and lactose intolerance. Today, mainstream medicine is starting to recognize leaky gut syndrome and beginning to realize how prevalent gluten and dairy intolerances are (in addition to other sensitivities). I found out that I was sensitive to milk, so I stopped drinking milk and eating anything made with cow's milk. I'm honestly not sure if I felt better because I was still dealing with postpartum depression, but I do know that Joshua stopped spitting up and therefore started sleeping better. That was a relief. As he slept more, Russ and I slept more. Our home was becoming more peaceful.

GEORGIA ON MY MIND

I stopped breastfeeding when Joshua was a year old and weaned myself off of the anti-depressant medication. I was feeling better. But at about that same time, we found out that the impending merger between Northwest Airlines and Delta Airlines could result in moving to Atlanta.

Before we had kids, I had told Russ that I was okay with moving to another big city—actually, moving sounded appealing and adventurous—but he liked Minneapolis and had no intention of looking for work elsewhere. But I remember being disappointed. Now it looked like we would have to move whether we wanted to or not, and I didn't want to go.

I was anxious about having to wait to see if Russ' job in the new organization would be in Minneapolis or Atlanta. I remember that after about eight months of waiting, I began crying out to the Lord about not knowing whether we would have to move and about whether I should start getting the house ready. My gut feeling after that prayer was to start getting the house ready even though I didn't know for sure if we would move, so I did. Just a few weeks later, we found out that we were moving.

In an effort to find a house in the city, I checked prices and commutes within Atlanta. I didn't like what I found, so we started looking south of Atlanta in small towns where most of the airline employees lived. When I realized we were not moving into the city of Atlanta but instead to a small town, I was even more unhappy about the move. I grew up in small towns, and I didn't like them. When my parents had moved us to the house near my high school, we were finally in a city, and I liked that. Now Russ, the boys, and I were not only moving across the country from the Midwest to The South, but we were moving from a metropolitan area to a small town. This was more change than I wanted.

We found a big house in a new subdivision. At least with the big house, my mom could stay with us during the winter, a more pleasant climate for her than all the snow and cold of Minnesota winters. We were moving from our beloved little city house built in the 1940s to a big suburban house that had just been built a few years before.

Russ and I were both stressed out by the move because neither of us wanted to go. We were grouchy with each other. I realize now that although I had learned not to worry about my brother, I hadn't learned to not worry about my own family life.

NWA PEACHES

One thing that eased the transition for me was meeting other wives of airline employees who were also moving from Minnesota to Georgia because of the merger. Russ told me that his boss' wife wanted to connect with other women. Then he told me about other wives. So, I invited these women to meet for lunch. We really enjoyed each other's company and had many of the same stresses in learning how to live in The South and in making new friends. We decided to meet again the following week ... and the week after that.

We became friends on Facebook, and I started a Facebook group for us. I posted invitations for lunch in the Facebook group so that everyone would know where we were meeting. The wife of Russ' boss was the first to invite everyone to her house, so then we started having potluck lunches in each other's homes. We brought our favorite Minnesota hotdishes and learned that in The South, a *hotdish* is called a *covered dish*.

I didn't know what to call the Facebook group, but one of the original women in the group started calling us "Peaches," which was a Georgia term. Somehow that turned into "NWA Peaches"—NWA for Northwest Airlines. The NWA Peaches grew and grew as we met more and more women and as our husbands would tell their coworkers about the group.

One NWA Peach was working at Target. Whenever she would see a debit card from the credit union that most NWA employees used, she'd tell her customer about NWA Peaches and invite them to join us for lunch. I loved that!

NWA Peaches were all women, but we were not all wives. Although most of the transferees were men simply because the airline industry is still a male-dominated industry, we made sure that all the female transferees were invited to the NWA Peaches, too. We were not exclusive. We even included several women who were from Minnesota but not part of NWA.

The NWA Peaches were such a joy for me. When we were together, we felt like we had a little Minnesota in Georgia. Many of the NWA Peaches were ahead of me in raising children, and I enjoyed hearing their stories. Even though several of us have since moved out of Georgia, we are still friends. And those who continue to live in Georgia still get together for lunch just about every week.

SCHOOLING THE BOYS

Daniel completed half-day kindergarten in Minneapolis Public Schools. Full-day first grade did not go well in Georgia for many reasons. I was in meetings at the school a lot, and I was frustrated to the point that I didn't want Daniel going to school there anymore. It took all that fall to convince Russ to let me homeschool Daniel. I did all sorts of research on homeschooling because I was determined to fix the situation. Russ and I argued about homeschooling. I remember that in the midst of one argument we both simultaneously remembered that I was a professional instructor. How could I forget my whole career? I knew how to help adults learn. I should be able to help my first grader learn. Russ finally said, "Yes" after Thanksgiving.

I brought Daniel home for winter break and kept him at home for school after that. We found a homeschool co-op, which not only provided Daniel and Joshua an opportunity to meet other kids their age but provided me a much-needed support network of other moms who had experience homeschooling their children.

Whereas I knew a great deal about teaching adults, whether college students or professionals in the workplace, I didn't know how to teach my child. I was especially concerned about writing because the school in Georgia said Daniel refused to write. As a result, I got to work learning about curricula options and how to structure our day.

Writing was the hardest subject to teach Daniel because I am a writer by nature and because Daniel's experience in school resulted in him hating to write, so I started researching how to teach elementary-aged boys and reluctant writers.[25] I learned all sorts of interesting things, like:

- Boys' hands (far more likely than girls') will cramp and literally hurt while handwriting.

- I could offer any number of writing tools to Daniel for writing, not just the yellow no. 2 pencil that school required. There is a myriad of grips that can be added to a pencil, or he could use a mechanical pencil, or he could use a pen. Since I was the teacher, I could decide.

- Boys (far more likely than girls) have a "one and done" attitude about writing, meaning that once they've written their first draft, they think the writing is done and don't see the point in rewriting. I quickly figured out that I needed to teach Daniel the writing process before he started to write. In general, that was Daniel's learning style anyway. He wanted to know what was going to happen before it happened.

- Writing is a complicated thing, especially for elementary students. It includes handwriting, generating ideas (pre-writing, brainstorming, etc.), organizing those ideas (outlining per the content, audience, and genre), written expression (the sentences, paragraphs, etc.), spelling, punctuation, grammar, and formatting (or spacing on the page). That's a lot to require of a six-year-old.

I started teaching Daniel at home—writing, math, history, science, etc. Joshua enjoyed joining us for science because we did experiments in the kitchen: They both enjoyed making liquids change colors and bubble.

Any homeschooling mom, if she's honest, will admit that patience is challenging, especially when you're spending the full day with your kids. Moms spent full days with their children for millennia before public school became a thing and now spending all day with our children stresses us out. How interesting. The boys and I had a different kind of relationship now, but we learned to work with each other and to take breaks from each other.

One big benefit I saw is that we no longer had homework in the evenings because all of Daniel's schoolwork was homework that could be completed during the day. This reduced my stress as I was getting dinner ready—a huge blessing given how stressed I already was about cooking dinner.

But overall, I was still stressed. Daniel did well because he is smart, but I was overwhelmed and never felt like I was doing a good enough job. I was striving to fix the schooling problem and, even though I can see now that we had a lot of schooling victories, at the time I felt completely overwhelmed.

After a year and a half of homeschooling, a charter school opened nearby. My friend was a teacher there and thought the school would be a good match for Daniel, so I enrolled him. After a long transition period as he learned to write the way the charter school wanted, he did well there. When Daniel was in fourth grade, Joshua was in kindergarten. He went to the charter school as well. But in Georgia, kindergarten is a full day, which was challenging for Joshua. He loved hanging out with his friends, but staying focused all day was difficult.

Daniel will tell you today that he liked the charter school. I don't think Joshua remembers much about it. Whenever we talk about it, I point out that the charter school was a good match for Daniel but not for Joshua. They have different learning styles, and one way of educating does not fit all students.

That year, Georgia was making changes to its legislation for charter schools, legislation that affected funding. Charter schools were in danger of closing. It became a big political issue leading up to the November vote. I got involved in promoting charter schools because I had finally found a good schooling match for Daniel. Besides, I had come from Minnesota where we had more school choice, so when it was time to advocate for school choice in Georgia, I shared information with friends, put up yard signs, and wrote letters to the editor. Once the legislation passed, we all sighed in relief that our school would stay open.

NOT ALL ROSY

While in Georgia, Russ was diagnosed with sleep apnea. In addition, we hated our mattress, which we had replaced twice, so sleep was a real challenge for him. As you know, when you don't get much sleep, you have a hard time making it through the day. Russ was grouchy. I was grouchy. I'm just thankful that the boys don't remember how grouchy we were.

There was a lot more going on in Georgia than I'm writing about because it doesn't really contribute to the story. I'll just add that we had crazy neighbors who were really annoying. We were not the only ones in our neighborhood annoyed by their love for dirt bikes and late-night skate boarding, so it was not just a difference in personalities between them and us. Now that I look back, I know that they needed a great deal of prayer, but it never occurred to me to pray for them.

All while living in Georgia, I strived. I strived to fix school. I strived to be a good mother. I really struggled emotionally and spiritually. I didn't like how I talked to my boys or my husband, and I didn't like how they talked to me. I could correct the boys, but I would argue with Russ.

I knew the fruit of the Holy Spirit is love, joy, peace, patience, kindness, goodness, faithfulness, gentleness, and self-control,[26] but I didn't know how to get them. I prayed and asked for them, but I didn't feel like God was answering my prayer.

A NEW JOB

That same year, Russ became interested in a new position near Washington, DC, and he asked me how I felt about moving. On the one hand, I was disappointed at the thought because we had just secured our school's continuation, and I liked how the school worked with Daniel. On the other hand, I wouldn't mind leaving our small Georgia town, which was not a good fit for me or for Russ. As a result, I started researching schools near his potential employer and found that they were quite good. This time I started preparing the house right away rather than waiting to see what would happen.

HEALTH

I gained a lot of weight while living in Georgia. I have learned that I am a stress eater. The move to Georgia was stressful, learning the new culture was stressful, schooling my kids was stressful. What I should have done was rely on the Lord rather than food, but even today I struggle with my addiction to sugary foods and drinks.

Russ wanted to lose weight in preparation for the interview, so we dieted together. The diet was vegetables and a much smaller portion of meat than we were used to eating. Russ had a little bit of wheat, but I chose not to have any wheat. I did all the food prep, which was a lot of work, but we were successful. Even though I had lost 20 pounds, I was still 25 pounds overweight, but I felt better. Russ was the thinnest I had ever seen him. He looked great! We were on a mission to get him the job that he wanted. We had come together for a purpose, and our relationship was so much better. The grouchiness went away.

As soon as we went off of the diet, I had a plate of noodles. About an hour after eating, I needed a nap—immediately! I fell asleep very quickly and had the deepest sleep that I could remember. The same thing happened the next time that I had wheat. As a result, I backed off of wheat and only had small amounts at a time. For example, I would have Chic-fil-A nuggets (who can resist Chic-fil-A?), but I would not have a piece of bread.

I did not think that I had celiac because I had had two colonoscopies and one upper GI scope while living in Georgia and plenty of conversations with more than one doctor about what could be causing my GI issues. None of the testing or conversations led to celiac. The whole thing was a mystery to me. I just knew that I felt better when I didn't eat bread or pasta, so I avoided them both while continuing to be dairy-free.

OFF TO VIRGINIA

For many months, we waited for the job to be officially posted and several more for the interviewing process to be completed, but Russ got the job, and we headed to Virginia.

Russ enjoyed his new job and being back in the city. I enjoyed being back in the city, too, but the boys and I missed our friends. Russ didn't seem to understand why we weren't as happy as he was. We were grouchy at each other again, but we were still on a mission together to find a house and get settled in, so we weren't too grouchy.

I homeschooled the boys for the last two months of the school year and then the boys attended our neighborhood school the following fall. Joshua was there for two years, and then we decided to homeschool him again. I now realize that traditional school with desks is not a good fit for him no matter in which state we live. That boy needs to move!

Daniel was in public school for four years, and then we were back to homeschooling him. I'm not sure how to explain why I chose to homeschool Daniel through high school. I just had a gut feeling that I shouldn't put him into the public high school.

Although I knew it would be challenging to homeschool both of them, I also knew that homeschooling Daniel would provide me insight into how to teach him to study. My biggest concern with Daniel is that he is too smart and therefore could slide through high school without much work. That's what my brother did. I wanted Daniel to learn how to study so that he would be prepared for college when the content would be much harder. Besides, if we homeschool, then we don't have to do homework in the evenings!

Daniel adored Joshua until he became that irritating little brother—as typically happens with siblings. Both boys are a joy, and I praise God for teaching me to become more like Him through parenting.

For a former feminazi, I've come a long way. Certainly, my former self never would've had children nor given up her career to raise them. Yet God continues to form me into the woman He designed me to be, which is so different than I ever imagined for myself. Although I was striving to fix things all during this part of my life, at least I wasn't just surviving.

> *My former self never would've had children nor given up her career to raise them. Yet God continues to form me into the woman He designed me to be.*

While in Georgia, I had decided to pray for our little town and the surrounding area because if the area were to prosper then we would prosper, as it says in Jeremiah 29:7.[27] I had chosen to be content in all circumstances.[28] Now I was heading to another area that was new to me, but I trusted the Lord:

"For I know the plans I have for you," declares the Lord, "plans to prosper you and not to harm you, plans to give you hope and a future. Then you will call on me and come and pray to me, and I will listen to you. You will seek me and find me when you seek me with all your heart." (Jeremiah 29:11-13 NIV)

7
WHY DON'T I HAVE SCHIZOPHRENIA?

As I stated in an earlier chapter, The American Psychiatric Association has now put schizophrenia on a spectrum. Their description of the Schizophrenia Spectrum Disorder includes delusions, hallucinations, disorganized thinking, and grossly disorganized or abnormal motor behavior (p. 87-88).

I have observed the following schizophrenic features in Nancy:

- Delusions that she will not reconsider, even when she is presented with conflicting evidence. For example, Nancy says that she went to Europe many years ago, yet she has never owned a passport.

- Erotomanic delusions, which are beliefs that someone is in love with the person who has schizophrenia, in that Nancy currently believes that she's getting married to a retired pastor who is older than our mom.

- Hallucinations, which I have described in this book as her imaginary friend. Today, she "sees" her "fiancé" at a coffee shop that she thinks he owns.

- Perhaps disorganized thinking. I find Nancy's talking to be disorganized in that she'll move from one topic to another and then stop for Acknowledgment even though I am lost as to what one thing has to do with the other. When I ask for clarification, she explains, and I am usually still confused.

- Abnormal motor behavior in that she used to hold her right hand very tightly. I haven't seen this for many, many years, though.

I have observed the following schizophrenic features in Paul:

- Persecutory delusions in that he has believed that police were following him, that people were reporting his whereabouts to the police, and that he was harassed, even by me.

- Referential delusions, which are neutral events thought to have a special meaning for the person with schizophrenia, in that Paul has thought that people looking at him, if only for a moment while talking on their own phones, means that they are talking about him.

- Auditory hallucinations in the form of voices that are perceived as distinct from his own thoughts, including voices in the hall outside of his apartment and voices telling him that Mom had died.

That's what the doctors say. There are Christians, however, that believe schizophrenia is demon possession. I don't know what to make of that. I have read every account of Jesus freeing people from demon possession, and I'm praying about it now. Some pastors and some of my solid Christian friends who share my beliefs do not rule out the possibility that my brother is demon possessed. I just don't know what I think.

However, I do keep thinking about how our human perspective is different than God's perspective, just like the biblical account of King David's life was likely different than the perspective of his Mighty Men or of the priests or of the Israelites of his time. I keep thinking that satan is the god of this world[29] in which we have all these medical terms for mental illnesses, and I know that satan is a liar.[30]

WHAT ABOUT ME?

When Paul was homeless, one of my friends—knowing my worries—looked me in the eye and said, "You don't have schizophrenia."

I can't tell you how nice it was to hear someone say that. I didn't think that I did, but it was nice to hear from someone who saw me every day at work that I showed no signs of schizophrenia.

Sometime after Joshua was born and before we moved to Georgia, my mom had a mild stroke. She lost sight in her left eye, but otherwise you wouldn't know that she had had a stroke. I did, however, find her a neurologist in the Twin Cities and took her there for a checkup, just to make sure that she was okay.

The medical history form asked about mental illnesses of family members. Of course, she wrote that two of her children had schizophrenia. The doctor came in, we all introduced ourselves, and I explained that although Mom had seemed to recover nicely from her stroke, I wanted to have a neurologist, not just her family doctor, check to be sure that she was okay.

The doctor went over Mom's medical history. She was a little surprised that two of mom's children had schizophrenia, so she was double checking her understanding of what Mom wrote on the form. "Yes, I have two children with schizophrenia." I noticed that the doctor was about to ask about my mental state, but she stopped herself. She didn't look me in the eye after that.

Even the neurologist wondered if I was mentally healthy. Honestly, I have often *not* told people about my siblings' schizophrenia because I have the perception that they are thinking, "What about you?" Is it possible to have a scarlet letter that shows I have family members with mental illness? A scarlet letter is a feeling of being labeled and judged. That's how I have often felt: labeled with "My family has mental illness" and judged as if people are constantly asking, "What's wrong with your family?"

Coincidentally, one of our Georgia neighbors had a 20-something year old son with schizophrenia living with her. When she told me, she assured me that he was non-violent. I assured her that I understood, told her about my siblings, and introduced her to Mom.

When we moved to Northern Virginia outside of Washington, DC, we invited my mom to move in with us. She was no longer responsible for Nancy's finances, and Nancy had moved to Minneapolis, so Mom was no longer involved in Nancy's day-to-day activities. Drew was on his own. Grandma had died before my Joshua was born. So no longer full of obligations in Minnesota, Mom moved into the in-law suite in our home outside of Washington, DC.

Even though Russ no longer worked for an airline, we were still able to enjoy his flight benefits with retiree status. As a retiree, he and his immediate family (the boys and me) fly standby for little or no cost. Flying standby takes a lot of patience, planning, and willingness to make last-minute decisions.

Although the money part of standby sounds good, the unpredictability can be very unnerving. Standby passengers get whatever empty seats have not been sold. Our names are on a standby list. We go to the airport and wait at the gate to find out whether or not we get on the plane.

Yes, that means we can pay for parking, check our bags, go through security, etc. and not get on the plane. What if we don't get on the plane? Then we check other flights to see if we can get on another plane. Sometimes we spend a whole day in the airport.

Sometimes we get a hotel room and stay overnight because we're stuck someplace that is not our destination or home.

I've done all those things for over 15 years with two boys in tow. Although it can be nerve-wracking, you have to remember that you don't have control, so there's no point in worrying.

I have learned to create contingency plans, to keep myself and the boys calm, and to be ready to make last-minute decisions. It can be fun, but many people don't like to fly standby because it's not predictable—including my husband. He remembers how much better it was to fly standby before 9/11 and rising fuel prices. Planes used to go out with more empty seats than they do today.

But every empty seat is lost revenue and with higher fuel prices, airlines have changed so that they send out full flights. It saves them money and keeps them in business, which we appreciate because we have retirement benefits tied to their profitability.

One year, I decided to use those standby benefits in August because I wanted to visit my dad and Lynn, the sister of my heart, before school started.

I emailed Paul to ask him out for lunch. He turned me down, which saddened me deeply. I had recently started a part-time job at our church helping with communications. Weekly, the staff would gather to pray as a work family. One coworker asked if I had a cold. I didn't. I was sniffling because I was upset that my brother wouldn't see me. They all prayed for me and for Paul.

Daniel was 12, and Joshua was eight. They knew more about schizophrenia than most adults. They knew their Aunt Nancy, and they asked really good questions about her behavior. While in Minnesota, the boys and I had lunch with Nancy to celebrate her birthday.

We picked up Nancy in downtown Minneapolis. I was enjoying being in my favorite city, so I purposely drove the long way to the restaurant in the suburbs, enjoying the scenery and memories along the way. After we ate, I let the boys play their video games. I didn't want the boys bothered by me asking Nancy questions that would help me discern if she were hallucinating again.

Nancy talked a lot about her "fiancé." She told us her fiancé's name years before this lunch date. My parents know the man to whom she claims to be engaged. Mom has tried reasoning with her, telling her that this man does not live in Minneapolis, but she will not be deterred from her story. It's as if she took a name from her memory and attached it to this fiancé hallucination. This is what I mean by "erotomanic delusion."

Nancy talked a lot about her church and her pastor. She did not like many of his sermons, but she said they were good when her fiancé gave her pastor sermons that he had given years before. It took a long time, but I was finally able to discern that her pastor and the man she thought was her fiancé have never met. I confirmed with her that they had never met. Then I confirmed with her that her "fiancé" had given his sermons to her pastor but not through email. She was clear that she meant mind-to-mind—from her fiancé's mind to her pastor's mind. I couldn't reason with her that this didn't make sense.

Then I just didn't want to continue the conversation because it was so disturbing. I paid the check so that we could leave. My emotions were rising up to my tear ducts, but I tried to hide them from Nancy. When the boys got into the car, I leaned in and quietly said, "Pray for me right now, please. I'm about to lose it."

I did not enjoy the scenery while driving back to downtown Minneapolis. I drove as fast and as directly as I could. I couldn't wait for Nancy to get out of the car.

After we dropped off Nancy, I drove out of the Twin Cities to the city where my dad, my nephew Drew, and Lynn lived outstate. I was quietly crying. Daniel asked if I was okay. "No," I said.

"Mom, listen to Christian radio," Joshua said. That's one smart boy. I found KTIS at 98.5 FM. Listening to Christian music helped me calm down.

Then Daniel asked, "May I ask you questions about what Aunt Nancy said?"

"Yes, of course."

"How much of what she said was true?"

"I'm not sure because she talked about many people whom I don't know. She did talk about some people whom I do know, but I don't know how much she said about them is true. But the whole story about her fiancé is not true."

Later while visiting with my dad, stepmom, and Drew, I asked them all sorts of questions about how Nancy and Paul were doing. In part, I was trying to figure out how much of what Nancy had said at lunch was real. Drew said Nancy had begun showing all sorts of signs of schizophrenia again, like talking to no one.

Dad said Paul would frequently hear voices, but he would check to see if what the voices said were true by periodically emailing Dad to check the facts. He was still hearing voices, but he was cognizant enough to realize that those voices might be telling lies.

I told Dad and my stepmom, Bea, that Paul wouldn't see me. Bea pointed out that there was nothing stopping me from knocking on his door. Hmm. Maybe I would do that.

I emailed my coworkers to ask for prayer. They all sent encouraging responses.

After having great visits with my dad, Drew, Lynn, and her family at one of the 15,256 Minnesota lakes, the boys and I drove back to the Twin Cities. I had worked out a timeline that allowed us to knock on Paul's door and still catch a flight back home, if there were open seats, that is.

The boys and I had lunch and then bought big cupcakes to take to Paul. We each chose a cupcake for dessert. For Paul, I bought German Chocolate. That was his favorite.

The boys did not know their Uncle Paul. They had seen some pictures of him although not many because Paul hated the camera and in most pictures he was obviously not himself. They had met him once about five years earlier, but they didn't remember him.

I prepped the boys for seeing Paul. I told them my plan, and I told them this may not work. I didn't know how Paul would respond, but we were going to try.

Paul lived in a secured building, so I used the phone in the entryway to call him so that he could let me into the building. He hung up on me. Just then, someone came through the door, so the boys and I went into the building and up to his floor. I told the boys what I was going to do. Then I knocked on the door. As Paul opened the door, I told him that we brought cupcakes, but he closed the door in our faces. My boys looked at me. "Well, we tried," I said, and we left the building.

I cried. The boys consoled me.

I took the boys to Veteran's Memorial Park near the airport because it has a big playground. Daniel and Joshua enjoyed the cupcakes and played while I cried and checked the flight. No seats. That was fine because I didn't want to pretend to be okay on the airplane when all I wanted to do was cry. I found a hotel for us to stay the night. I could've asked friends if we could stay at their place for one night, but I didn't want to talk to anyone.

We checked into the hotel. The boys played in the pool. I sat in the hot tub and cried inside. Sometimes I actually cried tears and then discretely touched my face with the hot pool water to hide my tears.

My boys were very sweet. They understood that I was upset. They let me be. But they also asked good questions. The best question was, "Mom, why don't you have schizophrenia?"

"I don't know that I will ever know the answer to that on this side of heaven."

But I know God says:

"For as the heavens are higher than the earth,
So are My ways higher than your ways
And My thoughts than your thoughts."
(Isaiah 55:9 NASB)

8
ALL THINGS WORK TOGETHER FOR GOOD

I often think of the 14 years from my abortion to my relationship with Christ as wasted years. That's not completely true because I can see how God used that time in my life to bring about loving relationships and preparation for what He is calling me to do. I first had this "a-ha" when I was 45 years old.

DETOXING MY BODY

I had just lost another 20 pounds while detoxifying my body. I was tired of all the colonoscopies and upper GI tests that told me what I already knew before the tests, so I decided to do something different by detoxing. I started with a juice fast and then alternated with homemade smoothies. I wasn't following anyone's plan. More than anything, I was just following my gut feelings (pardon the pun). The idea was to give my digestive system a break from working so hard and to get it all cleaned out. I thought I was going to fast for just one day, but surprisingly I easily made it to three days before switching from juice to smoothies.

About a week after starting the fast, I went to the doctor for a routine checkup. It was now about a year after we moved to Virginia, and I was finally getting around to taking care of myself. I gave my doctor my long history of GI and other medical issues, and she ordered a blood test. When she called me with the results, she said I had celiac. "Um, doctor, don't you need to have wheat in your system in order for celiac to show up on the test?" She confirmed that that was the case. "Doctor, I stopped eating wheat a week before you took my blood."

"Then wheat is likely a much bigger problem for you than my test shows," she said. I was dumbfounded. I explained to her that doctors had assured me that I didn't have celiac because of their tests while doing the upper GI scopes. She said if they took samples from healthy parts of my upper GI, then celiac wouldn't show up on the test results. A blood test. She solved the whole mystery with a blood test.

FASTING

Not too long into the detox, I was complaining on Facebook about dieting. Lent had just started, so one of my Georgia friends asked if I was fasting. "No, just a coincidence," I said.

"There are no such things as coincidences," he replied.

Shortly after that, my small group leader pointed out that I was fasting, so I should be studying the Word. I thought it interesting that two people who didn't know each other would point out that I was fasting. I didn't think of my detox diet as a fast, but they were right. I was giving up favorite foods and beverages.

So for the first time, I studied a book of the Bible on my own with highlighters and a prayer notebook. I chose the book of James. I had never realized how much that book had to say about anger. I looked up depression and found out that depression is basically repressed anger. I realized I was angry about several things, and through my study of James and my prayer journal, the Lord helped me work them out.

I did my detox diet for about 40 days—right up to Easter. I switched at some point to whole vegetables with some low-sugar whole fruits. Eventually I added fish, which I don't particularly like. I would much prefer to eat beef or chicken.

At some point I had a vegetarian meal at a fast-casual restaurant and got sick. I found out from a neighbor that her child who has celiac also got sick there. She figured it was from cross-contamination of the flour tortillas. I didn't think I had been off wheat long enough to have that big of a reaction.

I went to the restaurant's website and read about their allergens. Soy was in most of their foods. Then I remembered that when I first went dairy-free back when Joshua was a baby and tried soy milk, I got sick. As a result, I decided not to have soy any more, either. I was dairy-free, gluten-free, and soy-free—although I figured out that I could have gluten-free soy sauce, but I don't know why it didn't make me sick.

FOOD SENSITIVITIES

After the diet, I started drinking cocktails again, about once a week while on a date with Russ. My favorite drink was a cosmopolitan.[31] We would go out on Saturday night, and on Sunday I was tired and grouchy—like PMS grouchy. Somehow, I found out that the vodka in my cosmo was not made from potatoes: it was made from wheat! That's when I realized wheat did not just affect my GI, it made me tired and affected my mood. Soon after, I realized corn was bothering me, too, so no corn-based vodka, no corn meal, and no high-fructose corn syrup (which I was avoiding anyway). Between completely dropping both wheat and corn from my diet and releasing anger through prayer and study of the book of James, my depression was completely gone. I had thought it was gone when I was done with postpartum depression but looking back, I can tell that mild depression had lingered for many years after that.

Getting my body detoxed and my diet cleaned up seemed to help me hear from the Lord more clearly. I felt called to be a Christian speaker, but I didn't know what I would speak about. I just knew that I didn't want to speak about abortion because of how Christians had reacted to my story or about schizophrenia because it was so emotional for me. I didn't know what the Lord was calling me to do, but I was determined to seek Christ even more. I figured that I had another 45 years here on earth considering that both of my grandmothers lived past age 90, and there was nothing stopping me from serving God all the way to my last breath. That's when I'll retire—when I leave this earth for heaven. The second 45 years will be so much more effective for Christ because I will be a Christian in constant pursuit of His heart for the whole 45 years.

> *I didn't lose 45 years—that was just the beginning. I had another 45 years here on earth... and there was nothing stopping me from serving God all the way to my last breath.*

HOLY SPIRIT CONFIDENCE

After the detox, I had a gut feeling that I should try a product from my essential oils company called Sulfurzyme,® which contains dietary sulfur. I looked up everything I could find about dietary sulfur, and all the literature was about arthritis. I don't have arthritis, but I couldn't shake the feeling that I needed to take Sulfurzyme, so I ordered it and started taking it daily. After a couple weeks, my eczema cleared up and my fingernails, which had been breaking and chipping for many years, were strong and long. After about a month, I had energy that I didn't remember having since I was in high school. Now I could run for more than 10 feet without being absolutely exhausted. I noticed that following my gut instinct to take this supplement was the right thing to do.

About the same time, I was seeing a gynecologist for my heavy menstrual cycle. I mean heavy, like I didn't want to leave the house for two days without a change of clothes. The typical recommendation from a gynecologist today is a procedure called ablation, in which they destroy the lining of the uterus.[32] From my annual Pap smear, I found out that I had an abnormal cells;

however, I did not have HPV. I guess that usually when a woman has cervical dysphasia, she also has HPV.

Even though the doctors didn't tell me so at the time, I'm guessing that I had HPV when I had the cervical dysplasia that resulted in my laser cone biopsy of my cervix a year after marrying Arnold.

The doctor and I discussed ablation but given my history of cervical dysplasia with the addition of the heavy bleeding, he recommended a hysterectomy. My gut, though, was telling me that a hysterectomy was not the right solution.

In the lobby of the gynecologist's office, I found a pamphlet about heavy bleeding. The pamphlet explained that heavy bleeding was likely from having too much estrogen in my body. I started researching and found out that estrogen and progesterone work in balance but that women who were on estrogen-based birth control pills may have too much estrogen. Given that I had been on the pill for 14 or so years before getting pregnant with Daniel, I was not surprised that I may have had too much estrogen in my body. This may cause a number of health problems (you should look it up), one of which is the heavy bleeding that I was experiencing.

I got a second opinion on the hysterectomy, and the second doctor said it wasn't necessary. I could do it, of course, and therefore be done with menstrual periods altogether, but it wasn't necessary. That doctor recommended having the ablation instead. But ablation didn't seem like the right solution, either.

With that, I found a natural progesterone option and started using it. After two months of continual usage, my bleeding was less. Each month my bleeding was less and less.

The cervical dysplasia was still an issue, so perhaps a hysterectomy was a logical choice as my first doctor suggested. I had a gut feeling, though, that I needed to change the tampons I was using, so I switched from a commercial brand to a natural brand. Just a few months went by and my follow-up pap was normal. Now there really was no more reason to get a hysterectomy.

Russ called it a miracle—that I didn't need a hysterectomy after all. I called it obedience because I realized that my gut feeling was the Holy Spirit teaching and guiding me. I noticed that the more time I spend in prayer, bible study, and worship, the more gut feelings I get—even about how to do boring household chores like the laundry. Maybe that gut feeling is actually my Holy Spirit confidence.

My point is not to convince you to choose natural remedies instead of medical treatment. I am not a doctor or a medical professional of any sort. You *should* consult a doctor, as I did. Get a second opinion, as I did. My point is that you should be in continual prayer, bible study, and worship so that you are open to the Holy Spirit teaching and guiding you in all things from doing the laundry to your health. Honestly, if the natural remedies had not helped my body to do what it's supposed to do, I would have been back in a doctor's office scheduling an ablation or hysterectomy.

HOW ALL THINGS HAVE WORKED TOGETHER

The Holy Spirit has also shown me specific ways that my Lord has caused all things from my past to work together for my good.[33]

LYNN'S FAMILY IS MY FAMILY

For example, if it weren't for my marriage to Arnold, Lynn would not be the-sister-of-my-heart. Lynn's whole family is my family—my sister, my brother-in-law, my niece, and my nephews.

When the boys and I fly back to Minnesota, we usually stay with Lynn and her family. Her boys, even though much older than mine, hang out with my boys. They enjoy each other. In a weird sort of way, they are cousins.

Lynn's eldest, Lily, and her husband, Caleb, moved out east just before we did. She finished her teaching degree a few hours away from where we live near Washington, DC. As a result, they had holiday meals with us when they couldn't go back to

Minnesota. When Lynn and her family came out to visit Lily, I got to visit with them, too.

Lily also has a sister-of-her-heart who lives about four hours away from me. In our crazy way of thinking, I am *her* Aunt Cheryl, too. She was baptized and married recently, and I was there in person to celebrate.

Lily and Caleb had a baby girl, Ruby, while living out east. My boys are gaga over her.

Caleb and my husband Russ are both into cars. They became fast friends. We do miss them now that they have returned to Minnesota.

Therefore, not only do I have Lynn as the sister-of-my-heart, but I have her whole family as my family even though we are technically no longer related.

MORE GOOD FROM MY FIRST MARRIAGE

Because of Arnold, I learned how to treat grandmothers with chivalry. I saw him drop off and pick up his Southern grandmother at the door, hold open the car door for her, and offer a steady hand as she got up out of the car.

Now I do the same with my mom. It pretty much drives my independent Minnesotan mother crazy, but when her body is hurting, she secretly appreciates it. I think she realizes that I'm showing her respect and that I care for her well-being. Maybe someday she'll realize that she is worth it.

Because of Arnold, I gained a love for technology because he was such a geek. I ended up combining technology with writing and also with teaching and learning, all of which became my career in web-based training and other communication needs my employers had—and now I'm using those skills to write and speak about the sanctity of life and the sanctity of sex.

Because of Arnold, I have an interest in photography and a basic understanding of what makes a good photo. My eyesight is not particularly good, though, so I have to rely on autofocus. Although I really ought to take a photography class, I also know through Arnold how expensive photography equipment is. I may have gotten serious about becoming a better photographer years ago if it weren't so expensive, yet I take good enough photos to catch people's attention on social media.

Would I do those years over again? No way! But I do see God working everything out for my good and His glory.

For many years, I thought my testimony was complete. I had survived schizophrenia and everything in my life was going well. Little did I know my tests were not yet over and more tests were soon on their way.

THRIVING

9
PEACE THAT PASSES
ALL UNDERSTANDING

When I started working for the church, the church was just beginning a new journey of becoming more prayerful. What perfect timing for me because I was ready to be more prayerful. We read Daniel Henderson's *Transforming Prayer* book,[34] which reminded me to pray scripture as I had learned from Stormie Omartian's books (*Power of a Praying Wife, Power of a Praying Parent*, etc.[35]) and from Moms in Prayer[36] (an international prayer organization for praying for your child's school). Henderson took us even further than praying scripture. He taught us to worship God in prayer.

Henderson also met with the staff and volunteers to teach us himself. I enjoyed my shared Minnesota connection with Pastor Henderson—he used to pastor a church not far from where I lived in Minneapolis. But mostly I enjoyed learning how to change the focus of my prayers from my needs to God's glory, from seeking His hand to seeking His face first.[37]

Pastor Henderson teaches Christians to begin prayer with worship—not necessarily in song but certainly in our words. I have never been good about adoring God at the beginning of my prayers. I would just jump right into what I needed.

Who wants to be approached like that? When someone wants something from us, we don't appreciate them jumping right to what they want. We want to be greeted. We want to enjoy our relationship. If there is something negative between us, we would appreciate an apology. Aren't we much more interested in helping someone after a genuine apology? I finally understood that my relationship with God should be the same.

As a result, I began starting every prayer in worship of Him, seeking Him for Who He is rather than what He can do for me, and my relationship with God grew closer and closer. I began to really enjoy my prayer time. I would get up earlier and earlier so that I would have more time with Him before my family needed me.

I'm a night person! But it was as if the Lord was waking me up and sweetly whispering that He wanted to spend time with me. I felt so loved by Him.

I'm a night person! But it was as if the Lord was waking me up and sweetly whispering that He wanted to spend time with me. I felt so loved by Him.

Maybe half a year later, I remember taking a break from work and praying in an empty room. I was on my knees asking the Lord to change some family circumstances that had me heartbroken. At some point in that prayer, I felt tingling move through my body. Then I remembered this had happened before on occasion, usually when I was praying but on at least one occasion when I was discussing something biblical with a friend. I asked one of the pastors about it, but he didn't know for sure what it meant.

Another half year later, I was enjoying the breeze on my front porch one Friday evening in June. The next day was my dad's birthday. My cell phone rang. It was my dad!

I chose a custom ring for my dad's calls. It's a baritone singing "The Lord's Prayer" by Albert Hay Melotte.[38] I remember my dad singing "The Lord's Prayer" many a time while I was growing up. When he calls me, I imagine that it's my dad singing to me.

"Happy early birthday!" I said as my greeting. Dad thanked me. He wasn't overly cheerful. His voice was steady, thoughtful.

Dad had two pieces of news for me that night. He told me about my cousin first. Mitch had congestive heart failure. He was scheduled to have surgery on Monday. Mitch and I were close growing up. He's two years older than me, and we were a few years shy of 50. Was death knocking at his door?

Then the news that rocked my world: Paul was missing.

Dad explained that he had been calling and emailing Paul for a couple months but got no response. Paul had said he wanted to go to a linguistics conference in New Jersey, and Dad wanted to support him by providing travel money or by traveling with him, but Paul wouldn't answer the phone. He wouldn't respond to email, either.

Dad and Bea drove the 90 minutes to Paul's apartment, which was in St. Paul, but he wouldn't answer. The superintendent went into his apartment, but Paul wasn't there.

Dad contacted Paul's social worker, who met them at the apartment. She had the right to be let in whereas my dad did not. They looked around and found small indications that Paul had taken things with him, like his backpack.

While they were talking in the lobby, the postal carrier was putting mail in all the boxes. Dad and the social worker happened to see that Paul's mailbox was overflowing.

Through talking to one of Paul's neighbors and putting bits of information together, Dad and the social worker were able to surmise that Paul had been gone for about a month.

A month.

While Dad was talking, I was crying. I had my iPad with me, so I used it to text Russ, asking him to come out to the porch because Dad was on the phone giving me bad news about Paul.

Russ came out to the front porch to listen to what Dad had to say. Russ can think straight about Paul when I cannot, so he asks good, clarifying questions. I appreciate that about him.

After I composed myself, I went to my mom in our house's in-law suite and told her what I knew. She didn't sleep well that night—or for many nights.

Mom is rather good at hiding her feelings. She is also worn out, to say the least, from being tested by my siblings' schizophrenia. She worries. Typically, her worrying results in her not getting much sleep. Yet she knows there's nothing she can do.

She's exhausted.

I was an emotional mess for the next several days. At first, I was scared, but the Lord took away my fear. I don't know how to explain it. I cried to the Lord. I prayed as best I could. Within a day, the Lord had calmed my anxious heart.

I was no longer scared, so I was left feeling heartbroken. Paul really wasn't any more absent from my life than he had been for the last few years, but he was absent from my dad's life. I was heartbroken for my dad.

Before I knew about Paul disappearing, I had let my morning bible study and prayer time slip. My life showed it in that I was grouchy whenever I felt stressed. I began singing "Praise God, from Whom All Blessings Flow"[39] on my way to work. We don't sing that Doxology at my church, but our homeschool community sings it, and I had been missing it since community had ended for the school year. You may know the words:

Praise God from Whom all blessings flow!
Praise Him, all creatures here below!
Praise Him above, ye heavenly host!
Praise Father, Son, and Holy Ghost!

Now that I knew Paul was missing, I sang "Praise God, from Whom All Blessings Flow" even more. Every time I thought about Paul, I would sing. Then I added "The Lord's Prayer," the same version that is my phone ringer when my dad calls. I found a phenom, Jackie Evancho,[40] on YouTube who sings "The Lord's Prayer" beautifully and pretty much in my range. I listened to it over and over. And when no one else was in the car, I sang along with her. I would sing, and I would cry, often at the same time.

There was nothing else that I could do, even if I had been living in Minnesota, closer to Paul's apartment. There was no fixing—nothing that I could strive to do.

I was too sad, too emotional to pray, but God is good all the time. What else could I do but praise Him?

Rejoice in the Lord always; again I will say, rejoice! (Philippians 4:4 NASB)

This is the day that the Lord has made; let us rejoice and be glad in it. (Psalm 118:24 ESV)

Through Him then, let us continually offer up a sacrifice of praise to God, that is, the fruit of lips that give thanks to His name. (Hebrews 13:15 NASB)

Can you guess what I felt? I felt peace! Peace that passes all understanding.

Be anxious for nothing, but in everything by prayer and supplication with thanksgiving let your requests be made known to God. And the peace of God, which surpasses all comprehension, will guard your hearts and your minds in Christ Jesus. (Philippians 4:6-7 NASB)

Perhaps this is how Job felt when he lost his children and his wealth yet still bowed down to worship the Lord, saying:

Naked I came from my mother's womb,
And naked I shall return there.
The Lord gave and the Lord has taken away.
Blessed be the name of the Lord. (Job 1:20b NASB)

I made plans to fly to Minnesota the following week—after Mitch's surgery. Surgery had gone well. I was able to visit him twice on the trip. My dad and stepmom, Bea, picked me up at the airport, and we went right to the hospital. The next day, my nephew Drew and I went to the hospital before he dropped me off at the airport for my flight home.

In between, I spent time with my dad. I just wanted to comfort him. We just wanted to comfort each other. Only Mom could understand the depth of our sorrow, but she was hiding her feelings back in Virginia.

After another week or so, my dad was able to figure out that Paul had traveled to Boston. Paul had gone to Boston University his first year of college, so it seemed that he traveled to someplace he knew. We created a "missing" flyer and sent it to the university police and a few university departments, but we didn't hear anything during July nor August.

In the meantime, I made myself start studying the Bible again. About a year after moving to the Washington, DC area, I started reading the Bible book-by-book. Well, technically, I was listening to the Bible. A friend of mine from Georgia had introduced me to Dr. Bill Creasy's book-by-book studies.[41] I listened to them while walking the dog. I listened to them in the car. I listened to them while folding laundry. As a result, my Bible knowledge increased immensely.

If you study with Dr. Creasy or anyone else, be sure you are a Berean Christian. Berean Christians compare what they are learning with a good translation of the Bible (such as NASB or ESV), just as the Bereans of New Testament times compared what they heard with the scriptures, as told in the following passage:

> *The brothers immediately sent Paul and Silas away by night to Berea, and when they arrived they went into the Jewish synagogue. Now these Jews were more noble than those in Thessalonica; they received the word with all eagerness,* examining the Scriptures daily *to see if these things were so.* (Acts 17:10-11 ESV, emphasis mine)

For example, Dr. Creasy's explanation of Jesus' words on divorce in the Sermon on the Mount[42] didn't sit well with me. I think there's a reason Dr. Creasy stumbled over his words. His explanation did not match up with the Greek meanings, which I would not have looked up had he not stumbled over his words. Other than that instance, I like his in-depth studies.

My small group did a Beth Moore study of King David's life,[43] and I did every reading and answered every question. I had done that same study many years before when my firstborn was a baby, but I honestly didn't get all the homework done. This time the whole story fascinated me. I kept contemplating the perspective we get in the Bible, well, actually the perspectives, plural, since David's story is told with much more detail in First Samuel, Second Samuel, and First Kings than in First Chronicles. I started wondering what it would have been like to actually be there. How did David's Mighty Men view his story? How did the priests view his story? How did the people view his story? Who decided to give all those details about his scandal with Bathsheba? Isn't it interesting that Samuel anointed David to be the next king when he was about 17 years old, but he didn't become king until he was 30?

As a result of studying David's life, I started praying that, like King David, I would be a person after God's own heart.[44]

I took all the Bible classes at church. I learned Precept Ministries'[45] way of inductive Bible study. I bought a study bible[46] from Precept Ministries, and today it is full of highlighted words and of notes in the margin.

It was again time to get back into the Word. I was up early every morning, studying the book of Acts and asking the Lord for more of the Holy Spirit, which Luke 11:13 gives us permission to do,[47] so that love, joy, peace, patience, kindness, goodness, faithfulness, gentleness, and self-control[48] would be evident in my life.

During a staff meeting, our pastor invited us to join the Sunday morning prayer time. He didn't guilt trip us. I didn't feel bad about what he said. I felt a deep desire to be there. The problem was I couldn't be there at that time, and I took my problem to the Lord immediately, while our pastor was still talking. God pointed out that I could get up earlier. So, I did.

Now every Sunday morning, I was at church before dawn walking around the building at least seven times (like the march around Jericho except sometimes I do a "victory lap") praying,[49] even if it's cold, even if it's raining, even if it's snowing. I always start with worship. Sometimes I sing a praise song. I always ask for more of the Holy Spirit[50] for the church and for me. I pray for whomever enters my mind, which usually includes staff members, that Sunday's volunteers, and all who attend that week.

On the way home, I get breakfast from the McDonald's drive thru for my men. After dropping it off at the house, I take the dog for a run.

I trust that the church has benefitted from this prayer time, but I know that I have personally benefitted greatly. I feel so close to the Lord on those prayer walks. I crave my Sunday morning time with the Lord, and my week feels empty when I am not in town to do my prayer walk around my church.

Often, I wake up before my alarm, as if the Lord is waking me. When I get to see the sun rise, a huge grin fills my face. I feel like the Lord painted the sky just for me.

Worship-based prayer and bible study increased the Holy Spirit within me,[51] and I felt love, joy, peace, patience, kindness, goodness, faithfulness, gentleness, and self-control[52] in my day-to-day life. I was still concerned about Paul. I was still heartbroken for my dad and mom. But I was at peace and growing closer and closer to the Lord.

Dad paid Paul's rent all summer long. He wanted to be sure that Paul had a place to come home to. Dad continued to email Paul, but he never got a response.

In September, Dad decided to stop paying for the apartment. He, Drew, and two of our friends planned to go to Paul's apartment to clean it out so that Paul would get his deposit back.

I decided to go also and arranged to take the day off from work. My coworkers were already praying with me through the whole summer as I got a few more details here and a few more details there.

To help with Paul's apartment, I did an "in-and-out," meaning that I took the first flight into a city and the last flight out on the same day. I got up early that Tuesday morning, and Mom drove me to the airport because Russ was on a business trip.

Drew picked me up at the Minneapolis-St. Paul airport. We had breakfast. Drew was now 30-something and strong in his faith and worship leader at his church. (My dad is still the choir director at his church, and he is 81 years old.)

I told Drew that cleaning out Paul's apartment feels like a funeral, like we didn't think he was ever going to come back. He comforted me and reminded me to trust in the Lord. Then we agreed that we were going to sing praise songs anytime we got emotional that day.

Dad didn't know I had flown to St. Paul to help. When Drew and I pulled into the parking lot of Paul's apartment, Dad was talking to our friends. I hid behind Drew while he shouted, "Grandpa, I have a surprise for you!" Then I popped out from behind him.

I said, "hi" to our friends and gave Dad a big hug. I don't know how either of us were able to pull it together, but we did. Then I gave hugs to our friends and thanked them for helping us.

I went right to the kitchen and started cleaning out the cupboards. Dad, Drew, and the other two men started moving furniture and boxing possessions. Paul had left behind a spoon rest that I had given him. It looked like a bottle of Tabasco sauce. Paul loves Tabasco sauce. I put it in my bag so that I could take it home with me. When Paul got a place of his own again, I'd be happy to give it back to him.

We hadn't gotten emotional, yet, but Drew and I had the same idea at the same time. We started playing worship music on our phones. It certainly made the day easier.

Before we broke for lunch, Drew brought me Paul's prayer shawl (or tallit) and yarmulke (or kappa), which is a head covering that Orthodox Jews wear. Paul is not Orthodox, but he would have worn the yarmulke during prayers along with his prayer shawl.

Drew looked distraught. I looked him in the eye and sang, "Praise God from Whom all blessings flow!"

"But if he doesn't have his prayer shawl and yarmulke, then he must be... He wouldn't go anyplace without these," Drew said.

"He's been showing little signs of leaving his faith," I said. My mom had told me how Paul had given reasons for not following all the kosher food laws that he used to follow. "Let's believe that he is in Boston."

Drew found an updated version of "Praise God, from Whom All Blessings Flow" by Phil Wickham called "Doxology//Amen"[53] on his phone and turned up the volume.

It was a long day. It was an emotional day. But overall, we were at peace.

Our friends left at lunchtime, and Dad decided that he wanted to leave late in the afternoon but before rush hour traffic. He still lived 90 minutes away. Bea wasn't feeling well that day, so she had stayed home. Ironically, before that day, she had written in her prayer journal, "I wonder if Cheryl will be there to close Paul's apartment."

Drew also lived 90 minutes away, but he was content to hang out with me and drive home after rush hour. We went to the Mall of America, got Caribou Coffee, and talked. I was so tired that I tried to pay for our coffee using the Starbucks app on my phone. "I'm sorry," I said to the barista. "It's been a long day."

"A really long day," Drew echoed.

Drew took me to the airport. I got on the plane and went home. I was tired, but I was at peace. I was glad that I had gone to St. Paul to help my dad.

When I got to church the next day, it was time for staff prayers. I love our staff prayer time. I thanked God for my trip, for allowing me to be a blessing to my dad, and for keeping me healthy through the whole thing. My coworkers prayed for me and my family. Afterwards, I got a lot of hugs. Sweet coworkers! I love my coworkers.

A week after that, I fasted because I wanted to feel closer to the Lord. My family knew that I was fasting[54] because I would sit at the dinner table with them and only have water, but I didn't tell anyone else.

One of my coworkers found out because she tried to order dinner for me as well as several others who were working right up to the evening congregational meeting. She wouldn't take "no" for an answer about dinner, so I finally told her that I was fasting. "For your brother?" she asked. Well, yes, but not out of worry. I was primarily fasting because I wanted to be closer to the Lord.

A week later, I woke up earlier than usual because of a dream. Immediately, I wrote it all down in my prayer journal:

Oct 3

Lord, that was quite the dream! When the boys and I arrived in Minneapolis, Dad took us to a restaurant. I remember going in and seeing Dad's coworker walk from the back of the restaurant to the front but not toward me. Dad walked toward the back of the restaurant but stopped, waiting for me to notice.

Paul was in the back of the restaurant!

I didn't know what to do, so I fell to my knees and thanked God.

Paul was shy. It was clear that I shouldn't ask big questions. He wasn't sure about being near me and wouldn't talk to me directly.

I sat in a chair, a comfy chair by a fireplace like Starbucks, but it was not Starbucks. Paul would never go to Starbucks. If he was in a coffee shop, then it would be locally owned and full of character. I had my head in my hands, crying but then pulling myself together. I didn't want to embarrass Paul.

I explained to the boys who Paul was.

Paul's ex-wife was there for a brief time, but I didn't get to talk to her—she had to go.

Watching Paul was amazing. He was shy. He wanted to come near me but was timid. But he looked at me. He looked at me!

He was talking to Dad and joking around.

It didn't dawn on me until I woke up, but Paul no longer had schizophrenia! This was the Paul of the early 1990s.

He was getting closer to me but not talking to me. I understood. I didn't want to make him uncomfortable. I didn't want to ruin this opportunity to restart our friendship. But I didn't know what to say.

Then suddenly, I knew! "Paul, I have an idea."

Paul looked me in the eye. He looked me in the eye! He was timid, but he was listening. "I have two kayaks on the car. I have four life jackets and two paddles. They are ready to go. You can pick the gear you want. We could go kayak Minnehaha Creek." Paul agreed.

We made arrangements for Dad to take the boys and went as a group to the creek to drop off Paul and me.

And then I woke up—10 minutes before my 5:30 am alarm.

Thank You, Lord, for this dream! May it be a vision of what's to come! Although I can't imagine why I'd have my van and kayaks in Minnesota.

When Russ was getting ready for work, I told him about my dream. He stopped, looked at me, and said, "Wow! What do you think it means?" I wasn't willing to speculate out loud.

After I got Daniel off to school, I emailed my dad to tell him about the dream. He wrote back with a kind note. I also told my mom.

I was homeschooling Joshua by now. After a couple years in public school, I brought him home because he just couldn't concentrate on math among so many classmates. That day, he and I began working on his schoolwork. In the afternoon, I did some work for the church from home.

Not long before Daniel got home from school, I got an email from my dad. It was a forwarded note. At 1:30 that afternoon, the Boston University police emailed my dad to say that they had talked to Paul the Saturday before in a university food court.

My dad had found my brother!

The university police had the name of the homeless shelter where Paul was staying. Dad called and left a message for Paul, asking him to call at Dad's expense. Paul never called.

More and more, my prayers became scripture turned into my own personal prayer. For example, I wrote this in my prayer journal:

> *Be gracious to me, O God, according to Your lovingkindness. According to the greatness of Your compassion, blot out my transgressions. Wash me thoroughly from my sin for I know my transgressions, my rebellion, my self-righteousness all too well. Where I don't know it well enough, convict me. My sin is ever before me.*

That's what King David wrote in Psalm 51 with a few personalizations of my own.[55]

I asked my pastor about my dream. It wasn't the first time I had a dream that was a foreshadowing of what was to come. I had had a dream just a few months before that I was in a meeting with my pastor. As I got up to leave the meeting, I said, "Let me know if you are going to do a series on prayer because I could sing 'The Lord's Prayer.'" Within a couple days our pastor told me he was going to do a sermon series on prayer. I just figured it was a coincidence. After all, I was singing "The Lord's Prayer" while alone in the car *a lot* that summer.

My pastor didn't really look me in the eye when he answered me. He said, "With all the spiritual stuff going on in your family, I am not surprised. Besides, you've put a lot of prayer and fasting into this." How did he know that I had fasted?

I was dumbfounded. I didn't know what to do with that. "All the spiritual stuff"? Was he saying that schizophrenia was spiritual not mental or spiritual *and* mental rather than just mental? I wasn't sure, and I wasn't brave enough to ask.

Several weeks later, Dad was able to figure out that shortly after he had left the message for Paul at the homeless shelter in Boston, Paul went to Washington, DC.

I live near Washington, DC.

I talked to Mom about that at length. Wouldn't Paul make the connection between the return address on cards that Mom and I had sent and Washington, DC? Paul was very well learned, excellent at geography, and remembered everything. Certainly, Mom told him that she was moving to a town near DC when she had lunch with him right before moving. I mean, he did know we lived near DC, didn't he? He wouldn't avoid my mom, but he wouldn't seek her out, either. He would avoid me, though, so why would he be near us?

With my coworkers, I volunteered at the homeless shelter every month. It was organized by our Outreach Pastor, Dave. I asked Pastor Dave if he had any suggestions for where to look for Paul in Washington, DC. He didn't know DC shelters, but he pointed out that the shelter where we volunteer is the only one in the area that did not require proof that a resident is from the area. The tears began to flow. Would Paul make his way to our homeless shelter before it got cold? What would I do if he did?

If I went to DC, how would I possibly find him? If I did find him, he would probably bolt out of DC upon seeing me like he bolted out of Boston when Dad left a message for him there. I'd rather he be nearby when he needed help from me than be in another city somewhere in the USA. So, I just sang:

Praise God from Whom all blessings flow!
Praise Him, all creatures here below!
Praise Him above, ye heavenly hosts!
Praise Father, Son, and Holy Ghost!

I don't know how to explain it, but I had peace.[56]

I believed that my brother was alive. I believed that he was physically safe. I trusted the Lord to bring just the right people into his life, people who would help him and point him to Christ.

Unlike the first time Paul was homeless, I no longer asked small. I asked big. Really big.

Oct 21

Lord, Mighty One, Great Healer, I come to You as a sister who has sinned against her brother. I am sorry for not helping him with a plan that night (the night he was evicted).

Lord, soften my brother's heart to hear You and Your great love for him. Let light suddenly flash around him. May he suddenly hear a voice saying, "Saul, Saul, why do you hate me?" May he hear You say, "I am Jesus, the Christ." (Acts 9:3-5)

May my brother be a chosen instrument of Yours to bear Your name before the Gentiles and kings and sons of Israel. I don't want him to suffer. I do want him in a personal relationship with Christ. (Acts 9:15-16)

Give my brother his spiritual sight back and fill him with the Holy Spirit. May he get up and be baptized, take food, and be strengthened. (Acts 9:18-19) May he present his body as a living and holy sacrifice, acceptable to You as a spiritual service of worship. (Romans 12:1) Transform him by the renewing of his mind so that he may prove what the will of God is, that which is good and acceptable and perfect. (Romans 12:2)

Thank You, Lord, for doing so much more than I can think or imagine. (Ephesians 3:20)

In Jesus' Name,
Amen!

Nov 4

Lord, thank You for keeping my brother safe. Help him feel safe. Find him shelter that doesn't cost a lot. If it's Your will, bring him out here. Bring him into a personal relationship with Your Son, Jesus Christ, and heal him body, mind, and soul. (1 Thessalonians 5:23)

May Your will be done in all things. In Jesus' Name, Amen!

Since then, I've had a recurring dream about my brother walking into one of our church services. I see him and say to Pastor Dave, "That's my brother!" That dream hasn't come to be, yet. I don't remember having dreams like this before working at the church, and I've only had one other (which I'll tell you about later) at around the same time. I just thank God for teaching me, even in my sleep.

A CHANCE ENCOUNTER

My mom's leg was hurting and swollen. I took her to the doctor who then sent us for an ultrasound to check for clots. She didn't have any, but the purpose of telling you this is not to tell you about my mom's health but to tell you about the woman I met in the lobby while we waited for the ultrasound appointment.

A 20-something young man came into the lobby with his mother. He was pacing and mumbling. He played with the water cooler. His mom corrected him and cleaned up the water.

Clearly this man was not in his right mind, and his mother was distraught. I moved to sit down next to her and talked to her quietly. She told me that her son was there for yet another test and that he was stressed out about it. She freely admitted that she was really stressed, too.

I told her I understood because both of my siblings have schizophrenia. I pointed out who my mom was. "She's been through it all twice."

The woman clearly needed someone to talk to and was relieved to talk to someone who understood. She said her son had schizophrenia. She also told me she had two teenagers at home who were sick of the whole situation. I was about to say something about not neglecting the teens—I used to be them, after all—but she and her son were called in for his test.

I still pray for her today. I pray that God will bring her back into my life so that I can encourage her.

WHAT DID I LEARN?

With Paul close by but still missing, the Lord continued to remind me that I cannot fix this situation. It is in *His* hands. There was no point in striving to fix:

"Cease striving and know that I am God." (Psalm 46:10 NASB)

It's taken me a long time to realize that my siblings are not my responsibility. They are adults. They are on their own journey. I have not been invited by them to help, and even if they were to invite me, it would be my job to point them to Christ because He's the only one who can provide the direction and the healing that they need.

No medicine, no doctor, no government program can fix their lives. Only Christ can do that.

(If you need a song to remind yourself that you cannot fix things, listen to "King of the World" by Natalie Grant.[57] You can find the official lyric video on Natalie Grant's YouTube channel.)

I learned that there is hope because Jesus Christ is the Great Healer.[58] He is able to do whatever He wants, but He needs willing hearts that listen to Him and follow His directions to their straight path.[59] He will accomplish Romans 8:28—if we let Him.

And we know that God causes all things to work together for good to those who love God, to those who are called according to His purpose. (Romans 8:28 NASB)

It's also taken me a long time to realize that my responsibility for my parents is limited. I see now that Paul's situation is a test for my dad and my mom. My parents must learn to know themselves and to know God through this test. I cannot take away the pain of this test, and it's not my job to try.

I've learned my circumstances do not dictate what I do with my life. If I let circumstances influence my decisions, then I let satan win, and I suffer.

That's what I did in high school when my sister became mentally ill with schizophrenia. I did not turn *to* my Lord and Savior but instead I turned *away* from Him, blaming Him for my circumstances. As a result, I sinned through premarital sex, abortion, and living with my boyfriend before marriage. If I had been listening to God, I never would've married Arnold, saving both of us from the pain of loveless marriage and divorce.

As a result of my sexual sins and my abortion, my vitality was drained away.[60] I was in bondage.[61]

I used to describe my former self as "the walking dead" long before *The Walking Dead* became the name of a TV show. I was going about life, but I was dead inside until I chose Christ and confessed my sins.

King David elegantly described what happens with his uncon-fessed sin after he not only committed adultery but had a man killed to cover up what he had done:

When I kept silent about my sin, my body wasted away through my groaning all day long. For day and night Your hand was heavy upon me; my vitality was drained away as with the fever heat of summer. I acknowledged my sin to You and my iniquity I did not hide. I said, "I will confess my trans-gressions to the Lord"; and You forgave the guilt of my sin. (Psalm 32:3-5 NASB, emphasis mine)

Before I chose Christ and confessed my sin, only my sister was mentally ill. Now my brother *also* has schizophrenia, and now I *do* turn to God, believing that He will work all things out to His glory. Today I ask God what it is that I am supposed to learn from these circumstances and what it is that I am supposed to do or not do, say or not say.

For if I look to the Lord and seek His face,[62] concentrate on Him,[63] then I have peace that passes all understanding[64]—I'm not worrying, I'm not striving, I'm not fixing. Instead I make Godly decisions.[65]

My testimony[66] in just a few words:

If I turn away from God during difficult circumstances, I make stupid and life-changing decisions that drain vitality from my life.

If I turn to God through difficult circumstances, I have peace that passes all understanding and divine direction for my life.

C.S. Lewis said it even better:

Life with God is not immunity from difficulties but peace in difficulties.

WALKfm.org posted the following on Facebook:

Remember Shadrach, Meshach, & Abednego.[67] God didn't put out the fire. He just put Jesus in there with them. It's not about God "putting out your fires." It's about Who is in there with you.

Remember that Jesus did not come to bring peace on the earth,[68] but to be peace[69] in your heart:

"Peace I leave with you; My peace I give to you; not as the world gives do I give to you. Do not let your heart be troubled, nor let it be fearful." (John 14:27 NASB)

When people would ask me how I was doing back when I was going through my divorce, I would answer, "Fine," meaning Feeling Insecure, Neurotic, and Emotional. Today, when people ask me how I'm doing, I respond like this: "I have peace because I worship the Prince of Peace."[70]

I have peace because I worship the Prince of Peace.

10
HELPING AFRICA OR AFRICA HELPING ME

I thought I had finished writing this story. But once I got serious about getting published, God impressed on me that this book was not complete. As a result, here I am ready to tell you more.

At the point I left off, I had been working for the church for a year and a half. Pastor Dave organized the annual short-term mission trip to Uganda, which is on the north side of Lake Victoria in Africa, and I wanted to go. Dave's enthusiasm for mission work and compassion for our partners in Uganda was infectious. As a result, I signed up to be on the team. We were to leave for Uganda the day after Christmas.

SERVING REGARDLESS OF CIRCUMSTANCES

Whenever you do something for God, satan goes after you. He's crafty.[71] He steals.[72] He's a schemer.[73] I knew that satan could put my brother's situation in the way of my going to Uganda, but I wouldn't let him. I purposely put on my Armor of God[74] by studying the Bible and praying scripture. Here's one example from my journal:

Oct 27

Lord, I rejoice and am glad that salvation comes from You, from Your Son Jesus Christ. I rejoice in Your sovereignty, Your great plan and that I get to be part of it. How exciting it must have been for the Apostles to see so many come to faith in You while they watched and did Your will. How empowering it must have felt to have the Holy Spirit speak through them to the chief priests. I can only imagine that feeling of "wow, the Holy Spirit definitely put those words in my mouth." I want to be as on fire for You as the Apostles were in the book of Acts. My life may look different than theirs, and You may have very different plans for my evangelism and teaching, but You can still light the fire inside me and fan the flame. Lord, use me to do Your will.

Pull Russ and the boys closer to Yourself. Pull Mom, Dad, and Bea closer. Pull Nancy and Paul closer. Give us all discernment. Show us what is from the evil one and what is just our flesh. Give us direction. Make our paths straight and light the way. Bring the Uganda team closer to You. Give all of us a desire to spend time in Your word and in prayer with You. There's no better place to be!

My armor is on, Lord. Send me. Give me ears that hear and a will to obey. Here I am, Lord. Send me.

In Jesus' name, Amen!

While praying scripture, I also prayed to become a bondservant (sometimes translated bondslave) to God, like Mary was.[75] I vowed to the Lord that I would pierce my ears with a second hole in each as a sign that I was His bondservant. I got this idea from Exodus 21:5-6 where Moses explains that if a servant who was to be set free plainly says:

"'I love my master... and do not want to go free,' then his master must take him before the judges. He shall take him to the door or the doorpost and pierce his ear with an awl. Then he will be his servant for life." (NIV)

My plan was to get the piercings in January as soon as I got back from the trip.

I also prayed for more of the Holy Spirit[76] for Russ. Because I had seen my own behaviors change and improve once I prayed for more of the Holy Spirit for myself, I thought I would ask the Lord to give more of the Holy Spirit to Russ, the boys, and Mom. Evidently God answered my prayer because Russ said he was the calmest he had ever been leading up to Christmas. My jaw dropped. "Really?" I asked. Russ nodded his head. "I've been praying for more of the Holy Spirit for you."

My mom's leg problem had her sitting in her chair for six weeks leading up to Christmas. My husband's hip was hurting. My boys, ages 13 and nine, had never been without me for more than a day or two. But I was still going. They could get by without me for 13 days. And they did. They had a good time eating all the things that I wouldn't make for them, like store-bought lasagna and chocolate pudding. God took care of everything while I was gone.

Although there were many cool things about the mission trip, two stand out for me: teaching the Bible to children and a conversation about Down Syndrome and abortion.

TEACHING THE BIBLE TO CHILDREN

Three of our team members had been assigned to teach the children of pastors and ministry leaders who were at a pastors' conference led by Pastor Dave and our partner Pastor Cyrus, and I was one of them.

I kept thinking about a bible curriculum for kids that I had learned about over a year earlier. Previously, when we had decided to homeschool Joshua, I knew that we would use the Classical Conversations (CC) curriculum and join a local CC homeschool community. CC encourages the primary schooling parent to go to a Parent Practicum during the summer to learn about the upcoming year's curriculum and to be encouraged as we also went deeper in our knowledge, understanding, and wisdom.

Parent Practicum begins with a keynote speaker who addresses the entire group. Our speaker was Katharine Wang, Founder of Master the Bible Ministries[77] and herself a CC mom. Katharine mentioned that through her ministry she was writing a bible study curriculum for kids that taught key events in Jesus' life in chronological order, used songs to help kids memorize key facts and scripture, and taught the geography of the Bible as well. What she described sounded like a great way to teach my boys, so I signed up to get information about the curriculum as it became available.

I hadn't heard anything about a release date for the curriculum, but I couldn't get it out of my mind. I thought about contacting Katharine to ask directly, but I kept not writing the email. Then I had a weird dream.

In the dream, I was getting on an airplane to go on a trip. Russ was dropping me off at the airport, but the boys were not with me. The boys always travel with me, so this was unusual and really stuck out to me. Katharine was in the dream, too, following me around. She wasn't talking to me or anyone else. She was just there following me wherever I went.

When I woke up, I decided to email Katharine to ask about the curriculum. I told her that I was going to Uganda the day after Christmas, that I was going to be teaching children, and that I wanted to teach her curriculum. Katharine didn't have the curriculum completed, yet, but she agreed to send her draft with me to Uganda and asked that in exchange I give her feedback so that she could make it even better. "Absolutely!" I said. We were essentially beta testing her curriculum for her.

I needed to practice teaching the materials, so I invited my CC community to join me for several weeks so that I could practice with the kids. Then I took the curriculum to Uganda and taught it there.

It wasn't a perfect teaching experience. We thought we would be teaching children who knew English, but they did not know English well enough. We learned the high schoolers knew English, but younger children were not yet fluent enough to receive instruction in English. Swahili was the primary language where we were. We had a great translator, Ronald, and a wonderful helper, Timothy. They helped us as much as they helped the children.

We made changes to the curriculum on the fly so that the language barrier would not be as much of an issue. The second day went much better—so much so that they wanted more lessons than we thought we would teach that day.

With Katharine's blessing, I left her curriculum with the Bishop in that area and gave electronic copies to our partners in Kampala (where their primary language is Luganda).

When we came back from the trip, I met with Katharine to give her feedback on the curriculum. The drawings of characters worked well because the children had a visual to go with the story. They enjoyed participating in the story by holding the drawings. The bible verses were too detailed, especially for translating. The children best responded when there were short quotes. Katharine was inspired to make revisions. Now she has published her work for the USA and has a vibrant ministry with materials for both children and women. Find her ministry online at MastertheBibleMinistries.com.

TALKING ABOUT DOWN SYNDROME AND ABORTION

Before the Uganda trip, only one person in Virginia (other than my husband and my mom) knew about my abortion. A couple years before the Uganda trip, my neighborhood friend Erin sent me a private message via Facebook to say that she was following my example by advocating for life through comments on a Facebook post. My immediate thought was, "Oh, no. What did I do now?" I don't remember what I had posted on Facebook about abortion, but even when I stopped putting up articles about politics, I continued to post articles about abortion because for me it's not a political issue—and I would dare people to ask me about it. No one ever did.

I looked for the post Erin referenced and the conversation that was taking place in the comments. I went back to her in our private conversation and said, "Don't talk about the baby."

"What?" she said.

"Don't talk about the baby. The pro-choice don't believe it's a baby, and it's not worth the fight because they aren't going to change their minds. Instead, talk about the woman and all the reasons why abortion is not good for her."

And so, she did. I think I gave Erin other advice, too, and told her that I understood her audience very well because I used to be one of them. I also told her that I had had an abortion. She's Catholic. I had no idea how she would respond because my perspective of Catholics is skewed. But she continued to be my friend—and still is today.

Leading up to the Uganda trip, Pastor Dave was interviewing congregants who wanted to go on the trip. I asked him when he was going to interview me, and he said, "We don't have to meet. You work here, so I know that you will submit to my authority."

"But don't applicants have to share their testimony with you?"

"Yes, and the team will share their testimonies with each other at our retreat before the trip."

"Well, then we have to meet before the retreat so that you can hear my testimony. You have to hear my testimony before everyone else does."

For the first time, I told my story to someone in Virginia. Then I told the other team members at the retreat.

I don't know how to explain how difficult that was for me. Because if you remember when I told my story at my baptism back in Minnesota, I only got Acknowledgment from one pastor and no one else. I told my story at a women's Christmas tea for the same church, and I felt like I got the Christian cold shoulder.

While still in Minneapolis, Russ and I switched to a church in our neighborhood (not because of my experience at the previous church but because Russ felt that we needed to serve in our neighborhood). When my pastor at our new church asked me to give my testimony during a church service, I only agreed to do it because I was moving out of the state shortly thereafter. I don't remember anyone saying anything positive or negative to me. Some people seemed to avoid me, perhaps because they struggled with infertility and didn't know how to be around someone who didn't value the gift given her when they couldn't conceive at all.

However, one person was truly kind: Brianna. I met Brianna when she volunteered for Vacation Bible School (VBS), during which she helped my older son Daniel when he was stressed. She spoke kindly when she talked to him and then again to me when she explained what had happened at VBS.

After I gave my testimony, Brianna reached out to me. She asked if we could get together, so one night she came over to my house. We sat on the porch and talked for hours and hours.

Brianna told me she had been in a similar situation. I thought she was telling me she had had an abortion, but she wasn't. She was telling me that her son, who was about 10 years old, was born out of wedlock. Actually, he was a twin, but his sister didn't survive.

My heart broke. Brianna was telling me that she had also sinned by having premarital sex, but she wasn't there to judge me for choosing to abort but to let me know that I wasn't the only one who got pregnant from premarital sex. Brianna made the right choice and then had the sorrow of losing one of her babies, yet she showed me love even though I killed my baby.

We had a pleasant evening of sharing our life stories. We lamented that we had not gotten to know each other sooner. Now that we had bonded over a common experience, I was moving. I will forever treasure that night on the porch. Briana died from cancer less than a year later. Someday, we'll sit on our porches in heaven and share stories. I look forward to it!

A few weeks after Brianna's visit on the porch, we moved to Georgia. On a visit back to Minnesota, I had dinner with my women's bible study group. They all still loved me no matter my testimony. Yet I never told a soul about my abortion while living in Georgia. Even though my friends in Minnesota still loved me, I continued to feel like I was wearing a Scarlet Letter, and I hid it from all those I met in Georgia.

Why? Because I didn't want to experience the Christian cold shoulder again. People don't seem to know how to respond to someone who has had an abortion. The pro-life movement is so vocal about abortion being murder that we murderers do not feel forgiven by our church families even once we know we are forgiven by Christ. If people responded by giving us hugs after we give our testimonies, like Pastor Brendon did, then we would be less afraid to tell people how Christ has worked in our lives.

Oh, and that's just the abortion part of my story. Then there's schizophrenia. There are three of us and two have schizophrenia. Even if someone doesn't say the words, their body language says, "Do *you* have schizophrenia?" I just never know how people are going to respond to my story.

Before we went to Uganda, Pastor Dave and the congregants on the team all knew I had had an abortion. Pastor Cyrus did not. Nor did any of our team members who live in Uganda.

THE UGANDAN BOY WITH DOWN SYNDROME

On the first day of teaching the Bible to children in Uganda, we noticed a boy who was not like the other children. Clearly, he was developmentally delayed. I quickly guessed that he had Down Syndrome. My friend Jennifer has a boy with Down Syndrome, and I know many moms of boys on the Autism spectrum. He reminded me more of Jennifer's son than other boys.

There was another boy in charge of him, pulling him around and telling him what to do. It was sad to see how the children treated this boy, although not unlike how children in the USA treat children with special needs. The difference is that here we usually have special education assistants to guide and guard our children.

I tried to befriend the boy, whom I later found out was five years old, but he seemed afraid of me. Maybe I was the first white person he had seen!

Before we left for the hotel that evening, I saw the boy with his mom and asked to speak with her. Once we found a Swahili translator, I told her that God made her son perfectly and that God would be glorified through him. I told her I knew that parenting is hard and that parenting a child with special needs is harder but that God would strengthen her in the process. I wrote in my journal that night that I trust God had put those words in my mouth.

At dinner, I asked what would happen to the boy. Pastors Cyrus and Dave explained that he will never go to school. His parents will teach him how to harvest whatever they grow in the garden. We pray that he is not assaulted and left for dead.

Pastors Cyrus and Dave explained that we were blessed to know this boy is even alive. Many Ugandan mothers, upon seeing that their babies have an abnormality, drop them in the pit. By pit I mean an African outhouse, an outhouse with no seat, a squatty potty.

Let that sink in for a minute.

In the USA when a doctor tells us that the baby may not be "normal,"[78] we tear her apart using a vacuum. We call it abortion. Are we any better? No. We're all killing babies.

Then Pastor Cyrus told a story about someone's daughter who ran away with her boyfriend. Her parents were distraught, heartbroken. The mother sent an email to the daughter telling her that if she were to get pregnant, then she should come home, and they (her parents) would help with the baby. Well, the daughter wasn't pregnant when she read the email, but she got pregnant shortly thereafter. The boyfriend left her, and she went home to her parents. She credits that email from her mother for saving her child's life.

Pastor Cyrus pointed out that we need to choose our words wisely. When we say, "Don't come home pregnant," no matter where in the world we live, we are effectively telling our daughters to go have an abortion. He preaches on this in Uganda and other African countries because their dowry system means that pregnant daughters are "damaged goods" (his words), and the parents will not receive a dowry or as much of one for a daughter who already has a child. In a third-world country like Uganda, that's a big deal. However, as Christ followers, we are all called to obey His teachings no matter where we live.[79]

What Pastor Cyrus said reminded me of the other teen in my high school who got pregnant. I remembered how her high school counselor told her she had to go to the alternative school, even though she was at the top of our class. This could have influenced her to have an abortion, but she made the right choice instead.

I told the pastors that we need to have these same conversations at home in the USA. We women don't want to hear from men about abortion because as much as they try, men do not understand.[80] We women are the ones who can change things by talking woman to woman. We need to speak up.

The Holy Spirit was talking through me and to me. What I didn't know was how much this conversation was about to change my life. I saw Pastor Cyrus quietly nodding his head. I soon found out he told his wife that she needed to talk to me.

Later, I learned that one of our Ugandan drivers, Emmanuel, who was studying to be a pastor, had told his daughters not to come home pregnant. He thought he was teaching them to abstain from sex by saying this. He realized, after listening to us talk at the dinner table, that he needed to have a different conversation with his children. And so, he did.

A couple days later, the whole team was together again, having an interesting conversation about how our congregation might react to bringing someone to church who used to be in jail. I can't even remember how we got to that question, but I knew my response.

"What about me?" There was an awkward silence. "You have no idea how much your acceptance means to me. Everyone at this table except Pastor Cyrus knows about my abortion, although I'm sure he's figured it out by now. Many Christians are not accepting of me once they know what I did."

Later that day, my dear friend Pam gave me a hug, a purposeful reminder that she loves me despite my "big sin." I needed that.

BECOMING AN INTENTIONAL CHRISTIAN

After we got home from Uganda, I made a conscious effort to know the names of the women I saw every week in the McDonald's drive thru Sunday mornings after my prayer walk around the church building. One of the things that I had learned in Uganda was to treat everyone who was serving us well because you never know when you might get the opportunity to share the gospel. As a result, I took that thought home with me and became more intentional in the drive thru. Now I always approach the speaker and say, "Good morning," with a cheery voice no matter what the server on the other end sounds like. I remember working at McDonald's while in high school and in my early twenties. It's a long day with unhappy customers or with customers who are just indifferent. My goal was now to make the employees smile.

Susan is the employee I saw most frequently. We became friendly. She's from India, and she misses her home. When she realized I'm a Christian, I saw her smile diminish. How sad that her reaction to Christians is not a positive one. Well, I'm out to change her perspective, and so I engage her in conversation every week. My goal each Sunday? To make her smile. My long-term goal? To share the love of Christ with her. She would make a beautiful addition to the kingdom.

BECOMING CHRIST'S BONDSERVANT

Pastor Dave and his wife hosted dinner so that Pastor Cyrus could introduce me to his wife, Julie, who had started a ministry called Julie's Heart Cry.[81] Julie's Heart Cry aims to stop abortion one woman at a time both in the USA and abroad.

Julie was looking for post-abortive women to speak at her events. I didn't even want to be at this dinner, even though it was my idea in the first place. I organized the dinner to introduce Russ to Cyrus so that they could talk about a building project for our Ugandan partners, but the dinner became about Julie meeting me. I didn't want to tell more people about my abortion. But... since I told God before I went to Uganda that I was His bondservant, I said, "I will speak whenever you want me to."

Julie and I later got together and shared our stories with each other. Shortly after, she went to Africa by herself to meet with potential ministry partners. She went to Uganda and several other countries. She spoke to ministry partners and listened to women's stories. When she told me about her trip, I was excited about everything she had to say, and I was a little jealous. She said, "I wish I had someone there to record all the stories."

"I want to be that person!" I exclaimed. "Next time you go, I want to go with you to record stories. That's what I do."

Is that what I do? I guess I have done that in the past in various ways, like writing for my high school newspaper and writing for corporate communications. I have always dreamed of writing other people's stories, but I've never done it.[82]

While talking to Julie about her ministry's mission statement, I realized the Lord was nudging me to change the conversation about abortion—shifting the way that we talk about this sensitive issue. I didn't know exactly *how* the Lord wanted me to do that, but I knew it would involve telling people I had had an abortion, and I didn't want to do that.

In the months following the Uganda trip, I didn't sleep much. I would wake up multiple times in the middle of the night. I would have nightmares or just wake up and not be able to get back to sleep. I finally realized I was under spiritual attack. After all, satan didn't want me to obey God. He wants abortion. Realizing this, I started praying scripture-based prayers before bed.

I was finally able to sleep the whole night. Then Joshua started waking in the middle of the night with nightmares, so I was up with him. I realized this was also spiritual attack. It was as if satan understood that he couldn't get to me directly, so now he was going after my son. When he doesn't sleep, I don't sleep. When he and I don't get much sleep, we struggle to be kind and to get everything done.

Before I went to Uganda, I had told the Lord I would be His bondservant. I made this commitment before I went to Uganda, but now that the Lord was asking me to tell people about my abortion, I didn't want to keep my commitment.

Then I realized that the more resistant I was to fulfill my vow, the more I felt spiritual attacks. The Lord allowed the attacks. He was trying to get my attention. Would the Lord allow spiritual attacks on Joshua to get to me? I don't think so, but satan is a thief.[83]

I finally did it. I went to the mall and got my ears pierced. I took a picture of my newly pierced ears and sent it to Julie. I had to tell her that I was committed to doing whatever the Lord told me to do.

Submit yourselves, then, to God. Resist the devil, and he will flee from you. (James 4:7 NIV)

Joshua began sleeping the whole night, too.

Shortly thereafter, I was at a women's conference at my church. The keynote speaker was Jennie Allen, Founder of the IF:Gathering.[84] She cleverly led us through giving up our "large backpacks" of burdens and led us into whatever the Lord was telling us to do. On the second day, when we were ready to hear from the Lord, she asked what we thought the Lord was calling us to do but that we had not yet done.

One woman talked about starting a social group for parents of children with disabilities. The moms' disabilities small group all cheered. Then someone else shared another ministry idea.

Jennie enjoyed those stories but pointed out that we could share non-ministry ideas, too. Then someone shared that the Lord has been telling her to go running with her neighbor. "Great!" Jennie said. "Do you feel any resistance to obeying God?"

"Yes, I hate running!" Of course, we all laughed.

Then Jennie told us to write down three-to-five things that the Lord was telling us to do.

We were sitting behind the leader of the women's ministry, Roxy. She's the one who had organized this women's conference. I knew Julie had talked to her about having an event at our church about abortion. Talking to Roxy was the first thing on my list.

Then Jennie Allen had us share the list with our neighbor because once we share it, it becomes real. I shared my list with my friend Hassanatu. Then I tapped Roxy's shoulder and said, "I need to talk to you. You're the first thing on my list." She was so surprised!

When we all headed for breakout sessions, I went looking for Roxy. I didn't want to talk to her, but I knew that I needed to obey God. When Roxy had a few minutes, I told her I was a friend of Julie's, and I understood they had talked about having an event about abortion at our church. I told her I would offer my testimony.

Again, telling someone I had had an abortion was hard, but Roxy was kind. Several months later, Julie, Roxy, and I met to discuss ideas for an event and later hosted it at our church. Someone working with Roxy named it "Faces of Abortion."

After the women's conference, I read Jennie Allen's book, *Anything*,[85] which is basically about saying to God that you will do anything He asks. That is what a bondservant would do, right? She would do anything her Master says to do. Jennie Allen's book gave me practical examples of how this prayer affected her life, and I was even more encouraged to do anything for my Lord and Savior.

My early morning prayers continued. Every morning, the Lord would wake me for our prayer and bible reading time. I journaled my prayers. My requests were not about material things but about the Lord keeping me on His straight path[86] and being a lamp unto my feet.[87] Every morning, I would offer to do anything He asked.

Shortly after the women's conference, Julie asked me if I would speak to women and teens in June—in Uganda. Of course, I said, "Yes!" I love the people of Uganda and longed to see my new-found friends. What an incredible opportunity to encourage women and teens in Uganda and then return home to do the same in the USA.

Here's what I wrote in my prayer journal after receiving Julie's invitation:

March 16

Wow, Lord! Just wow! Talk about fast forward. No rest. Ok! Whatever You decide. I am all Yours.

My heart is steadfast, O Lord, my heart is steadfast. I will sing, yes, I will sing praises! I will give thanks to You, O Lord, among the peoples. I will sing, yes, I will sing praises to You among the nations! Psalm 57

May Your face shine upon me!

Lord, although I never wanted to tell others about my abortion, I am excited to speak! I know that's not humble, but it's true. I am so excited to see coming true what You told me so many years ago when you twice nudged me to be a Christian speaker. Please don't let me screw this up!

To Your glory, Lord, to Your glory! Thy will be done.

Jesus, my Lord and Savior, you are life. You are my Light. Your Light shines in the darkness and the darkness did not understand.

I come humbly as a witness, to testify about Your Light so that all may believe through me. Oh, how humbling that is. That You would send me, a huge sinner—full of pride and bitterness—to testify about You so that all who hear may believe.

Lord, thank You for speaking to me today, giving me Your words.

I talked to Pastor Dave about presenting to a smaller group of women over the summer because one of the women in leadership had a heart for the abortion issue. He said, "Don't wait. Talk to the women's daytime bible study this spring." Um. Okay. Honestly, I was not prepared to hear that. I would have protested about speaking so soon, but I remembered those second holes in my ears.

I realized that since I would be telling my story in my church, I needed to tell my boys. They needed to hear my story from me, not someone else.

I talked to Russ about telling the boys, who were now 13 and nine. He had a great idea—to tell the boys on Good Friday. After Good Friday dinner, we sat on our deck and each of us told the boys our stories. Both of the boys were blown away because they have only known us as Christians yet both of us did not become Christ followers until we were adults. Both boys were so sweet and loving. After we told them our stories, we had communion followed by s'mores. It's a memory that I'll always treasure.

That spring, our church decided to reduce staff. I prayed on whether I should be one of the staff to leave. I felt like the Lord wanted me to be home with my family, homeschooling both boys (not just Joshua), while simultaneously speaking boldly about abortion and purity. I had an incredible peace about it. As a result, I opted to leave.

My last day was a week after Easter. I worked extra hours both for Easter and to make sure that my coworkers knew where to find everything and how to do my job. I was exhausted. But instead of taking a vacation, I took a one-day prayer retreat. I had my favorite breakfast of corned beef hash and eggs at a local diner with my prayer journal in hand. Then I found a park, a place to be outside in God's creation, and sat at a picnic bench with my bible, my highlighters, and my prayer journal.

I praised God for He is good all the time. I studied the end of Isaiah, as my Holy Spirit confidence led me to do. I highlighted. I cross referenced. I asked God to open my mind to understanding the scriptures (which is from Luke 24:45[88]). God began opening my eyes to the straight path[89] that He had for me and to what He was calling me to do. It was that day Isaiah 58:1 became my theme verse, what I am called to do:

> *"Cry loudly, do not hold back;*
> *Raise your voice like a trumpet,*
> *And declare to My people their transgression*
> *And to the house of Jacob their sins." (NASB)*

I went home in time for dinner, feeling refreshed.

HIP REPLACEMENT SURGERY

Before my last day at work, we found out that Russ needed to have his right hip replaced. I thought the timing was perfect because I would be free from work to help him with recovery before going back to Uganda.

However, since it was unclear how much of Russ' pain was from his back and how much was from his hip, he first tried injections to relieve the pain. He seemed to be doing okay until the middle of May. The pain had gotten progressively worse. He was miserable.

In early June, Russ called to get surgery scheduled and got a doctor appointment to discuss whether to have surgery the day I was to return from Uganda, but the doctor's office was concerned about scheduling surgery so soon after injections. Evidently, there's increased risk of bone infection when surgery is too soon after an injection.

Russ is no wimp. The pain was bad, so the doctor called him in for a new x-ray. The x-ray showed that he had avascular necrosis or AVN, a condition in which poor blood supply to an area of bone leads to bone death. AVN was the reason he had increased pain despite the injections. They scheduled surgery for July 11.

Before surgery, I was doing more and more nursing for Russ so that he would be more comfortable. I was glad I was no longer working. The timing for leaving my job was perfect. Thank You, Lord!

But I was conflicted about going back to Uganda with Julie to speak. I wanted to be home for all of June to take care of Russ, but I also knew God was calling me to Uganda. It wasn't just that I wanted to go. I had Holy Spirit confidence that the Lord was sending me.

At the very least, I could shorten my trip by a day. I changed my flights so that I would leave Uganda as soon as my speaking obligations were complete. I'd be home Monday, June 26.

NEW WORSHIP MUSIC

I was still up early every morning to pray, and I was still singing "Praise God, from Whom All Blessings Flow" to myself whenever things were difficult, like when I saw Russ in pain (which was pretty much all the time). Then an idea popped into my head. I could create a playlist on my phone of worship music that was only praise to God, nothing about me or my difficulties. On my playlist, I put:

- "What a Beautiful Name" by Hillsong Worship[90]
- "Great Are You, Lord" by All Sons & Daughters[91]
- "There Is Power" by Lincoln Brewster[92]

I listened to my playlist while walking the dog. I listened while washing the dishes. I listened while in the car—and sang, too, if no one else was with me. I worshiped the Lord, and He gave me peace and patience.

I realized this is what Daniel Henderson taught the staff and volunteers at church—praise God in prayer and in song. The singing part didn't click in my mind until I put together this playlist. It doesn't matter whether you're praising through contemporary worship music, old hymns,[93] or Handel's "Messiah." We just need to praise Him!

FLYING STANDBY

When Julie had asked me to go to Uganda, the challenge was figuring out how to pay for the flight, which would've been about $1200 if I had purchased the tickets in March. Then it occurred to me that I could fly standby.

Remember that Russ is retired from an airline, so I can fly standby for little or no cost. Because I'd be flying with a different airline, there was a cost, but it was less than $500, which was much better than the $1200 ticket that guaranteed me a seat. My dad generously paid the standby cost.

Although the money part of standby sounds wonderful, the unpredictability can be very unnerving. Choosing standby when I have to be in-country at a specific time ready to speak was a risky choice, but I had complete peace about it.[94] As a result, I listed as a standby passenger on four flights: Washington, DC to Amsterdam, Amsterdam to Uganda, Uganda to Amsterdam, and Amsterdam back to DC.

Standby made Julie nervous—and understandably so. What if one of her speakers didn't make it to Uganda? Not only would she have to punt, but it would affect her reputation.

But I had absolute peace—no worries at all. I felt absolutely confident that I would get there on time.

CHANGE IN PLANS

It was one week before I was to leave for Uganda. Russ was in so much pain that he wanted to change his surgery to an earlier date. Although I hated seeing him in pain, I did not like the risk of bone infection. Bone infection sounded like worse pain and worse consequences than AVN, so we prayed. After prayer, we both had peace about asking the doctor if he would reschedule the surgery for an earlier date.

Later that day, Russ texted me with a new surgery date: Tuesday, June 27. I was scheduled to land on Monday, June 26—twenty-four hours beforehand as a standby passenger. I had a moment of panic. What if I didn't get on that plane? Then I realized God had planned everything. After just a moment of doubt, I had peace that passes all understanding.[95]

GETTING ON THE PLANE

Getting on the first plane was the hardest. Not because there were no seats but because I was leaving my husband behind, my husband who was in a great deal of pain.

Yet I realized I couldn't prevent him from falling. I couldn't prevent him from getting into a car accident. He was in God's hands. I had to trust Him.

Faith. The Lord was testing my faith.

At the gate, Julie wanted to know what the next option was if I were not to get on this flight. I didn't know. I hadn't looked up the next flight option. I had unbelievable peace and said, "I'm getting on this plane." And I did.

In Amsterdam, I still had absolute peace, and I got on the second plane.

Russ later told me that he didn't think I would get on the first plane. When I did, he heard God whisper, "Do you think I'd give her an assignment and not get her there?"

IN UGANDA

Julie had put together a speaking team of three: Julie herself, the founder of Julie's Heart Cry; Rhonda Darville, founder of the Bahamas GodParent Center,[96] and me.

We had a great time while God worked through us. We spoke to teens on Friday, women on Saturday, and churchgoers on Sunday. We encouraged one another, we learned more about Ugandan culture, and we laughed at ourselves.

I was blessed to hear from people who were encouraged by our honesty. Many were shocked that I, a white woman, had had an abortion. I was taken aback by their surprise. They think because I'm white on the outside, I'm white on the inside—that is, perfect. Say what!?! Oh, did I bust their bubble.

Another thing happened that bothered me. Whenever Julie, Rhonda, and I would get our picture taken together, they wanted to put me in the middle. I said, "No Oreo®!" There was no reason to put me in the middle. This was Julie's event. She should be in the middle. Several months later, I was at a fundraiser for our local pregnancy center. I had been invited by my small group leader, Jennifer, who works there. Our friend Hassanatu went, too. The three of us took a selfie. They were going to put me in the middle. I said, "No Oreo!" This was Jennifer's event. She should be in the middle.

Note to white people: Don't put yourself in a position to be elevated above others. Go out of your way to *not* be elevated. You know as well as I do that we are not white on the inside. Not only are we just as sinful, but we have a legacy of being colonizers[97] and oppressors. Go out of your way to be humble because humility glorifies the Lord.

GOING HOME

Julie was just as concerned about my getting home as she was my getting to Uganda. I was going to the airport—late at night in a foreign country, a white woman traveling alone in Africa. What a dear friend to be so concerned about me.

But, again, I had peace that passes understanding.[98]

Emmanuel, our driver and protector—the very same driver we had on the previous trip—very kindly saw me all the way to the door and watched me go through security.

When I went to check my bag, I got my seat assignment—I was getting on the plane to Amsterdam.

Once in Amsterdam, I had a seven-hour layover, which provided opportunity to pray and reflect on the weekend.

When I went to the gate, the gate agent told me that the flight was full and asked if I would take a jump seat. I had never been asked that before. It sounded exciting!

Again, I wasn't nervous at all. There's nothing I can do about the situation, remember? This was all in God's hands.

On Facebook, I requested prayer. Then I went to get cleaned up. After all, I had been dancing in church Sunday morning, perspiring in the Uganda heat all day, sitting on an eight-hour flight, then sitting in the airport for another seven hours. I didn't smell too good.

When I returned to the gate, I watched person after person get on the plane. The gate agents were all very efficient.

I amended my request for prayer on Facebook, saying that if they hadn't heard from me by 7:45 am, then assume I was on the plane.

It seemed like everyone was on the plane. The gate agent made a phone call. She was talking in Dutch, but I understood "Krichbaum." I tried connecting to the Wi-Fi so that I could quickly post on Facebook that I was getting on the plane, but I couldn't connect to the Internet.

The gate agent got off the phone and reached for my passport. I was getting on the plane.

Russ and my family and friends had to trust that "no news is good news."

After I got settled in a seat meant for flight attendants, I started crying while singing "Praise God from Whom all blessings flow" in my head. A flight attendant noticed my tears and asked me what was wrong.

"Nothing! I'm just so grateful you let me on the plane!"

I explained to her that my husband was having surgery 24 hours after I landed, and I was so appreciative that they let me on the plane. I really wish I had gotten a picture of the gate agent who asked the flight crew for permission for me to be in a jump seat and a picture of the flight crew who were so kind to me. Even though I don't have pictures of them, I have prayed for them many times.

Russ picked me up at the airport. When I got in the car, we both cried. I don't think we've ever been so happy to see each other, nor so grateful for God's providence.

SURGERY

Russ was scheduled for the last surgery the day after I got home, and it was delayed by a couple hours. Russ asked if I was still okay with going ahead with the surgery. "After this past weekend? Of course!" God had made it clear that *He* was in control.

Everything went perfectly.

After surgery, the nurses stopped Russ' gurney a couple steps away from the bed and had him take the two steps to the bed. Russ said, "That's all? I want to walk to the door!" The nurses looked surprised but led him across the room to the door and back.

It was late at night, so they kept him overnight. The next day, Russ did great with the physical therapy exercises and practiced going up and down stairs and in and out of a pretend car, so they let him go home.

They say that hip replacement patients will have a walker for two weeks. Russ stopped using his walker the first day. They expected Russ to be on a cane for two weeks after the walker, but he often walked without it.

Russ did use the cane for stability when walking on our block, and it worked really well for closing the back door after the dog came back inside.

To God be the glory!

GOD'S PLAN BROUGHT HIM MORE GLORY

My perfect plan would've been Russ having surgery in May and being fully recovered before my trip to Uganda. God's plan was a test for me and for Russ, and it brought Him more glory. Sometimes I think God just likes to show off.

Do you remember the story of Joshua and the Israelite army conquering the city of Jericho?[99] It made no sense that marching around the city for seven days and yelling would bring down the walls of resistance to God's plan. But that's what happened. And God got the glory!

Do you remember the story of Gideon and the Israelite army?[100] God reduced the army to 300 so that Israel would not "become boastful, saying, 'My own power has delivered me.'" (Judges 7:2b) And God got the glory!

Let me not sound boastful. This trip was not about me. It was about obedience and faith. To God be the glory!

Trust in the Lord with all your heart and do not lean on your own understanding. In all your ways acknowledge Him and He will make your path straight. (Proverbs 3:5-6 NASB)

I can't say my messages at Julie's events in Uganda were great or even that good, but they were the beginnings of what I was hearing the Lord telling me.

Daniel, Joshua, and I would continue to discuss abortion. This part of my life was still new to them, and they knew I went to Uganda to speak about it. Joshua, who was now 10, was proud of me and gave me hugs all the time. Daniel, now 14, had many questions. I expected him to be 100% pro-life with no exceptions, but he was wrestling with the difficulties that women face. I love that kid.

At one point, Daniel said, "I think a woman who has been raped should be able to have an abortion. She's already been through so much, and it wasn't her choice."

I replied by saying, "I am heartbroken for women who are raped. I can't even imagine. But as New Testament believers, we know that God is in control and that God is the Creator of life. We use birth control and think we are preventing pregnancy and to some extent we are. However, Abby Johnson,[165] who is a former Planned Parenthood Director turned pro-lifer, says that lots of women who use birth control, even the pill, get abortions. We know God is the One Who decides who gets pregnant. So, if a woman gets pregnant from rape, there must be a pretty powerful purpose for that child's life."

"Huh," he said. "I hadn't thought of it like that." Honestly, I hadn't either. Those words just came flying out of my mouth. It must have been the Holy Spirit guiding my words.

I continued writing this story but was making little progress. I was stuck. I couldn't get through the story about Arnold. I knew what I was going to write, but I just couldn't make myself do it.

I went to a prayer service. It was there that I realized I was mad at God for letting me get pregnant. I had just told Daniel that God decides who gets pregnant so according to my own words, God decided I would get pregnant.

Of course, this is not an excuse for premarital sex. How God knew all the days appointed for my daughter[101] when I should not have had extra-marital sex, I don't know. What I do know is that such knowledge is too wonderful for me; it is high; I cannot attain it. (Psalm 139:6 ESV)

I was quickly on my knees confessing I was upset with God's plan. I asked God to forgive me for my arrogance and for my desire to control my life by having an abortion.

After that, I felt free. Before that night, I thought I was completely free, but now I felt freer still.

I finished the book quickly after that, well through chapter eight, that is.

In September, Roxy hosted the women's event we had discussed the previous spring, called Faces of Abortion. Julie and I both spoke. The event went very well. Evidently my speaking improved because Roxy said I should consider presenting at a future women's conference.

For my part of the presentation, I had my friend click "record" on Facebook Live when it was my turn to speak. I had intended that the live video would go on my @CherylKrichbaum page, which had about 100 followers at the time, but because I wasn't clear as to what I wanted her to click, the Facebook Live was on my personal page instead—so the video went out to over 400 friends, about half of whom are from my non-Christian days.

I didn't realize that my presentation went out to my 400+ friends until after we went home. I received several private messages from friends complimenting me. It was so sweet. But then I thought it odd that all of those friends had seen the video since I didn't think they followed my professional @CherylKrichbaum page, so I went to look at the page. No video.

Oh, no! Oh, no! I found the video on my personal page. I chuckled. I really did! God must've wanted all those people to see the video. He's in control, after all. I'm quite sure that if I hadn't been at the prayer service the month before realizing God is in control, I would've been upset. But instead, I shrugged it off and thought, "Well, if my friends didn't know before, they certainly know now!"

Two of my Christian friends who sent me private messages told me they had also had abortions. Wow. Post-abortive women are everywhere.

GETTING GOD'S MESSAGE TO THE NATIONS RIGHT

Then I went to Uganda again, on our church's annual short-term mission trip the day after Christmas through early January. Pastor Dave gave me the opportunity to present all that the Lord had put on my heart.

Again, in preparation for the trip, the team shared their testimonies. However, schedules were challenging for two team members, so we shared our testimonies with each other with the exception of those two.

Well, that was a real problem for me. I did not want to go teach on abortion without my team knowing my story beforehand. One of the team members, Tim, is a co-teacher of a bible study that Russ and I attend together. I interacted with Tim every week, and he didn't know my story.

But God had a plan. We flew from the Washington Dulles airport to Dubai, but the flight left late because of a sick passenger.

We missed our connecting flight from Dubai to Uganda and had to stay the night in Dubai. Well, that provided us an evening to share our testimonies with the whole team, and so we did. Tim was gracious and kind, and he seemed to be in awe of God's power to turn me around. To God be the glory!

In Uganda, the Lord was compelling me to teach on the meaning of *worship*. My nephew Drew, who is a worship leader, had given me seven Hebrew words for worship (and I added one Greek word), but I didn't have time to study them in-depth before I left for Uganda, so I was going to talk about them generally.

---

shachah *(Hebrew)—to fall down flat, prostrate (see 2 Chronicles 20:18, Psalm 29:2)*

halal *(Hebrew)—base of hallelujah, to boast about the Lord in a kind of foolish way, meaning they were excited, giddy, and probably danced as if no one was looking (see 2 Chronicles 20:19, 21; Psalm 18:3)*

barak *(Hebrew)—to kneel while praising God (see 2 Chronicles 20:26; Psalm 16:7; 18:46)*

yadah *(Hebrew)—to give thanks (see 2 Chronicles 20:21; Psalm 7:17)*

zamar *(Hebrew)—to sing praise, make music (see 1 Chronicles 16:9; Psalm 7:17)*

tehillah *(Hebrew)—song or hymn of praise (see 2 Chronicles 20:22; Psalm 22:3)*

towdah *(Hebrew)—confession, thanksgiving (see Psalm 26:7)*

latreia *(Greek)—service for God (see Romans 12:1; Hebrews 9:1)*

I was meeting with Jennifer (who has a child with Down Syndrome and is a pregnancy center counselor), Tim, and his son because they were going to be co-presenters. I explained the outline of the presentation, including talking about the meaning of worship. Tim's son said, "These are the seven Hebrew words for worship" and proceeded to say them and their meanings. I chuckled. I guess the Lord really did want worship to be part of the message.

Tim's son was attending a Christian university and pursuing a degree in worship. I asked him to present the Hebrew words, these ways to worship the Lord, plus the Greek word *latreia* in Romans 12:1,[102] which means to worship God in a Levitical sense, that is, to worship Him while upholding all the laws including the sex laws since New Testament believers have not been released from the sex laws—see Acts 15:20 and 29.[103] We needed to teach that to the pastors and ministry leaders of our partner church in Katwe, which is a slum in Kampala.

Our time to present was shorter than we were originally told, so I narrowed the scope to Jennifer, Tim's son, and me presenting on abortion, extra-marital sex, and worship. It went really well. I felt the Lord brought it all together and used us to get His words to this church, a church that is in one of the largest slums in the world.

Before moving on to another part of Uganda, we visited a boarding school that our church supports. The children were on holiday break, but we got to tour the buildings and play with the orphaned children. While we were touring the elementary classrooms, we noticed signs on the outside of the building encouraging the children to abstain from sex. This was the equivalent of a school hallway in the USA, and they had signs up telling elementary children to abstain. You don't see that in the States.

Tim said we had to get a picture of me pointing to one of the signs. Then I started taking pictures of all the signs. The kind, quiet woman who was giving us the tour was waiting patiently. I said to her, "You don't see signs like that in the United States, not even for the older kids."

She had an almost indignant response saying, "Why not? These children need to know!"

How right she is. Certainly Mary, mother of Jesus, knew sex before marriage was forbidden and knew the consequences of

> *Abstain from sex until you get married.*
>
> *Have self control in sexual matters.*
>
> *Avoid alcohol. It affects you.*
>
> *School is a chance. Make use of it.*
>
> *Body changes are never a sign to start sex.*
>
> *Respect and appreciate your teachers.*
>
> *Say, "No" to gifts.*
>
> *Avoid walking in dark places.*
>
> *AIDS kills.*
>
> *AIDS has no age limit.*
>
> *Following your faith can help you to abstain.*
>
> *Avoid situations where you might be raped.*

pregnancy outside of marriage. Joseph knew, too. Why don't *our* young girls and boys?

Later in the trip, we spoke to pastors and ministry leaders in a more remote part of Uganda. This is the same place I had taught children the year before. I was hoping to talk to the mother of the boy with Down Syndrome again and to introduce Jennifer to her, but she wasn't there.

I was able to use Katherine Wang's bible study materials[77] again to teach the children about Jesus' life during Holy Week, and seven children indicated they wanted Jesus to be their Savior. What a wonderful thing to see.

This year, I was also able to present to adults: the pastors and ministry leaders. Instead of all three of us presenting together, I was tasked to present on my own. I always start with the message on abortion because people are pretty opinionated about abortion and are willing to listen. This group was fantastic. I started a prayer of repentance for the whole Church, and the translator had them repeat it. I said a line in English, the translator said it in Swahili, and the people said it again in Swahili. It was beautiful.

They clapped. They thought I was done speaking. I chuckled and said I wasn't done, yet. "We can't talk about abortion without talking about the very thing that results in abortions—sex."

I talked to them about teaching their children to abstain from sex before marriage. I said, "In my home, as you can imagine, we talk about sex pretty plainly. I have even wagged my finger at my boys and said, 'No sex for you!'" They laughed. (Of course, my boys and my Ugandan audience knew that I meant no sex before marriage.)

In addition to teaching about sex like I had in Katwe, I wanted to address a particular cultural issue. Many Ugandan women, feeling exhausted, tell their husbands to go get a "spare tire," that is, a young mistress so that he is sexually satisfied. I addressed this as unbiblical and pointed out that that kind of thinking didn't work out well for Sarah in the story of Abraham, Sarah, and Hagar.[104] Sarah became jealous and kicked Hagar and her son Ishmael to the streets. The result is that *today* we have two people groups who don't like each other (Jews and other Middle Eastern people).

I also called on the husbands to not exhaust their wives—a biblical concept in that if we love someone, we won't exhaust them. However, I did not support the concept with the right scriptures and therefore did not handle the Word of the Lord with care.[105] Pastor Dave and Tim pointed this out as soon as I finished. That evening over dinner, we talked it all through and they helped me see how to correct my teaching. I asked Dave for the opportunity to speak again the next day, and he said yes.

I thought this might be a good opportunity to encourage the ministry leaders to search the scriptures themselves to see if what their bible teachers were teaching is true, as the new believers in Berea did.[106] But it turned out that most of our audience didn't have bibles. Pastor Dave then made a commitment to send bibles. You see, in Uganda, they have far less access to the bible because bibles are so expensive and because not everyone has a smart phone and therefore cannot get the Bible app. (You can! I recommend Bible by Life Church or Bible Gateway by HarperCollins Christian Publishing or Blue Letter Bible by Blue Letter Bible.) Ugandan pastors do not go to seminary, because, again, they don't have the money to go. Feeding themselves and their families takes priority.

I started my presentation by saying, "I'm baa-ack!" They laughed. I said, "All the women are cheering, and all the men are saying, 'Great, I'm not getting sex tonight, either.'" They laughed again. Then I taught that 1 Corinthians 7:3-5 says not to deprive one another. I confessed to the women that this can be challenging, but it can also be pleasurable! I encouraged husbands and wives to talk about it today after the conference, to talk about their needs, and to come to an agreement that is loving for both of them. I caught the men looking at their wives with a "Yes, let's talk" look on their faces.

"Speak boldly," the Lord said. So, I did.

Later, we visited Sudanese refugee Christians in northern Uganda. At one point, the team was in a line shaking hands with the women. I went through the line, too, and at the end of the line, I was suddenly standing in front of a bunch of young girls. I'm guessing that they were 7-12 years old. I high-fived them.

One of our partners, Bishop Alex, turned and told me these girls were going back to Kampala to go to school. I wanted to encourage them, so I found a translator, a beautiful young woman who was going along with the children to help them with the language and with the transition from a refugee camp to a boarding school. I told the girls they were smart and strong. I also told them that God had gifted each of them with special skills and that it was their job to pray to God asking Him how He had gifted them so that they could pursue studies in those areas. I also told them that because the Lord had given them the gift of education, they should show appreciation to Him by studying hard.

Then I also said, "Keep yourselves pure. No sex until marriage." They giggled nervously, as did the translator. "God made you for one man. Pray that God reveals who that one man is and wait to have sex with him until *after* you're married." They laughed nervously again.

"Speak boldly," the Lord said. And so, I did. It seems like I will say anything to anyone.

Today, I mention my abortion in conversation as if it's just natural to talk about my story. I always talk about it in a repentant way, but I no longer worry about how people will react. They may not react the way I would prefer, but that's their issue to work through, not mine. I know that I am forgiven, white as snow. I rest in that.

Now to speak boldly in the United States.

11
CHANGING THE CONVERSATION ABOUT ABORTION

I met a woman recently through a mutual friend named Kim. My new friend said she is heartbroken over abortion and meets regularly with a dozen women socially, most of whom are non-Christians who are pro-choice. As we were talking, she said, "Kim says you know how to talk to pro-choice women."

"Yes, that's because I used to be one of them."

She looked surprised.

Not only did I have an abortion, but I advocated for women who wanted to have abortions. When my ex-husband and I were married, I volunteered for the Planned Parenthood Action Committee. I once protested against the Christians who were praying around an abortion clinic. I voted pro-choice without considering all the issues. The truth is, I was involved in the pro-choice movement because I wanted to justify what I had done.

My abortion went so "perfectly" that I could've been the poster woman for Planned Parenthood (although I didn't get an abortion in one of their clinics). I had little bleeding. I only had cramps the day of the procedure but not after that. I was still able to have children. I wasn't depressed. (I was in spiritual bondage, but I wasn't depressed.) Everyone around me reacted the way I wanted them to—not telling me what to do but supporting me in my decision.[107] My abortion was just as easy as the pro-choice movement advertises. But as I've learned, that's certainly not the case for all women: Many post-abortive women have anxiety, depression, and alcoholism, and many use and abuse drugs and become suicidal.[108]

Not only had I been one of the adamantly pro-choice, but my bachelors and my nearly finished master's degree from the Department of Rhetoric gave me a fair share of rhetorical theory and audience analysis classes, so I've been trained to consider my audience.

"Department of Rhetoric"? Yes, classical rhetoric. We hear people say, "That's just *rhetoric*," meaning, "That's just b.s." But classical rhetoric is the art of convincing people. We are most successful at our jobs if we are good at convincing people. That's what the study of rhetoric is about. It's from classical rhetoric that you may have learned the pattern of:

- Tell them what you're going to tell them

- Tell them

- Tell them what you told them

Classical rhetoric is a legitimate area of study. Hey, I almost got my PhD in rhetoric!

Not only did I study how to convince people, I learned that when the topic is emotional, as abortion is, people often do not address the same issues. In my Senior Seminar class, we looked at several controversial issues, including environmentalism and abortion. For each issue, we read two published articles, the second of which was a response to the first. If a person were responding to an article with an opposing viewpoint to prove that they are right and that the author of the original article is wrong, then they should refute each argument in the original article. They often didn't. They just argued their own points.

That was the case for the two articles we read on abortion. They didn't address the same points. I don't recall whether the first article was written by the pro-choice or the pro-life movement. It doesn't matter. Because even today, over 20 years later, rarely does either side of the abortion issue address the other's points directly. They just argue their own points. I often feel like they're just yelling at each other.

KNOW THY AUDIENCE

That's how I feel about the pro-life movement as a whole. We are not addressing the points of the pro-choice movement. We almost always talk about the baby, saying that abortion is the murder of babies, and it is; however, the pro-choice movement doesn't accept that they are babies. It doesn't matter how many times you argue your case that the pre-born are babies. It doesn't matter how good your argument is. Your argument falls on deaf ears. Their perception is that we are yelling at them about our religious beliefs. When was the last time that you convinced someone through yelling?

> "If we are negotiating with a mother who is holding a knife to her child's throat, do we convince her to put the knife down by yelling at her?"
> ~Julie Mad-Bondo~

My friend Julie, who took me to Uganda to speak about the sanctity of life and the sanctity of sex, gives a good example. If we are negotiating with a mother who is holding a knife to her child's throat, do we convince her to put the knife down by yelling at her? No, of course not.

Looking back at the controversy over my high school newspaper, I can see that the pro-life organization who sent the letter of complaint to the school district criticized us rather than fairly addressing our work. They yelled at us rather than entering into a conversation with us. Did they convince any of us to become pro-life? No. Did they look like fools to the whole city? Yes.

My degree in Scientific and Technical Communication from the Department of Rhetoric is all about the audience. We conduct audience analyses. We write for our audience. This degree program came under the Department of Rhetoric because classical rhetoric teaches us to consider the audience. The Apostle Paul, who was classically educated, also taught us to consider the audience:

> *For though I am free from all men, I have made myself a slave to all, so that I may win more. To the Jews I became as a Jew, so that I might win Jews; to those who are under the Law, as under the Law though not being myself under the Law, so that I might win those who are under the Law; to those who are without law, as without law, though not being without the law of God but under the law of Christ, so that I might win those who are without law. To the weak I became weak, that I might win the weak; I have become all things to all men, so that I may by all means save some. I do all things for the sake of the gospel, so that I may become a fellow partaker of it. (1 Corinthians 9:19-23 NASB)*

The Apostle Paul was one of the greatest rhetoricians of his time, as exemplified by the book of Romans, which is in a rhetorical form called "scholastic diatribe" complete with arguments and counter-arguments.[109]

If we who are pro-life want to convince the pro-choice not to abort, then we need to address *their* issues with arguments and counter-arguments. They are talking about women, so why don't *we* talk about women?

Because, after all, abortion is not good for women—nor is extra-marital sex.

Not all women have abortions out of convenience or because they think it's just as easy as birth control. Most have abortions because they are afraid. Those who say they use abortion simply as birth control, I would argue, are deceiving themselves.

Their stories are complicated and varied. It's not likely that you will find another woman who had an abortion because her family was stressed over her sister's mental illness, but you will find women who had abortions because they are:

- afraid of defying their boyfriends[110] or their parents

- afraid of their abusers

- afraid of what their parents will say if they were to find out

- afraid of what people will think

- afraid of potentially having a child with special needs

- afraid that they are ruining their futures or their unborn child's future

These are just some of the reasons that women abort. There may be as many reasons for aborting as there are abortions. Ironically, though, women *are* ruining their futures—their spiritual futures. They are inviting darkness over their lives—bondage—like I did. I was afraid of what people would think. I was afraid of delaying or ruining my education. However, having the abortion did not shield me from any of my worries. People knew anyway. Further, I didn't complete my bachelor's degree until eight years after I graduated from high school, so my education was delayed nevertheless.

Our lives are messy. Abortion is a symptom of the messiness. Jesus healed many people with messy lives. He did, after all, come to call sinners.[111]

THE GREAT COMMISSION

Like Emmanuel, my Ugandan driver and a pastor-in-training, we need to change the conversation about abortion. It's time for Christians to think and talk differently about abortion so that they can accomplish the Great Commission one hurting woman—and man—at a time.

How often do you think about the Great Commission? Perhaps you think about it when your pastor preaches on it or when your church supports a missionary or a short-term mission trip.

Do you remember what the Great Commission says? Some of us do. Most of us don't have it memorized, though. As a reminder, here is what Jesus said as recorded in Matthew:

> *"Go therefore and make disciples of all nations, baptizing them in the name of the Father and of the Son and of the Holy Spirit"...* *(Matthew 28:19 ESV)*

Most people stop right there, but that's not all. Jesus goes on in verse 20:

> *"...teaching them to observe all that I have commanded you. And behold, I am with you always, to the end of the age."* *(Matthew 28:20a ESV)*

When I hear the Great Commission, I hear "baptize them" and absolve myself of responsibility because it's the pastor's job to baptize (according to my church's practice), not mine. But the Great Commission says to make disciples, and that *is* my responsibility. If we are Christ-followers, then we are commissioned to make disciples, not just believers but disciples—fully devoted followers of Christ. The following dialogue from *Imaginary Jesus*[112] paints a picture of what it means to be a disciple:

> *"Do you understand what it means to be someone's disciple?"*

... "I thought it meant 'student.'"

"Yes, but not how you think of it. You're thinking of Y'shua [Jesus] like an algebra teacher. But to be a disciple means more than learning. It means to become like your teacher. It means transformation from what I am into what my teacher is. Y'shua said once, 'Everyone who is fully trained will be like his teacher.'"

... "You would eat when I eat, you would rest when I rest, and under the same olive tree. You wouldn't take the shortcut while I went the long way. We would be inseparable. You would live like my shadow, mimicking my actions until you could do what I do without thinking, until you had the same instincts, thoughts, and words."

Further, we often quote Matthew 28:19 without including verse 20—*teach* them. Our job is not just to go to all nations, not just to make disciples, not just to baptize, but to *teach* them to observe—follow, do—all that Jesus commanded. When we teach them, and they observe, follow, and do all that Jesus commanded, we are making fully trained disciples of our Teacher.

Do we need to "go" to another country to obey the Great Commission? No. The "nations" that Jesus was talking about here were the ethnic groups other than Israel, that is, the Gentiles—us! Jewish Jesus was in Israel telling Jewish Christians to make disciples out of everyone (not just Jews), baptize them, and teach them all that they learned from Him— "...in Jerusalem and in all Judea and Samaria, and to the end of the earth." (Acts 1:8 ESV)

Check out the definition of "nations"—ethnos—in the original Greek from the Blue Letter Bible.[113] *Ethnos* is where we get the English word *ethnic*, as in ethnic groups. Unlike the USA, a nation of Jesus' time was also an ethnic group. Remember also, that the boundaries between nations have changed quite a bit since the Bible was written.

We here in the USA are full of the nations, the ethnic groups, Jesus was talking about. We are the "melting pot" or "mosaic" of ethnic groups. Jesus was saying that salvation through Him is for everyone, not just Israel. We are part of "all nations," so those of us who are called to stay here are just as responsible for obeying the Great Commission as those who are called to be missionaries elsewhere (whether short-term like I did or long-term).

I love the people of Uganda, and I will continue to do mission work there and other places as the Lord calls me to do. We absolutely should be prayerfully and financially supporting missions work whether we are going or not simply because we are rich with resources (like water and bibles) and free to worship as we please.

As David Platt, pastor and author of several books including *Radical*, points out regularly, there are many unreached people groups (ethnos) who do not have access to the gospel, but our non-Christian neighbors and co-workers here in the USA do have access to us as well as to churches, Christian ministries, and bibles.

For that reason, we go outside of the USA if that's what the Lord has told us to do, and we stay home if that is what the Lord told us to do—and if we stay home, then we financially and prayerfully support international missions work. As Jill Briscoe said it: "You go where you're sent, and you stay where you're put, and you give what you've got."

So, whether we're at the grocery store or the drive-thru, we are responsible for obeying the Great Commission. Spread smiles wherever you go. Make the Christ in you attractive to everyone around you so that you can present the Gospel and God's truths about His love for women and men.

Think about women and men who are abortion minded as potential disciples. "Go and make disciples" of everyone—even those who are pregnant out of wedlock, even those who are considering abortion, even those who have had abortions, even the men who got the women pregnant, even men who pressured women into having abortions, even the babies who are born because the mom chose life: everyone, all nations, all ethnic groups. Go—don't sit around doing nothing—go and make disciples. Teach them all Jesus commanded, including His commands about the sanctity of *sex*, so that women don't get pregnant outside of marriage, thereby preventing the perceived need for abortion.

REMOVING THAT PLANK

However, we need to do some housekeeping before we talk to the nations. We need to take care of the planks in our own eyes. Jesus said:

> *"Judge not, that you be not judged. For with what judgment you judge, you will be judged; and with the measure you use, it will be measured back to you. And why do you look at the speck in your brother's eye, but do not consider the plank in your own eye? Or how can you say to your brother, 'Let me remove the speck from your eye'; and look, a plank is in your own eye? Hypocrite! First remove the plank from your own eye, and then you will see clearly to remove the speck from your brother's eye."* (Matthew 7:1-5 NKJV)

Russ and I had an exchange of ideas about why God has not moved on the politics around abortion, like de-funding Planned Parenthood and reversing Roe v Wade. I blurted out, "Because Christians don't want it! If they did, they would stop having sex outside of marriage!"

Seriously, friends, if we want God to move in the politics of abortion, then we need to repent of our own sexual sins because sexual sin is responsible for about 86% of abortions in the USA. Yes, there are abortions because of rape, but only about 1%.[114] Yes, there are abortions because medical tests predict Down Syndrome or some other imperfection. Those account for about 13%.[115] The rest are abortions because of unwanted pregnancy, most of those outside of marriage. How many Christians have had sex outside of marriage?

If we want God to move on the politics of abortion and, even further, to make abortion unusual, then we need to repent of our own and the country's extra-marital sex. God listens when we are obedient.[116]

> *"and My people who are called by My name humble themselves and pray and seek My face and turn from their wicked ways, then I will hear from heaven, will forgive their sin and will heal their land."*
> (2 Chronicles 7:14 NASB)

Notice that this verse is an if/then statement:

If God's people:	Then God will:
• humble themselves	• hear from heaven
• seek His face (not just His hand)	• forgive their sin
• turn from their wicked ways	• heal their land

If we want to heal our land of abortion, then we need to pray about abortion in humbleness while seeking His face and turning from our wicked ways. You may be asking, "Turning from our wicked ways? What did I do?" Maybe you are not one of the millions of women who had an abortion nor one of the millions of men who pressured a woman to have an abortion (or abdicated his responsibility in her "choice"). Wonderful!

Then repent on behalf[117] of The Church for we are not without guilt. Also repent for any premarital sex or adultery in your own life as well as any sexual immorality of your local church and The Church. We cannot ignore the connection between extra-marital sex and the high numbers of abortions. How can we, The Church, teach abortion-minded disciples all that Christ commanded (Matthew 28:20) when we are not following His commandments ourselves?

When we study the Bible, we see it's easier to make a case against sexual immorality than it is against abortion since the word *abortion* cannot be found in the Bible, but we find multiple words that are the same as *sexual immorality*.

Sexual immorality in Greek is *porneia*, which is translated to all of the following words in the New American Standard Bible (NASB):

- fornication

- immorality

- sexual immorality

- unchastity

We get our English word *pornography* from the Greek *porneia*. The sexual acts that are included in *porneia* are the forbidden sexual acts listed in Jewish Law, mostly in Leviticus (Jewish Law refers to the Pentateuch or Torah, also known as the first five books: Genesis, Exodus, Leviticus, Numbers, Deuteronomy):

- adultery

- homosexuality

- lesbianism

- intercourse with animals

- sex with close relatives

- sex with a divorced man or woman

- premarital sex[118]

Historically, the Church has looked down on *women* who have premarital sex. We know that even today women with crisis pregnancies are judged within the church and in society, but pregnancy is evidence of sex, evidence that is not found in men. We may not take women to the public square and accuse her as was done in Nathaniel Hawthorne's *Scarlet Letter*, but we still judge, and women still feel like they are wearing scarlet letters. As women living in a feminist society, we feel the hypocrisy—men are hallowed for their sexual conquests while women are quietly (or not-so-quietly) slut-shamed.

JESUS' KINDNESS

Have you ever noticed that when Jesus talked to women about their sexual immorality, He was kind? In contrast, whenever He talked to crowds of both men and women, He was direct about sexual immorality. Sometimes Jesus was angry, but I only see His anger when He was addressing the religious leaders—and He called them hypocrites.

JESUS TALKS KINDLY TO WOMEN ABOUT SEXUAL IMMORALITY

For example, when Jesus talked to the woman at the well about her sexual immorality,[119] He did not condemn her. He did clearly reveal Himself as the Christ to her, a woman. That was a big deal! At that point in His ministry, He was not even that direct with the 12 disciples about His divinity.

When the Pharisees brought a naked woman caught in the very act of adultery to Jesus,[120] He redirected their eyes away from her nakedness and down to the sand. Once all the accusatory men left, Jesus did not condemn the woman but simply told her to "go and sin no more."[121]

Jesus did not condemn either woman, but He was clear about their sin.

JESUS IS DIRECT ABOUT SEXUAL IMMORALITY

Jesus was also clear about *porneia* (sexual immorality) to all of His disciples (not just the 12 but the crowds). There are no parables about sex. Instead, Jesus outright says not to have sex outside of marriage. In three stories, Jesus uses the word *porneia*.

JESUS TALKS ABOUT SEXUAL IMMORALITY IN THE SERMON ON THE MOUNT

In the Sermon on the Mount, Jesus is direct about sexual immorality but since He talks about sexual immorality in the context of divorce, we often miss what He's saying about pre-marital sex.

But I say to you that whoever divorces his wife for any reason except sexual immorality [porneia] causes her to commit adultery [moicheuō]; and whoever marries a woman who is divorced commits adultery [moicheuō]. (Matthew 5:32 NKJV)

Notice that *sexual immorality* is the Greek *porneia* and that *adultery* is the Greek *moicheuō*. It wasn't until I studied this verse to understand what Jesus was saying about sex rather than what He was saying about divorce that I noticed the difference between *sexual immorality* and *adultery*.

Sexual immorality includes *adultery*. *Adultery* is sex with someone else's spouse. If you are having sex with someone when you are not married, then you are having sex with someone else's spouse, perhaps someone's future spouse.

Sexual immorality includes any type of sex other than heterosexual, consensual sex between one man and one woman who are married to each other. That tells me that if your spouse thinks you're a virgin when she or he marries you and then finds out you were not, she or he can divorce you. Jesus did not say that you must divorce, but He did say that it is permitted.

I hear you laughing under your breath. I know. I know—today, it would be unusual to find a couple in the USA who has not had premarital sex. But that tells us something about the context of Jesus' teaching. In Jewish society of His time, it was typical to be chaste until marriage.

Now, I'm not saying that you should divorce your spouse! Assuming you know each other's sexual history, The Church expects you to remain married, and God does, too. God hates divorce (Malachi 2:16).

There are many couples who stay together despite adultery because they chose forgiveness over bitterness. Certainly, if a couple can remain married as they heal from adultery, then they can stay together even if one lied about his/her virginity. I challenge you to remain married![122]

The fact that Jesus allowed couples to divorce because one of them had premarital sex (whether heterosexual or homosexual) tells us that He takes sex very seriously. Why do I say that? Because God hates divorce (Malachi 2:16).

JESUS IS DIRECT ABOUT DIVORCE AND SEXUAL IMMORALITY

On His way to Jerusalem for the final week of His life (known as Holy Week, from Palm Sunday to Resurrection Day or Easter), Jesus was followed by large crowds (Matthew 19:2) and some Pharisees came to test Him about divorce (19:3).

These Pharisees were trying to find fault in Jesus' teaching (19:3). They already knew what He said about divorce in the Sermon on the Mount or other places, since certainly He taught His commands wherever He went.[123]

These Pharisees wanted to discredit Jesus since He was preaching against what Moses allowed. Here, read the story for yourself. Note that anything in all caps is a quote from the Old Testament:

...and large crowds followed Him, and He healed them there.

Some Pharisees came to Jesus, testing Him and asking, "Is it lawful for a man to divorce his wife for any reason at all?"

And He answered and said, "Have you not read that He who created them from the beginning MADE THEM MALE AND FEMALE (Genesis 1:27, 5:2), and said, 'FOR THIS REASON A MAN SHALL LEAVE HIS FATHER AND MOTHER

AND BE JOINED TO HIS WIFE, AND THE TWO SHALL BECOME ONE FLESH'? [Genesis 2:24, which is before satan tricked Eve] So they are no longer two, but one flesh. What therefore God has joined together, let no man separate."

They said to Him, "Why then did Moses command to give her a certificate of divorce and send her away?" [a reference to Deuteronomy 24:1-4]

He said to them, "Because of your hardness of heart, Moses permitted you to divorce your wives; but from the beginning it has not been this way.

And I say to you, whoever divorces his wife, except for [sexual] immorality [porneia], and marries another woman commits adultery [moicheuō]." (Matthew 19:2-9 NASB)

As you have already read, Jesus is direct while repeating and reinforcing what he preached in the Sermon on the Mount.[124] Not only is divorce not in God's will, but sexual immorality is not, either.

JESUS GETS FRUSTRATED OR EVEN ANGRY WITH THE DISCIPLES

In another passage, Jesus gets frustrated, maybe even angry, with his disciples for their lack of understanding.

In the Gospel of Mark chapter 7, we read that the Pharisees and Scribes watched Jesus' disciples closely, found fault in them about the tradition of ritual hand washing, and challenged Jesus about it (7:1-5). Jesus calls them hypocrites (7:6), quotes the Old Testament prophesy about them (7:6-7), and goes on pointing out their hypocrisy (7:8-13).

Then Jesus turns to the crowd to declare all foods clean (7:14-16). Frustrated with the Jewish leaders, Jesus goes into Peter's house only to find that the disciples didn't understand either (7:17-19). Jesus then makes it clear that there's a difference between food laws and moral laws:

> *And He said to them, "Then are you also without understanding? Do you not see that whatever goes into a person from outside cannot defile him, since it enters not his heart but his stomach, and is expelled?" (Thus He declared all foods clean.)*

> *And He said, "What comes out of a person is what defiles him. For from within, out of the heart of man, come evil thoughts, sexual immorality [porneia], theft, murder, adultery [moicheuō], coveting, wickedness, deceit, sensuality, envy, slander, pride, foolishness. All these evil things come from within, and they defile a person." (Mark 7:18-23 ESV)*

So, yes, Jesus did talk about sexual immorality. Are we Christians keeping His commandments on sexual immorality and adultery? Jesus said, "If you love Me, you will keep My commandments." (John 14:15 NASB) Paul said, "The body is not for (sexual) immorality [porneia], but for the Lord, and the Lord is for the body." (1 Corinthians 6:13b NASB)

I am obeying this commandment now, but I have not always done so. I could not have written this book without first humbling myself before the Lord and asking Him to forgive me for both my abortion and my sexual immorality. I encourage you to do likewise before you post your next pro-life message on social media.

Before we, The Church, talk to abortion-minded disciples, perhaps we need to go before the Lord in humbleness, seek first His face (not His hand), and turn from our wicked ways.

TRUE WORSHIP
WORSHIP AHEAD OF THE BATTLE

While studying Hebrew and Greek words for *worship* and *praise* (see the list on page 171), I found King Jehoshaphat's unusual way of going into battle as told in 2 Chronicles 20:1-30.

Jehoshaphat was the king of Judah almost 100 years after King David died. Jehoshaphat is considered one of the good kings of Judah, but he went back and forth between seeking God and doing his own thing.

At the beginning of chapter 20, Jehoshaphat finds out that Judah will be attacked on all sides by its enemies. He is understandably afraid and turns his attention to seeking the Lord. He also called all of Judah to fast.[125]

Then Jehoshaphat stood in the temple with the assembly of Judah and worshiped the Lord (20:5-9) before asking Him to move on their behalf in complete humbleness and reliance on Him (20:10-13). The Lord answered them saying the battle was His not theirs, and they should not fear or be discouraged (20:14-17).

What was their immediate response? To prostrate themselves to the Lord as a form of worship. The word *worship* in verse 18 is the Hebrew word *shachah*, which is not just kneeling but falling down flat. God hadn't even done anything yet; He had just encouraged them, and yet they worshiped the Lord by falling down flat before Him.

Then the tribe of Levi stood up to praise God loudly. The word *praise* in verse 19 is *halal*, which is the base of our word *hallelujah*, and means to boast about the Lord in a kind of foolish way. That is, they were really excited, giddy, and probably danced as if no one was looking. And still, God hadn't done anything yet; He had just encouraged them.

The next morning, they went out for battle. King Jehoshaphat encouraged the nation and then sent a praise choir *ahead* of the army to give thanks to the Lord because of His everlasting kindness. The word *praised* in verse 21 is again the Hebrew word *halal*. They were singing and dancing ahead of their own army as if no one was looking. Can you imagine what their enemies were thinking?

When they began singing with joy and praising God, God ambushed and defeated their enemies (20:22-25). After the nation saw the defeated enemies, they assembled and blessed the Lord.

The word *blessed* in verse 26 is the Hebrew word *barak*, which means to kneel while praising God. They joyfully went back to the temple with their musical instruments after God won the battle.

MybodyMyworship

As I was studying this story, I felt the Lord nudge me to go to battle against abortion-minded Christians like Jehoshaphat and the nation of Judah battled—by sending praise out ahead of the battle—but with a New Testament twist. The Lord had already impressed on me that we are to worship in purity (Romans 12:1[126]) and with our whole bodies, which are temples of the Holy Spirit (1 Corinthians 6:19[127]), so we need to teach people what it means to worship in purity and what it means to be the New Testament temple of the Holy Spirit so that we can send worship ahead of the spiritual battle against abortion. The Lord was impressing on me that if we worship Him in spirit and moral truth,[128] then *He* will defeat the enemies in the war against abortion.

Why hasn't God moved in the war against abortion? Because Christians are not upholding His sex laws, because they are not worshiping Him in moral truth. Before we ask the Lord to change the minds of the abortion-minded, we need to change ourselves—humble ourselves, seek first His face (not just His hand), and turn from our sexual sins and sin no more.

MybodyMyworship was borne. Through teaching, prayer, and music, MybodyMyworship inspires spiritual acts of worship (Romans 12:1-2) by teaching biblically sound science of sexual integrity (1 Corinthians 6:19) and psychological effects of abortion (Psalm 32:3). Because current research supports God's Word, we will learn both science and His Word. If you would like to bring this teaching to your church, your Christian group, or your home, contact MybodyMyworship.org.

194

12
A DIVINE SURPRISE

A t the time that I wrote the first draft of this book, Paul was still missing. I was still sad. I was still heartbroken. But I trusted[129] that the Lord was watching over my brother, and I had learned to praise God in all circumstances.

In that year-and-a-half, the Lord called me into His plan for my life. It was if the Lord said, "Okay, good. You understand how to respond to life's tests. Now, pick up your cross and follow me."[130]

This is when God sent me to Uganda on my first short-term mission trip. While there, He convicted me that I needed to change the conversation about abortion.

Within a year, He sent me to speak on the sanctity of life and the sanctity of sex both at home and a second and third time in Uganda. Then He gave me His new ministry: MybodyMyworship, which inspires spiritual acts of worship (Romans 12:1-2) by teaching biblically sound science of sexual integrity (1 Corinthians 6:19) and psychological effects of abortion (Psalm 32:3) through teaching, prayer, and worship music.

I learned to obey Him more fully in this year-and-a-half. I learned to worship him in all circumstances. Honestly, I am on fire for the Lord. I'm so on fire for the Lord that I am annoying to my friends. They are going through difficulties, real and big life tests. My encouragement? Sing a praise song! I'm sure that response is annoying to them, but I try to remind them that life is challenging at my house, too, and that I have to take my own advice and sing praise songs even when I don't feel like it.

It's not always easy to worship God in the midst of a test, but doing so makes me feel better about enduring the test[131]—and makes it easier to understand how the Lord wants me to respond to the test. Sometimes I turn on Christian radio in every room of my house to remind everyone to praise God. The music is contagious. The boys start singing along with me. Then I notice that the atmosphere in our home changes because we changed our focus to Him.

Little did I know how soon I would encounter another big test. I returned home from my third Uganda trip on January 6. I went to the March for Life on January 19. I answered questions at church on January 21, which was Sanctity of Life Sunday.

Then on January 24, I got a phone call on my home phone just as I finished bible study with my boys at the start of our homeschool day. The caller asked for someone with my mom's first name and my married name, so I figured she was a telemarketer. I said, in an irritated voice, "There's no such person. Who's calling, please?"

The woman gave me her name and said she was a social worker at St. Elizabeth's Hospital in Washington, DC and that she was looking for Paul's parents.

I was in shock. I locked eyes with my teenager. I heard myself say, "I'm Paul's sister."

I'm not sure what she said after that because I was very emotional. I was still staring into Daniel's eyes. Both boys heard what I said and were waiting as anxiously as I was. We were all frozen. I couldn't believe what I was hearing.

The woman asked me if I was okay. I composed myself enough to say, "My brother has been missing for a year and a half."

"Take your time," she said kindly.

I took a deep breath and quietly told Joshua to go get Grandma. He ran out of the room.

I sat down and listened to everything the woman was saying. Mom had no idea what she was about to hear. When she sat down next to me, I politely interjected that my mom was sitting next to me, and I was putting the woman on speaker phone. I told Mom that Paul was in a hospital in Washington, DC.

The professionals may not be able to tell us much, but we have every right to tell them anything (which I learned many years before from the National Alliance for the Mentally Ill or NAMI)—and so we did.

After we got off the phone, Mom and I cried in each other's arms.

Then we called Dad and told him everything that had happened. I could tell that he was in shock and wanted to get off the phone to process everything.

I called Russ and told him the amazing news.

My nephew, Drew, had requested a Facebook Messenger video "call." He didn't know what was going on—he just wanted to talk. I used Messenger to text him that Paul had been located and that I would call via video as soon as I could. He was at an airport on his way to a worship event. All he could say was "Wow!" and "I need a place where I can go cry."

We were all astounded by the day's event. My brother disappeared from St. Paul, MN and ends up in Washington, DC, an hour away from my home. How does that happen? God. God is the only answer that makes sense.

THE FIRST VISIT

I had asked the woman if we could visit Paul. I said I didn't think Paul would agree to see me, but I'd be happy to drive my mom there. The woman said Paul was clear that he did not want to see me, but she would confirm if Mom could visit. She did call back to say, "Yes" to Mom visiting.

I was going to be out-of-town for Joshua's sporting event the next two days, so Mom and I went to Kohl's that very day to buy clothes for Paul. Then we drove into Washington, DC to see him. I dropped off Mom and watched her go through security and then sat in the parking lot, listening to my worship music playlist.

So Paul doesn't want to see me—that's okay. Paul was found. He was safe. He was physically okay. He was fed. He had a roof over his head. I was thankful. What else could I do but praise God?

Was Paul's situation ideal? No. But this was just step one. Things don't magically become perfect.

Mom visited with Paul for only 20 minutes. I guess 20 minutes was all he could handle. She said Paul, in his own words, had been 120 pounds and was now up to 160 pounds. He went from underweight to normal weight in two months. She said his hands were shaking and his legs were bobbing up and down. We later found out these were side effects of the psychiatric medicine.

Paul didn't have his glasses. He said they had been stolen over a year before. Paul has poor eyesight, and his glasses have thick lenses. He loves to read. How did he survive so long without glasses? He must have been miserable in that hospital without being able to read or watch TV. I was sad for him.

A Visit with Our Cousin

The next time I took my mom to the hospital, my cousin who lives in Washington, DC joined her. That visit was also about 20 minutes long. Mom pressed Paul to let me see him on a future visit. She did not like that I was driving all the way to the hospital but unable to see him. The last time I had seen Paul was two-and-a-half years earlier when he closed his apartment door on my boys and me.

But I Did Get to Visit Him

Russ' birthday was in the middle of these visits. I always make German Chocolate cupcakes because they are his favorite, and I have a pretty amazing recipe. I take a bunch of the cupcakes to Russ' work, too, because one of his co-workers has the same birthday. Then I realized we could take cupcakes to Paul because German Chocolate is also his favorite.

Mom and I drove to Washington, DC again, this time with cupcakes. After getting the cupcakes approved and getting through security, we sat in a large room full of tables and waited.

Paul entered the room quickly. I stood to greet him, and he came right up to me and hugged me. His hug seemed to be given out of obligation, but I was still amazed that he even acknowledged me. He looked down during the whole visit. He had no expression on his face (no "affect," as the DSM-5© says). He spoke quietly, which was typical since his mental illness, so I wasn't surprised by that.

Paul's left hand was shaking uncontrollably. Both of his legs were bouncing. His right hand was not shaking, but he didn't try to use it. I don't know if that is because he couldn't or because he's left handed.

Paul took the cupcake and said, "Thanks." He was polite. He ate the cupcake with his left hand. There were crumbs everywhere.

Paul only talked about getting out of the hospital.

I asked Paul what he needed, besides glasses. He said he needed shoes. I asked him what kind of shoes he wanted. He said, "11D."

"That's your size. What kind of shoes do you want?" He lifted his hands as if to shrug his shoulders but without shrugging them. I said I knew he didn't like tennis shoes, so I wanted to know what kind of shoes he would prefer.

Paul said, "It is true that I do not like tennis shoes, but tennis shoes would be sufficient for going back to Minnesota."

"Yes, but what kind of shoes do you want?"

Paul lifted his hands again as if to shrug, hesitated, and then said, "That's too much for me. I don't know how to answer that."

With that, he was done. I think we were there for 25 minutes.

Mom and I left with the impression that Paul would be compliant to anything as long as it resulted in his getting out of the hospital. We called Dad and Bea before we left the parking lot and told them about the whole conversation. Mom and I agreed that Paul was a flight risk. Everything was about getting out of the hospital, and we left thinking Paul would tolerate any of us as long it helped him get out of the hospital.

When we got home that night, I called the social worker's number and left a voice message saying that I wanted to tell him what I had observed. The social worker and I talked the next morning. After I told him everything, I asked about getting Paul glasses. He said if we were to take him to get his eyes checked, then he would get glasses faster. As a result, I arranged to take Paul out on a day pass the following Thursday.

THE DAY AT THE EYE DOCTOR

Russ was going to be on a business trip on that Thursday, but he asked his ophthalmologist to do the eye exam and set up the appointment. Mom was concerned about Paul walking away while we were out for the appointment. She was really worried. I told her that I wasn't worried and that it was okay if she didn't go. Mom decided to stay home with the boys. I would've been okay with them being home alone doing their schoolwork for the half day it would take for the appointment, but I was also okay with Mom staying home to supervise them.

Dad and Mom were both concerned about how Paul would react to being alone with me considering he was so adamant about not being around me for so many years. I was, too. I honestly expected to drop him off after lunch then sit in my car and cry. Nevertheless, this was the fastest way to get Paul glasses, so we were just going to have to trust God. I had complete peace about it.

I left early that morning so that I had time to find the ophthalmologist's office before going to the hospital to pick up Paul. I walked into the building and found the office door so that I would know how to go directly there in the next couple hours when Paul was with me.

On the way there, I sang along with my playlist. Since Christmas season, I had four songs on the list. They were:

- "What a Beautiful Name" by Hillsong Worship
- "Great Are You, Lord" by All Sons & Daughters
- "There Is Power" by Lincoln Brewster
- "Mary, Did You Know" written by Mark Lowry[132] and performed by Pentatonix[133]

I knew that Christmas was over, but "Mary, Did You Know" just speaks to me. When I sing along, I'm both confessing that Jesus is God and that the child whom I aborted had value because she was made in the image of God (Genesis 1:27). Speaking to Mary, the singer asks, "Did you know that when you kiss your baby, you kiss the face of God?" If I were to write new lyrics to Mark Lowry's melody, I would ask every pregnant woman, "Did you know that when you kiss your baby, you kiss the image of God?" (Genesis 1:26-27) This song has

> *Did you know that when you kiss your baby, you kiss the image of God?*

been so healing to me that I can't help but thank Mark Lowry.

Having recently studied how King Jehoshaphat sent a worship team ahead of the battle, I realized that's what I was doing. I was praising ahead of today's spiritual battle. Upon that realization, my disposition changed from one of discouragement to one of joy. God was battling the day for me.

I prayed in the car. I prayed for more of the Holy Spirit,[134] as I always do. The Lord's Prayer[135] popped into my head, so I prayed, "Thy kingdom come. Thy will be done on earth, right here in my car, as it is in heaven. There is peace in heaven, so there is peace in my car. There is no shaking in heaven, so there is no shaking in my car." I also prayed that Paul would feel peace when he is near me not so much because I wanted us to be friends again (I had given up on that long ago) but because I wanted him to experience the peace of Christ.

I picked up Paul from the hospital, and we began the drive to the ophthalmologist's office. I had no idea what Paul knew about smart phones and map apps, so I made sure to explain everything I was doing so he wouldn't be surprised by any noises. I didn't have any music playing because in the past he stayed away from anything Christian. I didn't have the radio on because I didn't want him to hear anything negative. I wanted to maintain peace in my car.

Paul didn't shake as much as usual in the car, but his hand was shaking some. I prayed that the shaking would go away, and it did. I thanked the Lord.

At the ophthalmologist's office, Paul had to fill out paperwork, but he couldn't because he was shaking and because he couldn't see to read. I hadn't asked the Lord to stop the shaking wherever we were, just in my car (probably because I didn't think of asking for more than that) so I wasn't surprised that he was shaking in the doctor's office. I asked Paul for permission to complete the form for him. I filled in everything that I knew, listing St. Elizabeth's Hospital as his address, but I did not make any assumptions. In the HIPPAA section, I asked him if he wanted Mom and Dad listed. He said, "Yes," so I wrote in their phone numbers. I asked him if he wanted me listed. He said, "No." I didn't expect him to say, "Yes," but I figured that it couldn't hurt to ask because the worst he could say is "No." I just moved on and didn't let myself feel hurt.

In the medical history section, I ask Paul about each item. I made no assumptions. When the form asked for surgeries, he said he had had two eye surgeries for lazy eye when he was six years old. I didn't think that was right. I was born the year he turned six. I didn't remember hearing anything about him having eye surgeries or any surgeries for that matter. Even though I was sure I was the only one who had eye surgeries, I wrote down what he said anyway. I even confirmed with him the year as the year I was born.

After I turned in the form, I texted my parents to ask about the eye surgeries. Mom confirmed that Paul did not have any surgeries and that I was the only one who had eye surgeries. I wrote a note to the doctor saying that those surgeries were false memories and held on to the note.

The office manager who had taken the paperwork said I needed to be added to the HIPPAA section so that I could be in the room with Paul during the exam. I said I was sure that Paul didn't want me on the form, but I would ask. I explained to Paul the situation, and he confirmed that he did not want me on the form nor did he need me in the room. I said, "Okay."

I said everything without emotion. Actually, I felt like a matter-of-fact special education teacher, who gently gets to the point without judgment in her voice.

When the nurse called Paul back, she motioned for me to follow, so I did. She showed me where to sit, but I didn't go into the room. From the door, I said Paul didn't want me in the room. She said someone had to be with him. I asked Paul if he was okay with that, and he said, "Yes." I pretended not to be surprised and sat down.

The nurse worked well with him. She was not overly talkative, but she wasn't scared off by his shaking or his scowl. When the doctor came into the room, I stood to shake his hand and handed him my note about the false memory. The doctor sat down essentially between Paul and me and turned to talk to me. He confirmed that Paul did not have surgeries. I guess the doctor didn't get the hint that he wasn't supposed to say anything out loud. I nodded my head. Paul said, "Yes, two surgeries when I was six years old for lazy eye." The doctor ignored him.

The doctor asked me, "So, he's at St. Elizabeth's now?" I think that anyone who has been in the Washington, DC area for any amount of time knew that St. Elizabeth's is a psychiatric hospital even though that was new information for me.

"Yes," I said.

"Do you know what his DSM diagnosis is?"

DSM is the Diagnostic and Statistical Manual published by the American Psychiatric Association. Remember, that book contains the diagnostic criteria for "psychiatric disorders." I own both the DSM IV and the DSM-5®, so I knew exactly what he was talking about.

I quietly answered the doctor: "Schizophrenia."

The doctor nodded his head. Paul said, "There is no such thing as schizophrenia." The doctor ignored him.

The doctor sent in the nurse to dilate Paul's eyes. That didn't seem right to me. They hadn't checked his eyes to write out a prescription, but I trusted them to do what they needed to do. We went out to the lobby to sit for 20 minutes.

They called us back again so that the doctor could examine Paul's eyes. The doctor said he wasn't going to check Paul's eyes for glasses. "Why not?" I asked.

"I can't now because his eyes are dilated," the doctor explained.

"That's why we came here. He needs glasses."

"If I were to check everyone's eyes for glasses for free, I'd have a line going out the door. I can't afford to do that."

"How much does it cost?"

"I can't check his eyes because they've been dilated."

"How much? I'll pay."

"It's $65, but I can't check his eyes because they are dilated."

I couldn't believe it. This was the whole reason for going to the doctor. How was Paul going to react?

"You can take him someplace else to get his eyes checked for glasses, but not for another five hours."

I texted Russ to tell him. He replied, "God's got a plan."

The doctor said Paul's eyes were healthy. I thanked the doctor and then the office manager, and we left.

When we got into the car, I said to Paul, "Well, I'm sorry. I thought we were getting your eyes checked for glasses. Now we have to figure out Plan B." I was looking at the calendar on my phone. "I can't come back out here until Tuesday."

Paul asked if Mom could drive him. I said, "No," and reminded him that Mom is 78 years old, she does not have sight in her left eye since her stroke, and she didn't feel comfortable driving in Washington, DC. Paul then asked about our cousin, but it just didn't feel right for someone other than Paul's immediate family to take him.

Then I realized that since Mom was at home with the boys, I didn't have to hurry home. I could stay in Washington, DC and take him to an optometrist late that afternoon. Paul was okay with that.

Paul chose McDonald's for lunch because eating a burger with shaking hands was easier than eating with a fork. When he was in my car, his hands and legs did not shake. When he was at the doctor's office and in McDonald's, they did. By the time we left McDonald's, he had ketchup all over the front of his shirt.

Paul was self-conscious of the shaking. He pointed out how problematic it was. I just acknowledged what he said. I asked him about going back to St. Paul. He said he didn't want to go to St. Paul. He wanted to go to Minneapolis.

Mom, Dad, and I had already talked about this. The best choice was for Paul to be in St. Paul where the social workers already knew him, but we also knew that Paul didn't want to go back to the building where he had been living. Minneapolis was not a good option because it is in a big county with a heavy caseload. Nancy lives in Minneapolis, and she is not getting the help that she needs. Paul doesn't like Nancy very much, so I referenced her, hoping that would discourage him from going to Minneapolis.

"Minneapolis is a big county with a heavy caseload, so they are not going to have as much for you there. Did you know that Nancy lives there?"

"I like Minneapolis because they're progressive," he said. In my opinion, Minneapolis is not any more progressive than St. Paul, but those were his words.

In retrospect, I can see how Paul would like that Minneapolis has a large caseload because that would make it easier for him to get lost in the system. He wanted to get lost in the system because he didn't want anyone telling him what to do.

We didn't talk for a while. I was okay with silence. It didn't feel awkward to me at all. Then I asked Paul what he wanted to do. "The pass is for all day. What would you like to do?"

"I don't know."

"We could buy clothes."

"I already have sufficient clothes."

Paul has two shirts and two pair of pants.

"No book shopping, right?"

"Since I have no glasses, books are problematic."

"How about walking along the water at National Harbor? Walking along the water always makes me feel calm."

"No." Paul kinda smiled. "I realize this is kind of a vacation."

"Do you want to go back to the hospital for the afternoon?"

"Yes."

"Okay, I'll plan to pick you up around four o'clock."

I took Paul back to the hospital and met with the social worker. He said Paul was actually in a good mood and smiled on his way back to his room.

"Really?" I asked. "I don't know what happened that would make him smile."

I told the social worker all that had happened. After I talked to the social worker, I went out to my car and called my parents to tell them everything. Remarkably, I didn't cry.

I found a coffee shop in which to do my bible study and pray and listen to my worship music. I almost forgot to make the appointment with the optometrist. I purposefully told the woman who answered the phone that I was bringing my brother and that he had a mental illness but that he was quiet and harmless. I thought it only fair to let her know ahead of time rather than watch her have a negative reaction when she saw him.

I picked up Paul and took him to the optometrist. The optometrist and the administrator were both women. They talked quietly. I was watching for their reactions, but they didn't give me an indication whether they were concerned or not. When the optometrist called Paul back to the exam room, she was great with him. She was in a good mood and treated him like he was perfectly normal. By the time we left with his prescription, he was smiling.

After that doctor appointment, we went out for dinner. While at dinner, I told Paul that Daniel reads like him (which means that they both read *a lot*). I also said Daniel was a walking calculator, like him. Paul smiled for a second.

I told Paul that Joshua takes after Grandpa, the one who tried out for the Olympics. I told him Dad had recently shared a story of Grandpa "walking" down the stairs in the family homestead on his hands. Evidently, this was a regular thing for him. He would do a handstand walk down the stairs in the family home—Paul would remember that home. I told Dad never to tell Joshua the story for fear that he would try it. Paul smiled for a second.

At some point during dinner, I told Paul about the dream I had about the two of us. It was the dream in which Dad had found Paul, the dream about which I told Russ, my dad, and my pastor on the day that Dad heard from the Boston University police over a year before. I didn't tell Paul the dream was about Dad finding him. I told him the dream was about the two of us kayaking—which was true. We did go kayaking in the dream. In the dream, we were putting my two kayaks on Minnehaha Creek in Minneapolis, but something wasn't right in my dream. I was fairly sure that the creek was flowing in the wrong direction.

"Oh," Paul said.

"We could go kayaking… or canoeing, if you prefer. What's the first river that you want to canoe when you get back to Minnesota?"

"I don't know," he said.

"Or we could go kayaking here on the Potomac River. I live near the Potomac River."

"Oh," Paul said, half smiling.

Paul knew Minnehaha Creek better than I did, so I asked him which way it flowed. He answered, but I didn't recognize the landmarks. I clarified that the creek paralleled 54th street for a while, then went over to the lakes (Hiawatha and Nokomis) and then went to Minnehaha Park before flowing into the Mississippi. "Did I get that right?"

"Yes." Paul seemed to appreciate being asked.

I asked Paul why he chose to go to Washington, DC. He said lawyers had called him to tell him he could practice law here. Paul is not a lawyer. This was a hallucination. Inside, I smiled and thanked the Lord for using a hallucination to get Paul near me. St. Paul to Boston to Washington, DC—my backyard. God is good.

Before we left, I heard myself saying, "I had a good time today."

"Me, too," he said.

I tried not to act surprised or excited, but in my head I thought, *Wow! I didn't expect that.*

When I brought Paul back to the hospital, I reiterated that I had had a good time and then said, "I hope that we can be friends again."

"We can see about that," he said.

That was huge!

Russ was right. God had a plan, and it was better than mine.

When I left, I got in my car and rejoiced! I put on my playlist and sang loudly in praise to the Lord! And I didn't cry.

On the way home, one of my girlfriends checked in on our little group. The three of us are constantly texting each other in order to encourage each other through life's tests. We're all going through big challenges.

I pulled over to reply: "Can't wait to tell you. Driving home. Been in DC all day with my brother. I'll be driving past your houses in about 20 min. Meet at Ridgetop Coffee?"

One girlfriend was able to meet me. When she walked in, I said with a big grin on my face, "See this?" pointing to myself. "This is peace!"

She wanted to hear all about my day. I told her I had been studying King Jehoshaphat's battle story in 2 Chronicles 20. That morning, I had started my worship music in the car like I always do but then realized this was a spiritual battle and that I should approach the day like the kingdom of Judah approached the battle—by sending worship and prayer ahead. Not only did I have peace, but Paul actually responded to me in a positive way.

From that day on, I realized the more I worship God in all circumstances, the more Holy Spirit peace I have as I live through all circumstances.

From that day on, I realized the more I worship God in all circumstances, the more Holy Spirit peace I have as I live through all circumstances.

ANOTHER VISIT AND BARNES & NOBLE

The next time Mom and I went to see Paul, we took him out for lunch then went to Barnes and Noble. Paul still didn't have glasses, but we were hopeful they would arrive soon. I helped Paul find a book. I asked at guest services where to find the kind of math books Paul wanted. They told us where to find the math section but suggested looking in a college bookstore for what Paul wanted. I smiled in agreement. In the math section, I read off book titles until Paul told me to look at one. I read the table of contents and confirmed that it was an anthology. He decided he wanted it.

Then I suggested we look online for the books he wanted, so we sat down near the café to do the search. I ordered the books then gave them to him the next time we visited. Unfortunately, Paul still didn't have his glasses by then.

RELEASE FROM THE HOSPITAL

Mom, Dad, Bea, and I talked a lot about what would happen when Paul got out of the hospital. We had to be careful not to do everything he wanted because he would probably disappear again. Although I've not read the book *When Helping Hurts,*[136] I do know the gist of the message from talking to my pastor co-workers at church. Whatever we did for Paul, it had to help him, not enable him to continue making poor decisions.

Six weeks after we got the first call that Paul was found, he was released from the hospital. Dad and Bea decided to drive out—and then it snowed in Minnesota. I started to get concerned they wouldn't get here in time. I didn't want to pick up Paul from the hospital without my dad, and I was concerned that my dad, already stressed by what was going on with Paul, may be distracted while driving on slippery roads. I asked all my friends for prayer, and I praised God.

Dad knew they wouldn't get to Washington, DC in time to pick up Paul from the hospital and asked if I would pick him up. "Yes, of course." By this time, I had peace about it.

I had been thinking about how the week would go, how we *wanted* it to go. I felt the Lord was telling me to receive Paul like the Prodigal Son[137] with joy, acceptance, and feasting. I thought about my dad and how much he loves Paul and how much he misses Paul and how much he has worried the last year-and-a-half. I wanted my dad to have time with Paul before we talked about what would happen next. God gave me a plan, and I communicated it to everyone.

- Wednesday, Mom and I would pick up Paul in the afternoon and bring him back to my home.

- Mom would make Reubens for dinner (Paul's favorite), and I would make German Chocolate cupcakes. *Everyone* was happy about the dinner plans!

- Dad and Bea would ideally arrive in time for dinner.

- We would defer Paul from conversations about what happens next, anything negative, or anything that was not real. We listen, but we don't agree. "Oh, interesting" may be our response, then we change the conversation to canoeing, kayaking, camping, hiking, music, or cribbage—anything positive and neutral. We were going to receive him with joy and feasting like the Father received his Prodigal Son.

- Thursday, we would have breakfast at the diner with a similar attitude of positivity and neutral conversations that have nothing to do with what happens next. Then I would send my boys home.

- We would have lunch at Chick-fil-A so that we could "talk business." If Paul says no to the conditions for riding back to Minnesota with Dad, then we would offer to take him to the Department of Family Services so that he could start the process for getting help from the county. If he says yes to that, then we would help him through the process.

- Friday morning, my dad and stepmom would leave for Minnesota. The rest of the day would depend on whether Paul was still at my home or with my dad.

I was supposed to lead class in our homeschool community on Friday, but since I had no idea how I'd be doing emotionally that day, I arranged to have someone else lead in my place.

Before Paul arrived at my home, I was intentionally prayerful that it would be a place of peace. I played worship music in every room all day long to remind all of us to focus on God. I prayed throughout the house but especially in the guest room where Paul would sleep. Before Mom and I left for the hospital, the boys, my mom, and I prayed prayers of forgiveness[138] and asked God for more of the Holy Spirit.[133]

When we picked up Paul from the hospital, he only had a jacket, a notebook, and the two books I had purchased for him. I asked about the second set of clothes that Mom had given him. The social worker said Paul didn't want them. I asked Paul why he didn't want the clothes. He mumbled something about the hospital. My guess is he associated them with the hospital, and he didn't like or trust anyone there. We don't think there was any rational reason for that because we were pleased with everyone we talked to.

Mom and Paul made it to our front door before I did. My boys met them in the entryway. Neither boy remembered Paul, except from the time he closed his apartment door in our faces. Mom introduced the boys to Paul. Paul was polite but didn't look up. I walked through the door just then. The boys looked at me. I nodded and gave them an I'm-proud-of-you smile.

Mom got settled in to her preparations for dinner. I took Paul to buy clothes. We got home shortly before Russ. Paul sat at the kitchen table while I helped Mom with dinner.

When Russ got home, he greeted Paul and said, "Do you remember me?" Paul said he did. They had a nice exchange.

Dad and Bea made it to town just in time for dinner. Lots of hugs were exchanged and then Dad saw Paul. Paul was polite and seemed pleased that Dad and Bea were happy to see him. Then Bea, sneezing because she's allergic to my dog, left to get her dinner. Bea was pleased to let us have family time.

We had a nice evening with laughter and stories. Russ and my boys received my brother with love, treating him like they would anyone even though Paul would not look them in the eye and seemed to have a scowl on his face.

Paul was sitting next to Dad. He scowled and looked down most of the time, but he would half smile at good memories. Maybe *scowl* isn't the right word. He had no affect, which means he had no expression. This is often seen in someone with a mental illness. He would answer questions when asked. He had even helped me set the table. One of my sons asked Paul to confirm whether he had really eaten eight Reubens on his 16th birthday. Paul half smiled and said, "Yes, that sounds about right."

I took a few pictures. I asked Paul if he'd smile for a picture, and he did. The weird thing is that Paul never smiled for pictures on demand. It was really hard to get him to smile or even to be in a picture years ago when he didn't seem to have an illness. Before Dad left, I asked for a picture of Paul, Dad, Mom, and me.

Paul smiled for that picture, too. That night, I sent the photos to Costco for printing.

THURSDAY

The next morning, Dad came over to use my Wi-Fi. He and Mom sat at the kitchen table and talked while I went to see if Paul was ready to go to breakfast. He was standing in the guest room near the door but not doing anything. I asked him if he was going to take a shower before we went to breakfast. He said, "There seems to be some confusion as to whether I should take a shower."

I said, "No confusion. Go ahead and take a shower. We'll go to breakfast when you're ready." I went back downstairs to visit with Mom and Dad.

About 20 minutes later, I went back upstairs to see if Paul was ready. He was standing in the same place in the guest room. I asked if he was ready to go. He said, "There seems to be some confusion as to whether I should take a shower."

I said, "It's up to you. Do you want to take a shower now or later today?" He answered by getting his notebook and books and followed me downstairs. We decided who was going in which car and left for the diner.

The food was good, as always. We gave Paul birthday cards, even though it was a month before his birthday, because we had missed so many of them. In the cards, we included Visa, McDonald's, and Burger King gift cards. I caught Paul half smiling at the birthday card that I gave him.

We enjoyed our conversations, but Paul didn't participate in any of them. He responded when asked questions, but otherwise sat at the table looking down and shaking. He had seemed better the night before. It was sad to see him like that.

After breakfast, Bea took the boys back to the house and went to rest at the hotel. Mom, Dad, Paul, and I went shopping for a phone, a watch, and toiletries. We stopped at Costco for the pictures. I gave a set to Mom, a set to Dad, a set to Paul, and kept a set for myself. Mom and Dad were both glad to have the photos. Paul simply said, "Oh," and put them in his notebook.

We ran a few more errands and then met Bea at Chick-fil-A for lunch. This is where we were going to talk to Paul about what happens next. I can't remember how Dad started the conversation, but he wasn't getting much of a response from Paul. Dad looked a little frustrated, like he didn't know what to say next. I broke in and said, "Dad is leaving for Minnesota tomorrow. We need to know if you're going with him. He's willing to give you a ride if you will agree to go back into the care you had in St. Paul."

"I'm not going back to St. Paul," he said.

"Well, if you're not going back to St. Paul, then we'll have to figure out how to get you services here. The Department of Family Services is the place to start. I know where the building is. May we take you there?" I asked.

"Yes, that would be okay," he said.

We decided to split up. Dad and I would take Paul to the Department of Family Services. Mom and Bea would go to an antique store downtown to explore. Why was my mom excited about taking my stepmom shopping? I have no idea.

I was going to break down. I needed to cry. I gave Dad the keys to the van and said I'd be out in a few minutes. I went to the ladies' room and cried. I knew in my heart this was how it would go—because God moved my brother from St. Paul to Boston to Washington, DC for a reason—but the responsibility made me cry. I'm not even sure why.

I composed myself and washed my face. When I went outside, Paul was sitting in the van. In my dad's car, Bea was in the driver's seat, my mom was sitting shotgun, and my dad was leaning in the driver's window talking to the two of them. I stopped short. Now that was an interesting scene. I wish I had taken a picture.

At the Department of Family Services, Paul was supposed to sign in using the computer. I started typing for Paul and then realized he had glasses now, so he could do it himself. He completed the form, took a number, and sat down. I asked him if he wanted us to stay. He said, "No."

Dad and I went back out into the hallway and sat down. We didn't know if we should leave the building or not. If we did, we didn't have a plan for where to go. We were talking about the pay-per-minute phone that we had just bought and realized that adding him to one of our cell phone plans would be cheaper. We chose mine because we had an old phone that could be reactivated and because it was a little less per month than Dad's plan.

Paul had taken all his purchases, his books, and his notebook with him, so Dad went back and asked him for the phone, the card with minutes on it, and the receipt. Paul gave them to Dad, so we took them back to Target. I called Mom to say I needed her old phone because we were going to reactivate it. My mom and stepmom met Dad and me back at the Department of Family Services. This time, Dad and my stepmom stayed with Paul while Mom and I got the phone and took it to Verizon.

As long as we were at Verizon, we had them transfer photos and contacts among the phones. The guy at Verizon was helpful and patient, but it took over an hour to get it all done. We all met back at the house. Paul went upstairs to be alone. Dad and Bea said they had been in the interview room with Paul at the Department of Family Services. Dad said the longer Paul was there, the more stressed he seemed, the more he looked like he wanted to get away. Bea said Paul had put the wrong last name on the paperwork but that they had gotten that corrected. Clearly, Paul didn't want to be in the county system or get their help. He was just doing what we told him to do.

That night we went out for dinner. I didn't take the usual route to the restaurant because I automatically started driving the road I always do for most of our activities. Mom pointed out that we needed to turn. Once we got on the road that I should have taken, I realized we were going by the homeless shelter. Since Paul would need to stay there, I pointed out the shelter along the way.

At dinner, everyone had a nice time talking, except Paul. He sat at the end of the table and didn't interact with anyone. At one point, I got up to show him some features on the phone. I was showing him how Google Maps works. I saved my address on there so that he could find my place. He said, "I don't want anything tracking my location."

I said, "I understand," and just continued showing him features.

FRIDAY

The next morning, Dad and Bea left reluctantly. It was a short visit. We all would have liked to spend more time together, but they had a choir rehearsal that they couldn't miss.

My younger boy, Joshua, had homeschool group that day, so we went but got there late. I normally "teach," so when my friend Tiffany saw me come in late, she immediately knew that something was not right. She pulled me aside. I gave her the full update. She was kind, and she prayed for me and for my whole family.

At lunch, I was sitting with Laura and Nahtasha. Laura caught me staring into space and said, "Cheryl, what are you thinking about?"

I do not usually stare into space. I am always thinking and moving. I said, "I'm trying to figure out how I'm going to get refilled." I meant refilled with the Holy Spirit, but she and Nahtasha knew what I meant.

Nahtasha said, "It's okay to rest."

Perhaps I needed permission.

In the afternoon, I looked into getting Paul a checking account. Dad had Paul's social security checks and left two of them with me. Dad had a checking account for Paul in Minnesota, but that bank didn't have any branches in my area. We considered showing Paul the one no-fee ATM that was nearby, but Dad wasn't able to add Paul's name to the account.

I found a low-fee banking option in town that required at least a $500 monthly automated deposit. Perhaps Paul's social security checks would make that minimum. We didn't know the amount of his checks, however, so I asked Paul if he would open one of the envelopes. He did. That was the first Paul knew about the checks. He didn't seem to know what to do with the two envelopes he now had in his possession. He set them down on the coffee table. Then he picked them up. Then he set them down again. So, I asked him if he wanted me to keep the checks someplace safe. He said, "Yes." By the time I had done all the research on banking options, it was 5 pm on Friday. We weren't going to get an account set up that day. That was okay, though, because my Holy Spirit confidence said something wasn't right.

We had dinner that night at home. My boys were well behaved, and we were even laughing. I was pleasantly surprised because my boys are not well behaved at the table—and I know that that's my fault. I have brought my memories of sitting at the table with my schizophrenic sister and toddler nephew from 30 years before to my table. I do not like sitting at the dinner table with children, not even my own. I can't stand whining at the table. My instinct is to escape. Russ has worked with the boys, and they have gotten a lot better, but they still seem to just tolerate the dinner table, much like I do.

But not that night. That night, they were talking and laughing. Paul just sat there looking down. It was sad but at the same time I was glad he was at the table with our family.

Unfortunately, after dinner, I had to take Paul to the homeless shelter. As I mentioned, we can't get help for our mentally ill loved ones who are adults when they live in our homes. I was also concerned that he may overhear our discussions and turn them into paranoid hallucinations—lies—that would divide the two of us even further. I didn't want more division. I wanted to be friends again.

The homeless shelter has two sections—the cold weather shelter, which was open through March 31st and the main shelter. To be in the main shelter, you need a referral from the Department of Family Services. I already knew that they were full, but even if they weren't, Paul would have to agree to get services from the Department of Family Services, but he wasn't cooperating with them.

The cold weather shelter requires the homeless to give them background information and an I.D. I completed Paul's paperwork because his hand was shaking so much he couldn't write. In addition to all the required information, I wrote in the margin that I am his sister and that I was a former co-worker of Pastor Dave. Pastor Dave knows many of the employees at the shelter because our church has been volunteering there for years.

Paul volunteered the I.D. that St. Elizabeth's had given him, but that didn't meet their requirements. As per their policy, they called the police to have them I.D. Paul. I was concerned about how Paul would respond to the police. I looked at the woman and shook my head. She said, "I know, but that's the policy."

The police simply asked for Paul's social security number, checked him out in their system, and then came back to give the staff a thumb's up.

I was dropping off Paul at the cold-weather shelter at 9 pm. At 7 am the next morning, they expected everyone to leave. I told Paul that. That afternoon, I looked at all the bus routes with Paul. I had never been on these buses, but it looked like there was no bus service on the weekends. I told Paul that either Russ or I would pick him up at 7 am. He said, "Okay."

On Facebook, I posted "#schizophreniasucks." My apologies for the choice of words, but I wanted to use much stronger language. Dropping off my brother at the homeless shelter was hard, unbelievably hard, but it was the right thing to do. I cried all the way home.

SATURDAY

When Russ went to pick up Paul the next morning, he wasn't there. Russ drove around the area and didn't see him. He called me and reluctantly told me. I was sad but not surprised. I said, "God, You took care of him for one-and-a-half years. I trust You to take care of him now." I figured this was the way life was going to be. I'd just have to trust God and praise Him every time I knew Paul was okay. I was sad all day. I think I was emotionally exhausted. I needed more of the Holy Spirit.

I listened to my worship music as I did my Saturday chores. I sang and worshiped God even though I was sad. I was not mad at God. I was not disappointed in God. I was just sad and worshiped God anyway because He is my Lord.

That night, Russ and I drove out of town toward one of our favorite restaurants for our date night. Russ noticed that the police car ahead of us saw a pedestrian on an unsafe part of the highway. He quickly assessed that the police car was going to go talk to the pedestrian and said to me, "Wait! What is Paul wearing?"

"A jacket, khaki pants, and tennis shoes."

"Does the jacket have a stripe?"

"Yes. Why?"

"I think that was Paul. That police officer is turning around. I think he spotted Paul. I'm going to follow him."

Russ followed the police officer through two U-turns. The police officer pulled over. Sure enough, the pedestrian was Paul. I said to Russ, "I'll talk to him."

The police officer got out of his car and was surprised to see us. Russ kept his hands on the steering wheel so that the officer could see we meant no harm. I had stepped out of the van but stayed near my door. I called out, "Paul, are you okay?"

"Yes," he said.

To the police officer I said, "He's my brother."

The police officer relaxed. I stayed back to give the officer the space he seemed to want while he talked to Paul. I was a little concerned that Paul would get upset because he had been paranoid of the police since he's had schizophrenia, thinking they were following him and harassing him even though there was never evidence of that. But he was calm, unemotional, and answered every question. He even volunteered his I.D., which was the card issued by St. Elizabeth's Hospital. The officer quickly understood because, of course, every police officer in the area would recognize that St. Elizabeth's is a psychiatric hospital. He was kind.

Paul said he was going to the homeless shelter. I asked him if that's what he wanted to do. He looked at me in the eye, a rarity, and asked, "Do I have any other options?"

I paused, contemplating my plan not to enable him, then said, "Why don't you stay at my house tonight." Perhaps my plan could start on Monday.

The officer took my name and address. I gave him my card. The officer nodded as if to show his understanding and bid us a good night.

Paul got in the van, and we took him home. On the way, I called Mom to tell her that we had Paul and that we were bringing him home to stay the night. When we walked into the house, Mom looked relieved. She and I talked briefly. She thought perhaps Paul chose his route because I had mistakenly driven that way the Thursday before on the way to dinner.

Russ and I still went out on our date, and I was still emotionally exhausted, but I was ever so thankful for Russ' keen eyes. I even tagged him on Facebook to make sure everyone knew how grateful I was.

JOY COMES IN THE MORNING

The next morning, I was up at 5:30 am to go to church and pray as I do every Sunday. I walked my seven laps around the building. The bible says, "Joy comes in the morning" in Psalm 30:5, and it's not kidding! My joy did return. I was thankful for my joy. I was thankful that Paul was safe and warm at my house. I was thankful that my dad and stepmom made it back to Minnesota safely. I had much to be thankful for.

I did my usual drive-thru at McDonald's and said "hi" to Susan. I dropped off breakfast and then took the dog for a run.

It was the first day of Daylight Savings Time. We would normally be at both church services (one for class and one for worship), but that day we decided to take our time rather than be more frazzled than we already were from the previous days' events. After our morning routine, we went to church service. I knew the person at the Welcome Desk. She asked how I was doing, not knowing my circumstances, of course. I smiled and replied, "Joy comes in the morning!" Someone else asked me how I was doing. I said, "I have peace because I worship the Prince of Peace."

I have peace because I worship the Prince of Peace!

That afternoon, I showed Paul around town so that he would know a safer route to the homeless shelter. He'd been homeless for the last year-and-a-half, so he was used to walking. If he was going to walk, then I wanted him to walk where he was less likely to get hit by a car. I showed him the bus route, which was about the same as the walking route. The route went to the library near my house. I knew that he liked the library.

That night, I had a meeting at church. As I left to go home, Pastor Dave stopped to see how I was doing. Just then, Russ called and told me that Paul left the house without explanation. I sighed, "Okay, I'll look for him on the way home."

I drove home on the route I had showed Paul, but I didn't see him. I drove to the library, but I didn't see him. As I drove out of the library's driveway, I prayed. I felt God encouraging me to go home to my family. I should spend time with my family rather than worrying about Paul.

When I got home, both my boys met me at the door to give me hugs. They were both so concerned about me. It was very sweet. Russ had a look on his face like, "I'm sorry that I lost your brother." I put my hand on his arm and said, "It's okay. I prayed and felt God tell me to go home to spend time with my family. I have a feeling that this is what life is going to be like for a while. I'm trusting God." Russ looked relieved.

13

FOLLOWING NOT STRIVING TO GET AHEAD

The next morning, Daniel and I had his homeschool community class. While Daniel and I were away for the day, Joshua would homeschool with my mom. As I was getting everything ready to go, I grabbed a fleece that Russ had offered for Paul, Paul's phone, and five one-dollar bills. I put them in the van.

When Daniel and I left, I purposely drove the route that I had showed to Paul. Within two minutes, I saw Paul on the sidewalk. I turned the van around and found a place to park with the flashers on so that I would not impede morning traffic. I crossed the street, walked up to Paul, and said, "Good morning!" He half smiled. I asked, "Will you take this fleece so that you're warm?" He put it under his arm. "And here are some ones so that you can take the bus." I didn't give him the phone because I didn't think he'd take it, and frankly I didn't want it lost or purposely left behind someplace. I reminded Paul where we live and that he was welcome there.

Paul said, "Thank you," and kept walking.

I got back in the van and called Russ, who was home that day to receive a furniture delivery, to let him know what had happened. Why were we getting a delivery? Because at the same time Paul reentered our lives, Russ' mom was moving from her senior living apartment into an Alzheimer's care apartment, both in Chicago. In her new home, his mom did not have space for the grandfather clock and curio cabinet, which he had made for her long before I had met him. So not only was our life tested with Paul's return but also with concern for Russ' mom.

I told Russ I saw Paul walking near our street and watched him while Russ and I were on the phone. "Looks like he's going to the library," I said. Then Daniel and I headed to class.

Daniel said, "Are you okay?"

"Yes, I'm happy to see him."

"It's a good thing you had that fleece for him."

"Yeah, I had a feeling I should have it with me just in case we saw him." My Holy Spirit confidence was at work within me once again.

Paul went to the library after I saw him but later went to the house. Mom made him sloppy joes for lunch. He was also at the house for dinner, and then he left.

The next morning, Paul was back at my house. He didn't ring the doorbell. Instead, he knocked and waited for someone to let him in. The dog went crazy until she saw it was Paul. Then she was sweet and calm.

Paul said he wanted to get his checks cashed. I said, "Okay, let me get homeschooling done then we can go to the bank to cash the checks." After lunch and schoolwork, Paul told me—without any prompting from me—that he wanted to get his checks cashed so that he could go back to Minnesota to get his I.D. He could then get a bank account set up and continue traveling to the University of California at Berkeley where he could do research in their library.

"Will you take your phone with you?"

"No, I don't want the phone."

"Then how will we know you're okay?"

Paul didn't have an answer. He simply said, "I just do what I do."

There are so many ways I could have said what I was feeling, what Mom and Dad were probably feeling. I could have said, "So, you're going to disappear again." I could have said, "So, you'll be homeless again and eventually picked up by the police like you were in Washington, DC and years ago when you were homeless in Minneapolis." I could have said, "You must not like us if you keep running away." I purposely didn't say any of those things.

I chose my words carefully. I thought about what I had learned so many years before from the NAMI class—no guilt trips; be short and to the point. So instead of saying what was in my head, I said, "So, you'll disappear again, and we won't know if you're okay." Fail. Try again. I remembered the language Russ suggested and said, "When you are traveling without a phone and not calling us to let us know you're okay, I worry."

Paul didn't respond.

I was upset. I wouldn't look at him. "I will not enable you to disappear again. I'll give you your checks, but I will not help you cash them."

I gave Paul his checks. They weren't mine to keep anyway. He said, "Thank you" and left.

I cried. Would we see him again?

I texted Dad, Mom, and Russ to let them all know what had happened.

The next morning, Paul showed up at my house again and sat on the couch all day. Evidently, he didn't find a place that would cash his checks.

That became the pattern. Paul would be at our house during the day, sitting on the couch in the family room. He would join us for meals and then sleep at the cold-weather part of the homeless shelter.

I showed Paul how to use the TV remote. He would watch TV until something violent was on the screen and then turn it off. One time I found him just sitting on the couch and asked him if he wanted to watch TV. He said there was something with sex in it, so he turned it off. I noticed he never watched the news, either. I found the National Geographic channel for him, and he watched hours and hours of shows about wildlife.

A week later, a wintry mix of snow and freezing rain was in the forecast. I explained to Paul that snow in Northern Virginia was icier than in Minnesota and that the sidewalks would be more dangerous. (Sorry, folks, but Minnesota is much better than Virginia about clearing walks and putting out salt and sand to deal with ice.) I told Paul to stay at our house so that he wasn't walking in his tennis shoes in the snow and on the slippery walks. He said, "Okay." He did stay several nights. On Monday, we had several evening activities, so I explained to Paul where we were going to be. Evidently, I was not clear that he was welcome to stay because when we got home, he wasn't there.

Russ saw my concern and said, "God has taken care of him so far." I nodded, turned on worship music in the guest room, and went to bed.

The next morning, Paul showed up again and sat on the couch. I said, "Hello" without judgment or surprise in my voice. I was getting really good at talking in a matter-of-fact way.

Paul said hello in return. I told him that we were surprised that he wasn't in the house when we got home. He said there was some confusion.

I waited until he looked me in the eye. "No confusion. You are welcome to stay here. Stay here through April 8th, and we'll figure out what to do after that." April 1st was Easter. April 8th was Eastern Orthodox Easter. I was praying the Lord would cause some sort of breakthrough on Easter, whichever Easter He chose.

SMILES AND LAUGHTER

One night that week, Russ was late getting home for dinner. I was hungry and wanted to leave for an evening bible study, so we started the meal without Russ. Paul had held hands with us while we prayed at every meal, although he never prayed with us. That night, I said, "Boys, have we showed Paul the 'Jaws' prayer?"

Joshua looked at Daniel as if to say, "I can't believe she's doing this." I smiled.

When Paul, Nancy, and I were growing up, we had the honor of choosing the table prayer whenever we set the table. Nancy and I almost always chose to sing "Johnny Appleseed."[139] But when Paul set the table, he would choose to say the prayer: "God is great. God is good, and we thank Him for our food. Amen."

Well, at our house today, we chant "God is great" to the "Jaws" movie theme song. "Paul," I said. "We put our hands together over our heads like a shark fin." Paul did it while looking down. He always looked down. "Then we chant the prayer to the 'Jaws' theme song like this."

The boys were still looking at each other like "I guess she's really doing this." I continued smiling.

Paul laughed and laughed—while still looking down.

I laughed, too. "I know! Funny, right!?!"

The boys still had bewildered looks on their faces, but they enjoyed Paul's reaction to the prayer.

The following week was Holy Week. At church on Palm Sunday, a friend stopped to ask me how Paul was doing. I gave her an update and said, "I feel like the Lord is pleased with how we welcomed him like the Prodigal Son." She nodded her head. "And I sense the Lord saying I should follow Him and not get ahead of Him."

"Oh, yes, that's a good one." I could tell she was contemplating that for herself.

That week, I fasted for Paul's salvation, healing, and reconciliation with our family Monday through Friday, that is, until dinnertime on Friday.

My friend Tiffany, from Joshua's homeschool community, had invited me to a Protestant church that had the Stations of the Cross open for 24 hours from Maundy Thursday to noon on Good Friday. I had never experienced the Stations of the Cross, and I was intrigued.

As a result of cancelations of our community because of snow from the previous weeks, we had community on Good Friday to make up for missed days. I knew I wouldn't make it to the Stations of the Cross on Thursday, but perhaps I could go early on Friday before community. Tiffany said she had been waking up at 3 am recently, so she would probably go then. Russ and I both had been waking up at 4 am that week, so I told her I may join her early in the morning.

When I woke up at 3:30 am, I wasn't the least bit surprised. I chuckled to myself at the thought that God woke me up, and I drove the 20 minutes to another town for the Stations of the Cross. On the way, I sang to my worship play list.

Each station included art provided by the church's congregation. The first one was interactive with a Polaroid camera. Several had beautiful paintings. One had music. It was magnificent.

In the yard of the church were three crosses. We nailed our confessions and prayer requests to the middle cross. There were benches near there. That's where Tiffany and I sat and talked about how moving the experience was. She was finished, so she headed home. I went back inside to experience the last few stations, which included one with an essential oil diffuser that contained Myrrh. I took pictures of most of the prayers I wrote because I didn't want to forget them:

Lord, in my convictions, may I never betray You nor sway from anything but Your perfect plan. I am Your bondservant. ~Cheryl

Lord, convict me with boldness to go to political leaders and to serve You even when I am afraid of the religious leaders. I ask in Jesus' Name. Amen. ~Cheryl

Lord, bring justice to those who provide abortions, promote abortions, force abortions, pressure women to have abortions, work to keep abortions, and look the other way while children are ripped from their mothers and while women are torn emotionally and spiritually. Bring justice for the women who have been lied to by the law. Amen! ~ Cheryl

Lord, I am sorry for denying You for so long. My soul weeps bitterly for all those years of denying You. Thank You for calling me out of the grave. Thank You for forgiving me and washing me white as snow. Thank You for adopting me into Your family. Thank You, Jesus. ~ Cheryl

Lord, may I always submit to Your will when I am accused. I know that I am a child of God. I stand firm on the knowledge of who I am. I do not need affirmation from others. Only You. May Your Name be praised forever. More of You and less of me. Amen. ~ Cheryl

Lord, no matter the wounds inflicted on me by people who think they are right, I will choose You. Amen. ~ Cheryl

Lord, I have picked up my cross, and I am following You. Your will be done. Amen. ~ Cheryl

Lord, give me strength to bear the anger of those who are not following You. May I carry Your cross—I only wish to serve You. Amen. ~ Cheryl

Lord, You said the time will come when women will say, "Blessed are the barren women, the wombs that never bore and the breasts that never nursed." Lord, are those the women who never were pregnant or are those the women who have aborted? Open my mind to understanding the scriptures. (Luke 24:45) Amen. ~ Cheryl

Lord, may Paul be "ripped" no more. ["Schizo" means "ripped."] Give him complete healing and reconciliation with You and with our family in Jesus' Name. Amen. ~ Cheryl

Lord, You are the Great Healer. You desire us to be in Your family. You call us by name. Call Paul by name. Call him into Your family. Do it because You love my God-fearing ancestors. Do it because of how my family has served You and will serve You. Do it because it glorifies You. May You get all the glory! I ask You to heal him completely and reconcile him with You and with our family. In Jesus' Name. Amen. ~Cheryl

Lord, all the way to my own death, I will confess Your Son as the Christ. I look forward to being in paradise with You when my time here is done. In the meantime, use me to bring glory to Your name. Use me to bring a multitude of this generation to Paradise as well. I ask in Jesus' Name. Amen. ~Cheryl

Lord, I thank You that Lynn is my family and that her children and their children are my family. I praise You for choosing me to be in Your family. Use me to bring more people into Your family. I ask in Jesus' Name. Amen. ~Cheryl

Lord, thank You for ripping the curtain to give all people access to You.[140] Thank You for giving me access to You, for accepting my prayers. Thank You for bringing me into Your Holy presence—sanctified and righteous because I have Your righteousness not my own. I praise You because You are worthy to be praised. With appreciation and adoration, Cheryl

At our homeschool community that morning, I was to lead the lesson on famous composers and although we were studying a composer from the impressionist era, I was reminded of our study of Handel, who is from the Baroque Period. I'm sure you remember Handel's *Messiah*.[141] Handel actually wrote it for Easter. When you listen to the words, you realize that makes sense. We associate the "Hallelujah" chorus with Christmas because it is a great performance for fundraisers, which are popular at Christmas and not-so-much for Easter, even back in Handel's time.

I found the "Hallelujah" chorus on my phone and worshiped God by singing it on the way home—I can really belt it out at 5:30 in the morning when no one is around to hear me!

That night at home, we had a Seder meal, which is the Passover meal that Jesus shared with His disciples on what we Christians call Maundy Thursday. Sundown that Good Friday was the start of Passover and therefore the day for the Seder. I was inspired by my friend Katharine Wang's bible study[142] on the Passover Meal. Since Paul used to be Jewish, he knew the Seder better than I did, but I wasn't going to cook traditional Jewish foods. I just wanted the ritual breaking of bread with the story of the Passover so that Russ and I could discuss the Christian meanings of this meal with the boys while fully knowing Paul was hearing everything we said.

I told Paul that Mom was making dinner, like she usually did on Friday evenings, but we were going to have a combination celebration of Maundy Thursday, Good Friday, and Seder with our oh-so-*not*-Kosher-Minnesota hamburger hot dish.[143] He laughed! And I laughed with him.

I found a Christian website that led us through the traditional meal. I tried to pronounce the Hebrew words, but with my Minnesota accent, my words didn't sound much like they should in Hebrew. Paul, on the other hand, knows Hebrew, Aramaic, and Mandarin and has no problem pronouncing words correctly, so I would check with him to see if my pronunciation was okay. He would smile and either say, "that will work" or he'd say the word correctly. I enjoyed asking him if I got it right. He smiled every time I asked and smirked every time I got a word wrong. I had no problem being corrected. It was exactly as I had hoped, and I enjoyed his smiles.

In the Seder meal, there are three pieces of Matzah (or unleavened) bread. The table leader takes the middle piece and breaks it in half. The smaller half is put in a white linen cloth and hidden for later in the meal. From what I understand, Jews have different thoughts on what the three pieces of bread represent, like perhaps they refer to Abraham, Isaac, and Jacob. Christians, however, see the three pieces of bread as the aspects of God: Father, Son, and Holy Spirit. The middle one, the Son, is broken. He is raised from the dead on Easter Sunday, represented by the larger of the two halves, and one day will return to Earth, represented by the smaller of the two halves. Daniel and Joshua seemed to enjoy the symbolism. They liked the ritual retelling of the Passover and did quite well in explaining it themselves, including how Jesus fulfilled the Passover by being the Sacrificial Lamb Whose blood protects us from eternal death. Russ and I were proud of them.

Paul heard all that, but I couldn't tell if he was moved by it. I didn't feel we were supposed to ask Paul about his beliefs but instead were to let all that was said sink into him.

I thanked Paul for his help. He smiled, "You're welcome" and left the table.

CONTENDING

That night as I was praying before falling asleep, I felt God was pleased with us, and I heard the word *contend*. Contend? How do I contend? "Now it's time to contend for Paul's faith."

Beloved, although I was very eager to write to you about our common salvation, I found it necessary to write appealing to you to contend for the faith that was once for all delivered to the saints. (Jude 3 ESV)

My prayers that Saturday morning became more declarative. "Thank You, Lord, for bringing Paul into a personal relationship with Your Son Jesus Christ."

I had an opportunity to talk to Paul alone Saturday morning. The Lord had given me this conversation starter. I said, "I have a question for you."

"Mmm hmm?" Paul responded.

"When I took you to the eye doctor, you said that there's no such thing as schizophrenia."

"There isn't."

"I'm not disagreeing with you. That's a human perspective." I wanted to explore with him whether schizophrenia was a spiritual issue.

"Bad doctors."

"But what do you think is going on?" Paul was searching for an answer. I continued, "I looked up the word: *Schizo* is Greek, and it means ripped in a violent way. So, when Jesus died on the cross, the veil around the Holy of Holies was ripped, *schizo*, from top to bottom.[144] And when Jesus was baptized, the skies were ripped open, *schizo*, and the Holy Spirit came down like a dove.[145] So what do you think is ripped?"

"I don't know."

"Hmm. Well, how do you feel about Jesus?"

"Jesus is not for me," and with that Paul got up and left the room.

I wasn't surprised, disappointed, or upset. I had done what God told me to do. I rested in that.

I stayed up late Saturday night reading blogs and listening to sermons about the meaning of *contend*—not a good decision on my part. I am the mom, after all. I had to prepare Easter breakfast, Easter lunch, and Easter baskets. I set my alarm for 5 am so that I could get my prayer walk done before I started the food prep. Then I went to sleep after 11:30 pm. Ugh.

The next morning, I woke up at 6:30. Oh, no! Why didn't my alarm go off at 5 am? I checked to make sure that I had set up everything correctly. I had. That was odd. Why didn't my alarm go off? Maybe it was God giving me a little more rest. "Thank You, Lord!"

We were only going to one service that day, so I went ahead with my plan for the morning. I went to church to pray. Because I was there later than usual, I saw several volunteers arrive, including the worship team and one of my former co-workers.

At one point in my prayer, I was prostrate in the grass behind the building where no one could see me crying for Paul's salvation. When I got up, I couldn't find my glasses. I didn't remember taking them off. When I found them, the left lens had popped out. I tried to get it back in, but it was not quite in place. God nudged me to start walking again. I did and then stopped to work on the lens again. "Walk," He said. So, I continued walking.

I got around the corner to the office door where someone was trying to get into the building. I told her that I could help her. She said, "Is this where the event is?"

"Well, we have church services today at 9, 11, and 1."

"Yes, the event. We need to set up for the event." I didn't know what she was talking about, but I figured she needed the front door, so I told her how to drive around to the front door then walked there myself. By the time I got to the front door, she had driven up to that entrance, so I opened the door for her. She found someone in the lobby who knew what she needed, and I went on with my walk.

When I got in the car, I found a text message from my former co-worker saying, "I'm guessing that you are praying. Please pray that we have enough volunteers today." And so, I did.

On the way home, I stopped by McDonald's like I always do on Sunday morning. I'm sad they are open on Easter, but I had a plan. I asked for the manager. You know that look on the manager's face when you ask for her, right? I had once been that manager, and I knew what it was like to deal with unhappy customers.

But I surprised her when I said, "This is for you and your crew." I handed her a gift bag filled with Easter candy and an Easter card addressed to "Susan and all those who work on Sunday mornings." I enjoyed seeing the smile on her face. This time I didn't buy breakfast from McDonald's—they weren't supposed to be serving me that day because it was a holiday. I was not going to encourage them to be open by spending money.

When I got home, I took the dog for a quick run. Then I made breakfast. I was late, so I changed my meal plan to something faster than the oven breakfast casserole I had planned. Somehow, we managed to finish breakfast, shower, get dressed, and head out the door on time. But before we left, both Russ and I invited Paul to join us. He declined.

After the service, we got in line to have our picture taken. It was fun and silly! This caused us to get home later than planned. Thankfully, dinner was simply for our family, so we didn't have to hurry for guests.

Because we live near the only Catholic Church in town, we usually avoid going downtown through the heavy traffic but instead drive through the neighborhood. But we forgot. I said to Russ, "I know you just passed the turn, but you may want to avoid driving downtown."

"Yeah, I just realized that. Well, if the traffic is bad, I'll turn around."

Just as we noticed traffic was not an issue, we also noticed a young African American man limping across the street. He was carrying two cloth grocery bags that were clearly full. Getting across the street was exhausting for him. He looked relieved to put the bags on the curb as he got out of the way of the cars. Russ said, "That man needs help," and he turned the car around.

I said, "Yes, he does. Invite him for lunch. We have plenty of food."

Russ lowered his window: "Can we give you a ride somewhere?"

"Um, yeah, sure. Thank you," the young man said.

Joshua moved into the far back, and Daniel moved all of our coats out of the way so that the man had room to sit in the van. We introduced ourselves. His name was Elijah. He said the night before was the last night the cold-weather shelter was open, which was true. After March 31, you needed to receive services from the county to be given a place at the year-round homeless shelter. He said he needed to figure out where he was going to sleep that night.

All I could think is that Elijah needed the help of the Department of Family Services, which didn't open until the next morning.

Elijah said his mom had died the night before in the homeless shelter. Wow! Really? I wasn't sure whether to believe him or not, but I knew how to find out. I texted Pastor Dave because he had a relationship with the homeless shelter and could check Elijah's story.

Elijah simply requested a ride to the main bus stop since that is where he was headed when we found him. Russ pulled over and looked at me for confirmation. I said, "Well, how about if you come home with us for Easter dinner? The Department of Family Services is not open today, so I'm guessing that you are not in a hurry."

Elijah looked surprised. "Thank you. That would be nice."

We took Elijah home with us. I knew Mom had started making Easter dinner, so I called her to let her know we were bringing home one more person. "Okay," she said.

When we got close to home, I said to Elijah, "Just so you know, my brother is staying with us. He is also homeless and has a mental illness, but he is quiet and keeps to himself."

Daniel carried Elijah's bags into the house. I quietly pulled Mom aside to tell her that Elijah was homeless. We introduced Elijah to Mom and Paul. Elijah recognized Paul from the cold weather shelter. They exchanged friendly greetings.

Elijah sat at the table while Mom and I made dinner (which we Minnesotans define as the largest meal of the day eaten mid-afternoon on holidays). I was really looking forward to serving dinner to Paul because it included many dishes that we had growing up, like ham and broccoli with hollandaise sauce. Every holiday, we have broccoli with hollandaise sauce. Mom, Daniel, and I always look forward to it. I was glad that Paul, too, was there to enjoy one of our favorite dishes.

I asked Paul if he had ever made hollandaise sauce[146] with a blender. He said, "No," so I told him that I had found this technique that was nearly foolproof and explained it.

After dinner, Paul, Elijah, and I watched the 2009 version of *Star Trek*—the reboot with Chris Pine. Paul hadn't seen any of the recent *Star Trek* movies, and he used to enjoy *Star Trek*. I told Elijah that I was trying to get Paul caught up on the new movies. "I understand. I understand," he said with a smile and a nod.

I was tired. All I wanted to do was take a nap.

Over dinner, we had found out that Elijah had three younger brothers who were in the custody of social services in the adjoining county. He was trying to figure out how to meet up with them to give them the news about their mother. Russ and his big heart went to a grocery store and got Easter candy for Elijah's brothers and for Elijah. Elijah was grateful, but his reaction was also a little odd. I can't explain it, but he wasn't excited about giving his brothers the candy.

Pastor Dave didn't have any additional information about Elijah's mom nor any ideas for where he could sleep that night. Russ and I talked about Elijah's situation and decided to have Daniel sleep in Joshua's room so that Elijah could sleep in Daniel's room.

Elijah was surprised at the invitation but gratefully accepted.

Daniel and I changed the sheets and removed all the valuables. I gave Elijah clean towels and showed him Daniel's room. Finally, everyone was going to bed.

I was exhausted from the long day and the short amount of sleep from the night before, but all day I had paid attention to what Elijah said. I didn't react very emotionally because I didn't know what was true and what wasn't, but I knew things didn't add up. I wasn't sure if he was lying or mentally ill. He never tried to take advantage of us, though. The most he asked for were cotton swabs. I just didn't want to consider that I might have a second mentally ill homeless man in my house. I prayed and fell asleep.

Thankfully, I got a good night's rest. I was up early, getting everything ready so that Daniel and I could go to his homeschool community and so that Joshua knew what schoolwork to get done while he stayed home with Mom. I bought everyone McDonald's breakfast because it was faster and less messy than making breakfast for the houseful. Before Russ went to work, he and I prayed.

I didn't want to leave my mom alone with a stranger, so I told Elijah I would drop him off at the Department of Family Services. He talked about meeting his brothers at the library, but I pointed out that the library wasn't open until 10 am and also that he needed help from his case manager to figure out where he might sleep that night. He agreed.

I texted Pastor Dave again, asking that he check with the cold-weather part of the homeless shelter about whether Elijah's mom had died there that weekend. Then Elijah gathered up his things, and we got in the van. As we were driving, I reminded him that he needed to tell his case manager about his mom and to get suggestions for where he could sleep. In the middle of my sentence, Elijah interrupted, saying, "The kids are sitting down."

"What?" I said.

Elijah was kind of chuckling and said, "The kids are sitting down."

"Oh," I said. *Disorganized thinking—sounds like he may be mentally ill,* I thought to myself. "Remember to ask your case manager for ideas for where you can sleep tonight."

"Okay," he said.

I dropped him off at the Department of Family Services and watched him go inside. His limp was better. Evidently the decent night's sleep helped.

I drove home, still tired. I don't know how much was physical exhaustion and how much was emotional exhaustion. I was wishing I had gone to bed earlier Saturday night so that I could handle everything better.

When I got home, I got a text from Pastor Dave: No one had died at the shelter recently. By this time, I was thinking more clearly than the day before. *Confirmation,* I thought. I wondered if his mom had died at a shelter at some point, but he couldn't remember when. Was it even this shelter? I didn't want to know. I didn't want to get involved. Taking care of one mentally ill person was enough for me.

I talked to the boys about the possibility of Elijah coming back looking for help and made it clear they were not to let him into the house. If he came by, they were to get Russ or me, not Grandma. If we were not home or if we were busy, they were to say we were not available without giving a specific time for when we would be available. Although they may be tempted to say we weren't home, they were to remember that Elijah could see whether our vehicles were in the driveway.

I said, "I don't think that he's dangerous, so this is a precaution. I think he has a mental illness. He could have been lying to us, but he didn't try to take advantage of us."

"Yeah, I noticed that," Daniel said.

I continued, "Our job is to protect our family. We're essentially doing the same thing with your uncle Paul. His behavior is fine right now, but if that were to change, we would protect our family first. Understand?"

"Yeah," they both said.

I told Daniel I was sorry we would be late to his homeschool community. He was really tired himself because he didn't sleep well in his brother's room. I said, "We're not going until the afternoon because I need a break." The boys were concerned about me, but they understood.

I told Mom what had happened and that Daniel and I would be leaving at lunchtime.

I went up to my room and closed the door. I cried. So much of the homeless population is mentally ill, so why was I surprised that the one homeless man we invited home for dinner was also mentally ill?

I texted Russ to tell him what Pastor Dave said and to tell him I thought Elijah had a mental illness. Russ was taken aback because he hadn't picked up on it but said it made sense. We wondered whether the younger brothers were real.

I drew a hot bath with Epsom salts and essential oils, specifically one called Release.™ Oh, did I need to release! I turned on my worship playlist and sank into the tub. I cried. I worshiped. I prayed for more of the Holy Spirit. I needed a refill.

After community, we came home and got ready for our next guests. My cousin Marvin and his husband were going to be our dinner guests that night. (Yes, my cousin is gay. He and his husband are active in their church, but their church does not adhere to the scriptures like we do. We both know the other's beliefs, but I love my cousin even though we don't agree.) Easter

Sunday was my cousin's birthday. He's two days older than Paul, so I invited Marvin for a joint birthday dinner. Mom made Reubens and German potato salad. I made hot fudge pudding with "hard" sauce.[147] Hot fudge pudding was another of Paul's favorites—and mine, too. Oh, so rich!

They arrived early, so Paul could teach our cousin how to play cribbage. We reminisced about Grandpa playing cribbage with his pals in between pumping gas at the gas station he owned and operated and marveled at how my cousin never learned to play. That was the most engaged I had seen Paul. He didn't participate in the stories about Grandpa, but he seemed happy as he taught Marvin how to play cribbage.

After Russ got home, we savored Mom's Reubens. We continued talking, but Paul only participated when we asked him questions directly, which was typical of any dinnertime.

Marvin brought Paul a gift of notebooks and a gift card to Starbucks. We gave Marvin birthday cards. Right after that, Paul went upstairs to his room without saying goodbye. Evidently, he had had enough.

Marvin and his husband asked how Paul was getting along. Mom and I told them that Paul mostly sat on the couch all day and that he would turn off the TV when there was violence or sex. Marvin is interested in pastoral care for the mentally ill and said, "He's probably avoiding stress." That makes sense. I just hadn't thought of it that way.

Marvin and his husband left for their hour drive home, and I went right to bed to catch up on some sleep.

The next day was Paul's birthday. I made more of Paul's favorite foods for dinner. We had Steak Diane with rice and more broccoli with hollandaise sauce. We were all once again delighting in the foods. I had asked Paul what kind of wine he likes. I don't know anything about wine, and I wanted to get some that Paul liked for this special occasion. I wrote it down and asked for help at the store. I was pleased with the assistance once I saw the smile on Paul's face at what I brought home. We got Paul to smile several times that evening.

Paul's smiles warm my heart. This is a man who shut me out of his life for 14 years, who literally shut the door in my face two-and-a-half years before. Now he was enjoying my cooking and Mom's cooking in my own home. I was grateful and thanked God often.

After Holy Week, Easter, helping Elijah, and birthday celebrations, I was exhausted. I was both physically and emotionally exhausted. I needed more of the Holy Spirit, but for some reason I didn't take time to pray, worship, or study the bible. I was still writing this book but couldn't figure out where to end the story. I lost focus for a while.

When I did finally sit down to continue writing, I felt the Lord wanted me to tell the story you just read about Elijah. When I tried to write, I couldn't get it out. I was too emotional. I realized I needed more of God and less of me,[148] so I spent time in worship and prayer, asking the Lord why I was having such a hard time writing. Then I realized I was sad there were so many people in the world with mental illnesses. I can't help them all, but I could give Elijah a place to rest his head for one night.

The Lord reminded me how differently I responded to Elijah than I had to Malek so many years before and how differently I was responding to Paul compared to when he was homeless back in Minneapolis. Now I had boundaries that I had not created before. Rather than dashing in to fix every problem, I confirmed what I heard. I considered the consequences of helping rather than assuming I had to help in every way. When I talked to the boys about being precautious with Elijah, the words just flowed out of my mouth as if they were from the Holy Spirit and not from me. I realized I had never said anything like that before. I had never set boundaries before. I felt the Lord was pleased with my growth—and so am I.

I am glad I listen to the Lord because if I were to forge ahead without Him, I would be worried, exasperated, and emotionally exhausted all the time, and my family would feel neglected.

But even more, I am glad I listened to the Lord because if I were to forge ahead without Him, I would be worried, exasperated, and emotionally exhausted *all* the time, and my family would feel neglected. Following Him is so much better than getting ahead of Him because His plan is always better than mine.

Easter had come and gone. Orthodox Easter had come and gone. I wasn't disappointed that Paul was the same. Perhaps his healing was not the breakthrough that the Lord had planned. I had a breakthrough, though: I knew the Lord had spoken to me after my fast about contending, but I still didn't know what that meant I should do.

When Paul first got out of the hospital a month before, I was sure the Lord did not want him to stay with us. Perhaps it was a reminder to Paul that his situation was difficult, providing him a reminder that he needed help. When I asked Paul to stay through the snow storm and then through Easter, the Lord was leading me to show Paul love by providing shelter. Now I felt that the Lord was pleased with us and that Paul should continue to stay so that we could continue to show him love. After talking to the boys about boundaries, I knew that I would ask Paul to leave if needed.

I needed to know Russ' thoughts. He said, "I'm not going to kick the guy out." Great! We were in agreement. Paul was to be in our home for now. We discussed how we would continue to watch his behavior and reconsider if needed.

One night, not too much later, I was pondering again what it meant to contend. The verse Christians most often quote is Jude 1:3 in which Jude, Jesus' half brother, says:

Beloved, while I was making every effort to write you about our common salvation, I was compelled to write to you [urgently] appealing that you fight strenuously for [the defense of] the faith which was once for all handed down to the saints [the faith that is the sum of Christian belief that was given verbally to believers]. (Jude 1:3 AMP)

But does that mean I talk to my brother again about Who Christ is? I didn't think so. Certainly, if the Lord led me to do so, I would, but He has been clear that I should follow Him and not get ahead of Him. I didn't sense that He was leading me to share the Gospel with Paul again anytime soon.

I was at Ridgetop, my favorite coffee shop, while Joshua was at sports practice, researching what it meant to contend. Then I realized I should ask Pastor Dave. Why didn't I think of that before? I sent him an email right before I had to leave to pick up Joshua.

After I picked him up, we headed back to town. We often listen to worship music from my playlist or WGTS 91.9 FM, our local Christian radio station, while in the car. I noticed the peace on my son's face as he listened and sang along with the music.

My mind wandered back to this book, and the story about how Russ led me to Christ by being an example of Jesus and by praying for me. That's when it hit me—Russ *contended* for me. Since Russ successfully prayed me into accepting Christ's gift,[149] then I should contend through prayer for Paul to believe that Jesus is the Christ.[150] To *contend* means to go to *battle*. In Ephesians 6:12, the Apostle Paul says that our battle is not against flesh and blood but against the spiritual forces in heavenly places.[151]

I was crying with happiness, and I couldn't wait to get home! While Joshua was getting ready for bed, I searched the bible for verses about believing Jesus is the Christ. I found several long lists on reputable Christian websites. I copied the Bible verses and customized them for Paul. Here are some examples:

For God so loved the world, that He gave His only begotten Son, that whoever believes in Him shall not perish, but have eternal life. For God did not send the Son into the world to judge the world, but that the world might be saved through Him. He who believes in Him is not judged; he who does not believe has been judged already, because he has not believed in the name of the only begotten Son of God. (John 3:16-18 NASB)

For God so loved Paul that He gave His only begotten Son, that Paul believes in Him and shall not perish but have eternal life. For God did not send the Son to Paul to judge him but that Paul might be saved through Him. Paul believes in Him and is not judged. Paul believes in the name of the only begotten Son of God.

Jesus said to him, "I am the way, and the truth, and the life; no one comes to the Father but through Me." (John 14:6 NASB)

Jesus is the way, the truth, and the life. Paul comes to the Father through Jesus Christ.

Now to Him who is able to do far more abundantly beyond all that we ask or think, according to the power that works within us, to Him be the glory in the church and in Christ Jesus to all generations forever and ever. Amen. (Ephesians 3:14-21 NASB)

Now to Him who is able to do far more abundantly beyond all that we (Russ, Cheryl, Daniel, Joshua, Dad, Mom, Bea, Drew, and Drew's wife) ask or think, according to the power that works within us, to Him be the glory in the church and in Christ Jesus to all generations forever and ever. Amen!

Contending! Okay, Lord, I understand. I will follow the examples that I had read so many years before in Stormie Omartian's *Power of the Praying…* books.[35] I will contend for both Paul *and* Nancy.

Russ was out of town for work and called to say good night. "How are you?" he asked.

"I'm super excited," I said. "I just figured out what God meant by contending." Then I gave Russ all sorts of examples.

"Good! I'm glad you got the answer you were asking for."

I emailed Pastor Dave to say, "Never mind. I figured it out!" and I sent him my obnoxiously long list of verses customized for Paul.

POSSIBILITIES OUT OF IMPOSSIBLE SITUATIONS

A friend of mine who also was fasting leading up to Easter asked me to read Isaiah 58. "Gladly!" I thought since Isaiah 58:1 is the calling the Lord has put on my life.[152] It's probably been nearly a year since I read the whole chapter. As I read it again, many of the verses pierced my heart in a new way.

Most of the chapter is about fasting. Essentially, the Lord is saying that we often fast in a way that does not honor Him and then we wonder why we feel God doesn't notice our sacrifice (58:3). God goes on to say we fast to please ourselves while making others continue to serve us (58:3). I thought about the times I've fasted and yet continued to go to shopping, which is today's equivalent to making others continue to serve us.

What God wants is for us to fast in such a way that we take burdens off of others (58:6) by sharing our food with the hungry, bringing homeless into our own homes, and providing clothes to those who lack (58:7). Then I read the words that struck me at the end of verse 7: do not hide from your own relatives when they need help.

Wow! Well, that certainly matched up to our Easter week. Without planning ahead, we brought a homeless man into our home to feed him and give him rest all the while helping my own brother by providing him with food, clothing, and shelter.

"Then you will call, and the Lord will answer; you will cry for help, and he will say: 'Here am I.'" (Isaiah 58:9a NIV)

"The LORD will guide you continually, And satisfy your soul in drought, And strengthen your bones; You shall be like a watered garden, And like a spring of water, whose waters do not fail." (Isaiah 58:11 NKJV)

Lord,

I am calling out to You for my siblings! (Isaiah 58:9a) And I thank you for guiding me continually, for satisfying my soul, and for strengthening my bones (Isaiah 58:11). I trust in the name of Jesus Christ that soon we will hear both Paul and Nancy confess with their mouths that Jesus is Lord and believe in their hearts that God raised Jesus from the dead (Romans 10:9). Paul and Nancy pray and ask for healing, believing that they have received it, and healing has been granted to both Paul and Nancy (Mark 11:24).

And just in case schizophrenia is more than a medical condition:

Jesus, my Lord and Savior,

Thank You for saying to all unclean spirits within Paul and Nancy, "Come out!" (Mark 5:8). Thank You for giving Legion permission to go into the swine and therefore out of Paul and Nancy (Matthew 8:31-32) in Jesus' name. Lord, I have faith the size of a mustard seed, believing that Your rebuke of the demons results in my brother and sister being cured at once (Matthew 17:18, 20). Amen!

I pray these things, and I thank you for praying with me because I believe as my friend Tiffany says:

"I believe in the God who can make possibilities out of impossible situations."
~Rev. Tiffany Towberman

14
NAMING HER

Paul left. He had been walking around town during the day, probably going to Starbucks to spend the gift card Marvin had given him for his birthday. As he was walking out the door on Friday, May 11th, I noticed he was wearing his jacket. I told him it was nice outside, so he didn't really need a jacket. "Okay," he said, not turning to look at me, and walked out the door still wearing his jacket. He didn't come back.

On Sunday evening, my neighbor saw Paul walking near the library, so I drove around looking for him. When I found him, I invited him to go to McDonald's. He said, "I'm not talking to you," and crossed the street.

I called out to him saying, "You are always welcome at my house. I love you!"

The following week, we had thunderstorm after thunderstorm. The homeless shelter was not open for drop-ins. To have a bed at the homeless shelter after April 1st, people have to go through the Department of Family Services. I knew Paul wouldn't do that. I wondered where he was sleeping and prayed he was safe and healthy.

Just over a week after I saw him on the street, on Monday, May 21st, I really wanted a Coca Cola.® I had been drinking Mexican Coke,® which is made with sugar instead of high fructose corn syrup, but we were all out. My desire for a cold Coke overtook my desire to not drink high fructose corn syrup, so I went to McDonald's. On the way there, I realized I didn't have any cash to give to Paul if I were to see him, so I bought a gift card, too.

A couple hours later, it was time to take Joshua to his sports practice. I usually drive through the neighborhood to get to the highway, but this time without even thinking about it I drove Paul's usual walking route. As we drove by the main bus stop downtown, I saw Paul sitting on a bench. I found a place to park, told Joshua to pray, grabbed the McDonald's gift card, and walked up to Paul.

"Paul! Hi! Here's a gift card for you," I said as I sat down. He looked up to see who I was, took the gift card, and then turned away from me. He was sunburned. His shirt was stained as if he had been caught in one of the recent downpours.

I invited Paul back to the house. He said I had brought a flower into the house and that he would not be in the house as long as the flower was there. I had a hard time understanding him because he was facing away from me and talking quietly, like he usually does. I asked him what the flower was so that I could get it out of the house, but he was tired of repeating himself. "I already told you." He was done talking.

I told Paul he was always welcome at my house, even if just to shower and wash his clothes or to eat. He was irritated, indignant. "I'm not going to be stuck in this town. I'm catching the 505 bus to DC."

I don't know if such a bus exists. I certainly wouldn't expect a bus to be going to Washington, DC in the afternoon, and I don't know how he would pay for the bus, but I also wouldn't be surprised if he were to walk to DC. He walks everywhere anyway, and as evidenced by his shirt, he was already sleeping outside so what difference would it be to him to sleep in our town or one of the towns on the way to DC?

There was only one thing left to say: "You are always welcome at my house. I love you."

Joshua was late for practice.

TWO YEARS AND TWO MONTHS

Two years ago, I got the call from Dad saying my brother was missing. It's been two years of learning to worship God anyway, to rest in the fact that God is in control, and to follow Him rather than strive to fix the situation.

My brother was once again missing, but I enjoyed two months with him—two months of good food, laughs, and just loving him. Yes, I'm sad he once again walked away from the love his family offers, but then I realize that's exactly what God experiences every day.

My brother has the free will to stay at our house and receive our love, but he has chosen to be alone and homeless. Every person on this planet has the free will to choose God's house and receive His love.[153] God's house is full of good food,[154] good company,[155] and great love.[156] Yet most of us have chosen to be alone and without an eternal home.

> *Why people don't choose God is as baffling to me as my brother not choosing to stay with us.*

Why people don't choose Him is as baffling to me as my brother not choosing to stay with us.

POST-ABORTION HEALING CLASS

A month after Paul left, I took a post-abortion healing class through my local pregnancy center. As my friend says, the post-abortion healing class is the best-kept secret. She's right. Until a year ago while in Uganda talking with Julie and Rhonda, I had never heard of such a class. I considered taking the class in the spring, but with all that was going on with my brother, homeschool, and Joshua's sports, I just couldn't add one more thing. So, I took the next class, which started in June.

On the one hand, I didn't know why I was there. I felt healed from the abortion when I gave my testimony at my baptism 16 years before. Then a year ago, I realized I was mad at God and repented. I honestly felt free after that. But on the other hand, I wanted to make sure I had dealt with everything, so I went.

There were two leaders and three of us taking the class. We used *Surrendering the Secret*,[157] which is an eight-week video and workbook study packed full of scripture. I think most of it could be used for healing from any number of things.

When I started the class, I told Russ I was feeling overwhelmed without any good reason. Our schedule was much lighter than it had been in the spring, so I wasn't sure why I was feeling overwhelmed. Now I see that satan was attacking me as I was taking this class because he didn't want me healed.

A few weeks into the class, I got frustrated because I realized I was bitter, but I didn't think my bitterness was from the abortion. I started delving into bitterness, beginning with scripture:

> *See to it that no one comes short of the grace of God; that* no root of bitterness *springing up causes trouble, and by it many be defiled.* (Hebrews 12:15 NASB, emphasis mine)

I did some internet searches and found that bitterness is a form of anger. One website says it is the result of not dealing with hurt. One thing I already knew, to get rid of anger I need to forgive. Ephesians 4:31-32 says that, too:

Let all bitterness and wrath and anger and clamor and slander be put away from you, along with all malice. Be kind to one another, tenderhearted, forgiving each other *[emphasis mine], just as God in Christ also has forgiven you.*[158]

The Lord's prayer says, "forgive us our trespasses as we forgive those who trespass against us."[159] In the Matthew version, Jesus goes on to say:

For if you forgive others for their transgressions, your heavenly Father will also forgive you. But if you do not forgive others, then your Father will not forgive your transgressions. (Matthew 6:14-15 NASB)

I wanted to be forgiven! I began writing to the Lord asking Him to bring up all my bitterness, to show me why I was bitter. One by one, I prayed through each source of bitterness and forgave each person I held responsible for whatever went wrong. I spent a whole afternoon just forgiving people. Among them were all the Christians who didn't seem to welcome me after I gave my testimony.

Then I thought about every story of bitterness I had ever heard from my parents and my grandparents. I realized I had agreed with their bitterness, so I identified the people whom I blamed for each instance, and I forgave them. I even forgave my pastor grandfather, who died almost 40 years ago, for not teaching my mom to study the bible or pray at home. Then I realized that his parents hadn't taught him to study and pray at home and neither did his seminary, so I forgave all of them, too.

I wanted my joy back so badly that every time I forgave someone, I asked the Lord to replace the space that bitterness had left with joy. By the end of the afternoon, I felt lighter!

Although I felt like I had thought of everything and everyone against whom I had harbored bitterness, I wanted to make sure I was completely clean of unforgiveness. I asked the Lord again to reveal to me any root of bitterness.

Search me, O God... and see if there be any hurtful way in me,
and lead me in the everlasting way. (Psalm 139:23a, 24 NASB)

Before bed, I prayed that the Lord would teach me in the night. A few days later, I woke up at 5 am from a dream in which I was really mad at Russ. I didn't want to be awake, but the Lord whispered to me to go pray. I was going to sit in the recliner when I felt He was telling me to kneel. I probably would've fallen asleep in the recliner, but I wouldn't fall asleep on my knees. I forgave Russ. Back to bed I went and got another three hours of sleep! Oh, how I love summer's easy schedule. When I woke up, I couldn't remember why I had been angry with Russ in the dream, and I still don't remember today.

The same afternoon I spent forgiving everyone, the Lord impressed on me that I had gotten my daughter's name wrong. Her name is not Elizabeth Marie or Mary Elizabeth, which were the names I considered before Joshua was born. Her name is Joy Marie.

The next time I went to class, the topic was all about anger and forgiveness. Oops, I guess I worked ahead.

Even though I felt healed before I started the post-abortion healing class in June, the class helped me to value life even more and to give dignity to my baby girl, who had a name. She is a person. And she is in heaven serving the Lord.[160]

Here is the letter that I wrote to her:

July 28

You are beautiful, tall and slender like your dad with beautiful blue eyes and long hair, wavy hair about my color. You are deeply loved by our Heavenly Father and by me. I know that sounds odd because I once hated you, but I realize now that I hated my life, not you. My anger was misplaced. I am sorry I took out my anger on you.

I am sorry I took you away from the world and from adoptive parents who would have loved to raise you. You would have done great things here on earth.

I am sorry you didn't get to experience camping and canoeing and hiking in the Father's beautiful creation. I'm sorry we didn't get to walk and talk here on earth. I'm sorry I deprived you of relationships with your cousins Drew, Lily, and the boys. I'm sorry I deprived you of relationships with Daniel, Joshua, and Russ. You would have been a great big sister. Please forgive me.

I trust that the Father and the angels are taking good care of you. I trust that heaven is more beautiful than I can imagine. I trust that we will be reunited when I leave this world.

In the meantime, I trust that you are in the cloud of witnesses surrounding me (Hebrews 12:1[161]). I promise to honor you by speaking boldly and raising my voice like a trumpet[162] so that fewer and fewer babies join you and so that more and more mothers choose Christ so that they, too, are someday reunited with their babies.

I love you, Joy Marie.

Love,
Mom

Being in the class also helped me to see the connection between my choice of not following God to the consequence of my unplanned pregnancy. Rather than turning to God during that first life test, I turned away and looked for love through sex, resulting in a crisis pregnancy. No matter the words and actions of those around me, *I* was responsible for turning *away* from God rather than turning *to* Him.

I am ever-so-grateful that God convinced me to come back, that He showed me that His love is unconditional, that He taught me His word and how to pray, that He has forgiven me, and that He has healed me and set me free.

The best news of all:

I have my joy back!

For Joy

You formed my Joy Marie.
My daughter was fearfully
And wonderfully made.
I was afraid.

No joy. Wasted years.
Always looking for my worth.
Fake smiles. Pretending.

Now friendship with Christ.
"Let us contend together."
What did I do wrong?

My body. My choice.
My responsibility.
No blaming. My choice.

I see scarlet sin
for I know my transgressions.
Cleanse me from my sin!

Purify me. Wash! Scrub!
with the blood of Jesus Christ.
Restore me! Renew!

My clean heart restored.
My steadfast spirit renewed.
My spirit sustained.

Joyfully singing
Your praises! Your righteousness!
My joy has returned!

My body. My worship!

My Joy Marie
My Joy Marie

AFTERWORD

WHY I WROTE THIS BOOK

I wrote this book first and foremost because my Lord told me to. It was an act of obedience. I didn't want to tell you all about my sins, but writing this book has provided me a great deal of healing, and I continually thank God for that.

Second, I wrote this book to dispel satan's lies.

I did not write this book to justify my abortion. What I did was wrong. I murdered my daughter. Thankfully, she is in heaven waiting for me just like so many aborted babies who are in heaven waiting for their mommies and daddies. But will their mommies and daddies go to heaven? Or will those babies cry until God wipes every tear?[163]

I wrote this book so that you would understand what led me to the abortion clinic because the more you understand what leads women to abort, the more you understand what you can do to intervene.

SHAME

I aborted because of shame. The lie that I believed is that I should feel shame for getting pregnant. The truth is that I should feel shame for having sex outside of marriage, but there's no shame in pregnancy because God decided that I would get pregnant. The lie is that *pregnancy* outside of marriage is a sin. The truth is that *sex* outside of marriage is a sin. Pregnancy is the evidence of the sin, but many people sin by having sex outside of marriage without getting "caught" pregnant.

Even with all our medical knowledge and access to pharmaceuticals that prevent pregnancy, women still get pregnant when they don't want to be. If you were to talk to Abby Johnson, a former Planned Parenthood Director,[164] she would tell you that many women who were on the pill and took it as prescribed came into her clinic for abortions.

Ironically, a large number of church-goers have sinned just like me by having sex outside of marriage. They did not get pregnant, but I did. Who decides who gets pregnant? God. God decides which consequences we get from extra-marital sex. If we don't sin by having extra-marital sex, then God can give us those babies at the right time.

So why doesn't The Church address the sin of extra-marital sex to stop abortion? There is, after all, more sex education in schools than in The Church.

Do not be deceived: God cannot be mocked. A man reaps what he sows. (Galatians 6:7 NIV)

STRESS

I aborted because of stress. The lie is that my family had to deal with my sister's schizophrenia and my pregnancy on our own. The truth is that God wanted us to follow Him, but we

The lie is that my family had to deal with my sister's schizophrenia and my pregnancy on our own. The truth is that God wanted us to follow Him.

rejected His leadership and strived to fix my sister's schizophrenia on our own. If we had acknowledged Him in all our ways, He would've shown us the straight path that He paved for us (Proverbs 3:5-6). Instead, we chose an unknown path that was winding, full of rocks, and with a great deal of obstacles that we thought required our own strength to overcome.

EDUCATION

I aborted because I thought my education would be delayed or ruined if I went through with the pregnancy. Ironically, my education was delayed anyway. The truth is that because I live in the USA, I have access to education. As a citizen of the United States, I can have as much education as I'm willing to work for.

Unfortunately, education is not accessible to women throughout the world, so pregnancy is a real education stopper in other countries. Pray for these women! (And remember to financially support Christian missionaries who go to help these women, such as Julie's Heart Cry.[81])

ABORTION IS ABOUT WOMEN & MEN

I wrote this book so that you would understand that abortion not only kills babies, but it kills women's souls. It is heartbreaking to think of so many dead babies resulting from abortions around the world (for this is not just an issue in the USA).

But it should be just as heartbreaking to us that women are dead inside because of their abortions. The men, parents, friends, and doctors who pressured the woman or allowed the abortion

It is heartbreaking to think of so many dead babies. It should be just as heartbreaking that women and men are spiritually dead. Non-believers will be separated from their babies forever. Are we going to let those babies cry until God wipes every tear at the time of the new heaven and the new earth?

are dead inside, too. Women and men who don't believe that

Jesus is the Christ will be separated from their babies forever. Are we going to let those babies cry until God wipes every tear at the time of the new heaven and the new earth?[165] Or are we going to make disciples[166] of their mommies and daddies?

Those who do believe in Christ but are not yet healed live with their secret in shame and therefore are not living in Christ's freedom[167] and likely not living their God-designed purpose or even volunteering at their church.

Thankfully, there are post-abortive healing classes, like *Surrendering the Secret*[168] and *Forgiven and Set Free*.[169] Contact your local Christian pregnancy center[170] or church to find a class. For men, look for *Healing a Father's Heart: A Post-Abortion Bible Study for Men*.[171]

Women who abort are likely to abort again.[172] If you want to stop abortion, get post-abortive women healed and empowered to tell other women that abortion *does* hurt women and that women *are affected* by their "choice." The #shoutyourabortion movement is out to justify and normalize abortion. This Faces of Abortion Series is the pro-life response—not to justify but explain our thinking and share God's great healing.

> *The #shoutyourabortion movement is out to justify and normalize abortion. This Faces of Abortion Series is the pro-life response.*

ReTested is the first in the Faces of Abortion series. In the next two books, you'll read many more stories of post-abortive Christian women who have agreed to let me interview them. We have a voice, and we will raise it like a trumpet[173]—a warning to other women.

We also need to get post-abortive men to tell other men that abortion hurts them. I pray that someone reading this book will take up that mantle and partner with me to reach the world with the truth.

The pro-choice movement is:

- full of women who have aborted.

- full of women who are bitter toward men, whom they blame for the perceived unfairness that men can have sex without consequences and leave women bearing the consequences of extra-marital sex.

- full of women who can sympathize with being caught with an unplanned pregnancy or with expecting a special needs child or with being raped.

What better anti-abortion voice is there than women talking to women? And men talking to men?

MENTAL ILLNESS

I wrote this book to shed light on schizophrenia and mental illness in general—what it's really like and how it affects families.

How different lives would be if people knew they could go to church for support as they survive, strive, and thrive through mental illness.

Kudos to churches who do support families with mental illnesses!

SPECIAL NEEDS

I wrote this book to shed light on the stress of raising special needs children. Today, abortions because of Down Syndrome and other "different abilities" is on the rise.

How different things would be if people knew they could go to the church for support as they survive, strive, and thrive through parenting children who are not typical.

Kudos to churches who do support families with special needs![174]

THE TEST IN TESTIMONY

You can't have a testimony without a test.

Remember the book of Job, the righteous man of the Old Testament? Job was tested and retested. When he was tested the first time by losing his wealth and his children, he responded by worshiping God.

Then Job arose and tore his robe and shaved his head, and he fell to the ground and worshiped. He said,

"Naked I came from my mother's womb,
And naked I shall return there.
The Lord gave and the Lord has taken away.
Blessed be the name of the Lord."

Through all this Job did not sin nor did he blame God. (Job 1:20-22 NASB)

Job, however, had a firm foundation that I did not have even though I attended church throughout my childhood. I went to church once or twice a week. I knew all sorts of bible stories, but I didn't understand the whole story.

I didn't understand why the Old Testament Jews made sacrifices or why Jesus was the sacrifice for our sins. I was told that Jesus died for our sins, but I didn't think I was that bad so why would He need to die in such a horrific way?

I didn't know what happened to the Jews after King Solomon became wise and rich. I didn't know why, during Jesus' time, the Jews were under Roman rule. I didn't understand why the Jews didn't recognize that Jesus was the Christ. I didn't know that the Jews were expecting a political Christ who would rescue them from Roman rule.

I didn't know that Mark and Luke were *not* two of the 12 disciples. I didn't know that Luke was the only non-Jewish writer of the bible. I didn't know that Peter, James, and John were closer friends of Jesus than the other nine disciples. I didn't know that the book of James was written by Jesus' half-brother, not the disciple named James. I didn't know that there were more than 12 disciples, including many women.

I didn't know that Paul had been a bad guy before God talked to him on the road to Damascus. I didn't understand that when the apostles were creating churches, there were Jewish Christians and Gentile Christians or how big of a deal that was.

I didn't know anything about Armageddon. I didn't have the books of the Bible memorized (and still don't) nor any Bible verses. Other than the Ten Commandments and being nice to each other, I didn't know what it meant to be a Christian.

> *I knew* about *Jesus, but I didn't* know *Him.*

I knew *about* Jesus, but I didn't *know* Him. As a result, I was not prepared for life's tests.

RETESTED

Shortly after I chose to have a personal relationship with Christ at age 31, I read Rick Warren's book *A Purpose Driven Life*,[175] in which he says that everything is a test. I remember how reading that statement really made me stop to think. Yet I didn't let it fully impact how I lived.

When I was a student, my teachers gave me tests in order to see whether I knew what I had been taught, but ultimately the tests were for me to see whether I had *learned* what I had been taught.

But when the Lord allows a test, He is not checking to see whether you know what you were taught. He already knows what you know. The test is for *you* to see whether *you* learned what *you* were taught.[176]

Although I have been through many tests, many of which you read about in this book, the test that I keep retaking is of siblings with schizophrenia.

SURVIVING

When I was tested the first time, I chose to feel unloved by my parents (even though the truth was that they did love me) and to look for love elsewhere. Then although I knew that I shouldn't have sex outside of marriage, I did it anyway. When I got pregnant, I sinned again by killing my baby. Instead of worshiping the Lord in all circumstances, I turned my back on Him and blamed Him for my family's circumstances. I survived schizophrenia, but I got a big, red F on the test.

When Job was tested the second time by losing his health, he defended God to his wife, who was in pain right along with him for she also lost all of her children and all of her wealth. In addition, she was tending to her sick husband and mourning his misery. I know that helplessness a wife feels when her husband is not well and there's nothing she can do but care for him and pray. Job, though, still responded well by saying:

> *"Shall we indeed accept good from God and not accept adversity?" (Job 2:10b NASB)*

STRIVING

Shortly after I chose to accept God's love for me, I was tested the second time. I was born again into a living hope[177] shortly before my brother became homeless and showed signs of schizophrenia. I did not blame God nor leave Him as I had the first time but instead sought wisdom from the Bible and from other Christians. However, instead of focusing on God, I chose to worry (see Matthew 6:33a[178] for what I should have done). I strived to fix schizophrenia and got perhaps a C- on the test.

After this test, I struggled and strived through our two cross-country moves while trying to be a good wife and mother. Even though I had learned to pray scripture, I didn't put it into practice when my home life was challenging.

Many years later (in my mid-40s), I began to study the Bible and then I knew the answers to all those Bible questions, and I began praying scripture in a worshipful way rather than a worrying way.

THRIVING

When Job was tested a third time by his well-meaning friends, his trust in the Lord waivered. Job was depressed,[179] and understandably so. He defended his righteousness to his friends and justified himself before God.[180] Then the young Elihu rebuked Job for justifying himself before the Lord.[181] At the end of the story, God taught Job that His wisdom is far beyond what we humans can comprehend.[182] Job finally yields to the Lord's power saying:

"I know that You can do all things, and that no purpose of Yours can be thwarted." (Job 42:2 NASB)

When I was tested a third time, I finally learned to worship God in all circumstances as Job did. My brother went missing, and I was sad. I was heartbroken—but I was not worried. I began praising God even though I was crying. I started praying for more of the Holy Spirit, which Luke 11:13 gives me permission to do.[183] As a result, I grew closer to the Lord, and He began opening my eyes to His purpose and plan for my life. I began thriving despite schizophrenia and got perhaps a B+ on the test.

However, I didn't like part of God's plan for my life. I did not want to speak about abortion or schizophrenia, but I also didn't want to lose my close relationship with Jesus by breaking my vow to serve Him. The peace I get from being in His will is precious and worth everything, so I agreed to His plan.

My bible study changed from just learning to also teaching. I began writing and speaking God's truth about abortion and about sex and found that I was not alone but that many women have struggled through extra-marital sex and abortion. My prayers included much more listening than ever before.

Then my brother became homeless right in my town and right in my home. I worshiped the Lord and prayed scripture, starting early every morning. With the strength of Christ,[184] I was able to welcome my brother into my home with love and acceptance, to offer him the love of Christ, and to follow the Lord rather than fix the situation myself.

Ultimately, my brother left and became missing once again. But I trusted in the Lord and rejoiced that He has a plan and that He is in control. Perhaps I got an A- on this test.

As I grow closer and closer to God through the increasing of the Holy Spirit within me,[185] I am following Him more than striving to fix my situation, and I am trusting Him more than worrying. I am not perfect in my walk, but I do my best to live in hope because I know that God can do all things abundantly beyond what I can ask or think according to the power that works within me.[186]

Will there be a fifth test of schizophrenia? Yes, of course, because my sister and brother are not yet healed, but I am trusting that they will be. In the meantime...

Blessed be the God and Father of our Lord Jesus Christ, who according to His great mercy has caused [me] to be born again to a living hope through the resurrection of Jesus Christ from the dead (1 Peter 1:3 NASB)...

In all this [I, Cheryl] *greatly rejoice, though now for a little while* [I] *may have had to suffer grief in all kinds of trials. These have come so that the proven genuineness of* [my] *faith— of greater worth than gold, which perishes even though refined by fire—may result in praise, glory and honor when Jesus Christ is revealed. (1 Peter 1:6-7 NIV)*

This is my body, and with it I will worship my Lord and Savior!

My body My worship!

This is my voice, and with it I will speak boldly and not hold back. I will raise my voice like a trumpet!

A Few More Thoughts

I've known for many years that I would write this book. I used to say that I was waiting for a good ending to the story, but the Lord made it clear to me that I was to publish the book without a fairytale ending because life isn't like that of a fairy princess—that is, until we have the great happy ending and new beginning in Paradise as the bride of Christ.

Though I believe that Paul and Nancy will truly trust in Christ and be healed of their schizophrenia, I am not waiting for that ending before telling you my story because I know that whether my prayers are answered or not, it is well with my soul.

God is good all the time. I may not understand His ways this side of heaven, but that doesn't stop me from worshiping Him.

I pray that you live your life the same way: not surviving your circumstances, not striving to fix your circumstances, but thriving no matter your circumstances. May you follow Jesus, not strive to get ahead of Him.

In Christ,

ACKNOWLEDGMENTS

Without Russ, there would be no book. He shared the gospel with me and didn't give up when I scoffed at him. He contended for my faith through prayer. He helped me realize my value in the eyes of God. He supported me in my transition from professional to homeschooling mom. He provided so that you can read this book. Thank you, Russ, for your great love and your support through all the drama that you were not expecting in marriage. Thank you for allowing the Lord to use you. Your always and forever love abides in my heart.

Thank you to my boys for their love and encouragement and for being brave in this conversation right along with me.

Thank you to Pastors Dave and Cyrus for encouraging me to be brave and bold in what God has called me to do.

Thank you to Julie Mad-Bondo for taking a risk in bringing me to Uganda to speak and continuing to collaborate with me in bringing a voice to post-abortive women.

Thank you to both Uganda mission teams for supporting me and loving me despite my scarlet stain.

Thank you to Katharine, Kim, and the Destiny Prayer Group for countless prayers and encouragement. And an extra thank you to Kim for giving me a little boot every now and then to get this book done!

Thank you to Adina, Katharine, Kim, and Laura for reading early manuscripts and providing deeply insightful suggestions and encouragement.

Thank you to Terry for lending her editing skills.

Thank you to Erin, "that Catholic friend," who is not only my editor but also my encourager. From now on, let me be known as "Erin's Protestant friend"!

Almost all of the names in this book have been changed. Special thanks to "Lynn" for providing most of the pseudonyms.

I purposely chose "Paul" as the pseudonym for my brother. Do you remember that he was once Jewish? I have often prayed that he would have a Road to Damascus[187] experience, so it seemed appropriate that he would have the name of Saul turned Paul. My brother certainly is smart like Paul was.

Thank you to Ridgetop Coffee for providing a godly environment in which to write. Most of this book was written while sipping coffee or tea in one of their big, comfy chairs. May the Lord continue to bless their business.

CHERYL'S CONTENDING LIST

Below are Bible verses and prayers for contending for the faith of those who do not yet believe that Jesus died so that they could have abundant life.

> *For God so loved the world, that He gave His only begotten Son, that whoever believes in Him shall not perish, but have eternal life. For God did not send the Son into the world to judge the world, but that the world might be saved through Him. He who believes in Him is not judged; he who does not believe has been judged already, because he has not believed in the name of the only begotten Son of God. (John 3:16-18 NASB)*

For God so loved _____ that He gave His only begotten Son, that _____ believes in Him and does not perish but has eternal life. For God did not send the Son to _____ to judge _____ but that _____ might be saved through Him. _____ believes in Him and is not judged. _____ believes in the name of the only begotten Son of God.

Jesus said to him, "I am the way, and the truth, and the life; no one comes to the Father but through Me." (John 14:6 NASB)

_____ comes to the Father through Jesus Christ.

Jesus answered, "Truly, truly, I say to you, unless one is born of water and the Spirit he cannot enter into the kingdom of God. That which is born of the flesh is flesh, and that which is born of the Spirit is spirit. Do not be amazed that I said to you, 'You must be born again.'" (John 3:3, 5-7 NASB)

Unless _____ is born again, s/he cannot see the kingdom of God. _____ is born again and will see the kingdom of God.

Unless _____ is born of water and the Spirit, s/he cannot enter into the kingdom of God. _____ is born of water and the Spirit.

That which is born of the Spirit is spirit. _____ is born of the Spirit.

These things I have written to you who believe in the name of the Son of God, so that you may know that you have eternal life. (1 John 5:13 NASB)

_____ believes in the name of the Son of God so that s/he knows that s/he has eternal life.

But the Scripture has shut up everyone under sin, so that the promise by faith in Jesus Christ might be given to those who believe. (Galatians 3:22 NASB)

But the Scripture has shut up everyone under sin so that the promise by faith in Jesus Christ might be given to _____, who believes.

I have been crucified with Christ; and it is no longer I who live, but Christ lives in me; and the life which I now live in the flesh I live by faith in the Son of God, who loved me and gave Himself up for me. (Galatians 2:20 NASB)

_____ has been crucified with Christ; and it is no longer _____ who lives, but Christ lives in him/her; and the life that s/he now lives in the flesh s/he lives by faith in the Son of God, Who loved _____ and gave Himself up for _____.

But he must ask in faith without any doubting, for the one who doubts is like the surf of the sea, driven and tossed by the wind. (James 1:6 NASB)

_____ asks for healing and reconciliation with _____ without any doubting.

But as many as received Him, to them He gave the right to become children of God, even to those who believe in His name, who were born, not of blood nor of the will of the flesh nor of the will of man, but of God. (John 1:12-13 NASB)

_____ received Christ. To _____, Jesus gave the right to become a child of God, even to _____ who believes in His name, who was born, not of blood nor of the will of the flesh nor of the will of man, but of God.

For God so loved the world, that He gave His only begotten Son, that whoever believes in Him shall not perish, but have eternal life. For God did not send the Son into the world to judge the world, but that the world might be saved through Him. He who believes in Him is not judged; he who does not believe has been judged already, because he has not believed in the name of the only begotten Son of God. He who believes in the Son has eternal life; but he who does not obey the Son will not see life, but the wrath of God abides on him. (John 3:16-18, 36 NASB)

_____ believes in the Son and has eternal life. _____ obeys the Son and sees life and is freed from the wrath of God that formerly abided on him.

> *Jesus said to them, "I am the bread of life; he who comes to Me will not hunger, and he who believes in Me will never thirst. All that the Father gives Me will come to Me, and the one who comes to Me I will certainly not cast out. For this is the will of My Father, that everyone who beholds the Son and believes in Him will have eternal life, and I Myself will raise him up on the last day." (John 6:35, 37, 40 NASB)*

Jesus is the bread of life. _____ comes to Him and will not hunger. _____ believes in Jesus and will never thirst. _____ comes to Christ, and He will certainly not cast out _____. For this is the will of the Father, that _____ beholds the Son and believes in Him and has eternal life. Jesus Himself will raise up _____ on the last day.

> *Now on the last day, the great day of the feast, Jesus stood and cried out, saying, "If anyone is thirsty, let him come to Me and drink. He who believes in Me, as the Scripture said, 'From his innermost being will flow rivers of living water.'" But this He spoke of the Spirit, whom those who believed in Him were to receive; for the Spirit was not yet given, because Jesus was not yet glorified." (John 7:37-39 NASB)*

_____ is thirsty and goes to Christ and drinks. _____ believes in Christ. From _____'s innermost being will flow rivers of living water. _____ has received the Spirit because Jesus has been glorified.

> *And Jesus said to him, "Go; your faith has made you well." Immediately he regained his sight and began following Him on the road. (Mark 10:52 NASB)*

Jesus said to _____, "Go; your faith has made you well." Immediately, _____ regained his/her sight and began following Jesus Christ.

> *"Therefore I say to you, all things for which you pray and ask, believe that you have received them, and they will be granted you. Whenever you stand praying, forgive, if you have anything against anyone, so that your Father who is in heaven will also forgive you your transgressions." (Mark 11:24-25 NASB)*

I pray and ask for healing and for reconciliation with _____, believing that I have received these things and that they will be granted. _____ forgives all that s/he has against anyone so that our Father who is in heaven will also forgive _____ his/her transgressions.

> *"He who has believed and has been baptized shall be saved; but he who has disbelieved shall be condemned." (Mark 16:16 NASB)*

_____ has believed and has been baptized and is saved. S/he no longer disbelieves and is no longer condemned.

> *That if you confess with your mouth Jesus as Lord, and believe in your heart that God raised Him from the dead, you will be saved; for with the heart a person believes, resulting in righteousness, and with the mouth he confesses, resulting in salvation. For the Scripture says, "WHOEVER BELIEVES IN HIM WILL NOT BE DISAPPOINTED." For there is no distinction between Jew and Greek; for the same Lord is Lord of all, abounding in riches for all who call on Him; for "WHOEVER WILL CALL ON THE NAME OF THE LORD WILL BE SAVED." (Romans 10:9-13 NASB)*

_____ confesses with his/her mouth that Jesus is Lord and believes in his/her heart that God raised Him from the dead;

therefore, _____ is saved. With the heart, _____ believes, resulting in righteousness, and with his/her mouth, _____ confesses, resulting in salvation. _____ believes in Him and is not disappointed. Lord is Lord of all, abounding in riches for _____ who calls on Him for _____ calls on the name of the Lord and is saved.

"Now may the God of hope fill you with all joy and peace in believing, so that you will abound in hope by the power of the Holy Spirit." (Romans 15:13 NASB)

Now the God of hope fills _____ with all joy and peace in believing so that _____ will abound in hope by the power of the Holy Spirit.

We are Jews by nature and not sinners from among the Gentiles; nevertheless knowing that a man is not justified by the works of the Law but through faith in Christ Jesus, even we have believed in Christ Jesus, so that we may be justified by faith in Christ and not by the works of the Law; since by the works of the Law no flesh will be justified. (Galatians 2:15-16 NASB)

Knowing that man is not justified by the works of the Law but through faith in Christ Jesus, even _____ has believed in Christ Jesus so that s/he may be justified by faith in Christ and not by the works of the Law.

Jesus said to her, "I am the resurrection and the life; he who believes in Me will live even if he dies, and everyone who lives and believes in Me will never die. Do you believe this?" (John 11:25-26 NASB)

Jesus is the resurrection and the life. _____ believes in Him and lives even if s/he dies. S/he lives and believes in Jesus Christ and will never die. I, _____, believe this.

For this reason I bow my knees before the Father, from whom every family in heaven and on earth derives its name, that He would grant you, according to the riches of His glory, to be strengthened with power through His Spirit in the inner man, so that Christ may dwell in your hearts through faith; and that you, being rooted and grounded in love, may be able to comprehend with all the saints what is the breadth and length and height and depth, and to know the love of Christ which surpasses knowledge, that you may be filled up to all the fullness of God. Now to Him who is able to do far more abundantly beyond all that we ask or think, according to the power that works within us, to Him be the glory in the church and in Christ Jesus to all generations forever and ever. Amen. (Ephesians 3:14-21 NASB)

For this reason, I bow my knees before the Father from Whom every family (genealogy!) in heaven and on earth derives its name, that He would grant _____, according to the riches of His glory, to be strengthened with power through His spirit in the inner _____ so that Christ may dwell in _____'s heart through faith and that _____, being rooted and grounded in love, may be able to comprehend with all of us saints what is the breadth and length and height and depth, and to know the love of Christ which surpasses knowledge, that _____ may be filled up to all the fullness of God. Now to Him who is able to do far more abundantly beyond all that we (_____, _____) ask or think, according to the power that works within us, to Him be the glory in the church and in Christ Jesus to all generations forever and ever. Amen!

CHERYL'S PLAY LISTS

B elow are lists of all the worship music that Cheryl mentions in this book plus a few more.

MY DAILY WORSHIP

"I Surrender All" by Newsboys
"Holy Spirit" by Francesca Battistelli
"Great Are You Lord" by All Sons & Daughters
"What a Beautiful Name" by Hillsong Worship
"There is Power" by Lincoln Brewster
"Mary, Did You Know?" by Pentatonix

MY FAVORITE HYMNS

"All Creatures of Our God and King"
"All Hail the Power of Jesus Name"
"Holy Holy Holy"
"I Surrender All"
"It Is Well"
"Jesus Paid It All"

"Joy to the World"
"Praise God from Whom All Blessings Flow" (Doxology)
"What a Friend We Have in Jesus"

A FEW MORE THAT MOVE ME

"Glorious Day" by Passion featuring Kristian Stanfill
"King of the World" by Natalie Grant
"Hello, My Name Is" by Matthew West
"My Story" by Big Daddy Weave
"What Scars Are For" by Mandisa
"Day One" by Matthew West
"Restart" by Newsboys
"The Lord's Prayer" composed by Melotte
"Hallelujah," the chorus in Handel's *Messiah*

ABOUT THE AUTHOR

Cheryl Krichbaum has a burning passion to change the conversation about abortion so that abortion-minded women and men know the vitality draining consequences of abortion on themselves. In response to the #shoutyourabortion movement, the Faces of Abortion Series boldly speaks the truth about the death that abortion causes to not just babies but also to women's souls.

Cheryl invests her time writing, speaking, and designing Bible studies to help Christians know what both the Old and New Testaments say about the sanctity of life and the sanctity of sex, how to pray for the end of abortion in The Church and in our communities, and how to talk to the abortion-minded.

The Lord has impressed on Cheryl the books that belong in the Faces of Abortion Series, of which *ReTested* is the first. The second and third books will tell other women's stories to help Christians understand how abortion-minded women think. As a writer and instructional designer, Cheryl knows that you must know your audience, so let's get to know our abortion-minded audience.

Cheryl has a Bachelor of Science in Scientific and Technical Communication from the University of Minnesota and worked professionally as a technical and professional writer, project manager, and instructional designer. Today, she is the Founder of MybodyMyworship.

Connect with Cheryl at CherylKrichbaum.blog.

NOTES

CHAPTER I

1   American Psychiatric Association. *Diagnostic and Statistical Manual of Mental Disorders, 5th ed.* American Psychiatric Publishing, 2013, London.

CHAPTER 2

2   Gloria Loring and Carl Anderson. "Friends and Lovers." written by Jay Gruska and Paul Gordon, USA Carrere, 1986.

3   "Feminism: Belief in and desire for equality between the sexes. As Merriam-Webster noted last month: 'the belief that men and women should have equal rights and opportunities.' It encompasses social, political and economic equality. Of course, a lot of people tweak the definition to make it their own. Feminist activist Bell Hooks calls it 'a movement to end sexism, sexist exploitation, and oppression.'" Quoted from a March 16, 2017 article in USA Today titled, "A Feminist

Glossary Because We Didn't All Major in Gender Studies," which you can find at usatoday.com/story/news/2017/03/16/ feminism-glossary-lexicon-language/99120600/

4   I am not telling you that my joy was gone to get your sympathy. I don't deserve anyone's sympathy. I came to understand that what I did was wrong. I am telling you all these details so that you do not believe the lie that abortion is no big deal. It is a big deal. Babies are dead, but thankfully, they are in heaven. Post-abortive women, however, are hurting. I am telling you all these details to compel you to never have an abortion if you're a woman. If you're a man, I say this so that you never pressure a woman to abort nor to abdicate your responsibility by saying, "whatever you want." If you are a parent of a teen, whether girl or boy, read this book with them so that they can see the personal reality of their "choice" to abort. Do it before they leave your home. Mary, the mother of Jesus, may have been as young as 14 when the Lord called her to become the mother of Christ. She knew the Jewish Law and therefore the severe societal consequences of pregnancy before marriage. If your teen is receiving sex education at school, at home, or at church, then certainly you can choose to make the truth of abortion part of that education.

5   As you'll read in a later chapter, I no longer think of *pregnancy* out of wedlock as shameful.

CHAPTER 3

6   Today, the degree and department names have changed. For more information, contact the Department of Writing Studies at the University of Minnesota Twin Cities for the Technical Writing and Communication degree programs.

CHAPTER 4

7   I have always thought this was a great concept for mega-churches. How cool would it be for a church to have a single volunteers ministry in which they had the same number of men and women sign up to serve the community together? Do feel free to take that idea and run with it!

8   Well, I *didn't* like coffee—past tense. Now I like a sweet latte, preferably from Ridgetop Coffee & Tea, which is where I've written a good portion of this book.

9   "Feminazi: A derogatory term for a radical feminist." Quoted from a March 16, 2017 article in USA Today titled, "A Feminist Glossary Because We Didn't All Major in Gender Studies," which you can find at usatoday.com/story/news/2017/03/16/feminism-glossary-lexicon-language/99120600/

10   Where can I go from Your Spirit? Or where can I flee from Your presence? (Psalm 139:7 NASB)
"Who can hide in secret places so that I cannot see them?" Declares the Lord. "Do not I fill heaven and earth?" Declares the Lord. (Jeremiah 23:24 NIV)

11   And even if our gospel is veiled, it is veiled to those who are perishing. In their case the god of this world has blinded the minds of unbelievers, to keep them from seeing the light of the gospel of the glory of Christ, who is the image of God. (2 Corinthians 4:3-4 ESV)

12   "He who has ears, let him hear" (Matthew 11:15; 13:9, 43 NASB)—a statement made many more times in other gospels. Jesus was teaching his Jewish audience concepts they had heard before, but they had heard them so many times that they had grown deaf to them. Jesus was telling them in a new way so that perhaps they would understand and let His words change them. This was true for me. I had heard

all while growing up that God was omniscient, but I didn't let that knowledge change me.

13   God was in Christ reconciling the world to Himself not counting their trespasses against them (2 Corinthians 5:19a NASB). For God so loved the world that He gave His one and only Son that whoever believes in Him shall not perish but have eternal life (John 3:16 NIV). I chose NIV for this citation of John 3:16 because this is the version I have memorized!

14   I want to acknowledge that some people consider Landmark to be a cult. That was not my experience. Even to this day, I do not find anything that I learned in Landmark classes to be contradictory to my faith.

15   FamilyLife Marriage Conference "A Weekend to Remember." Arkansas: Campus Crusade for Christ, Inc. 1999, pages 69, 73.

16   Linda Dillow. *Creative Counterpart: Becoming the Woman, Wife, and Mother You Have Longed To Be*, Thomas Nelson, 1986.

17   And although "white as snow" is not in the following verse, we cannot forget Who makes us white as snow:
The next day (John the Baptist) saw Jesus coming to him and said, "Behold, the Lamb of God who takes away the sin of the world!" (John 1:29 NASB)

18   Kristian Stanfill. "Glorious Day" written by Kristian Stanfill, Jonathan Smith, Jason Ingram, and Sean Curran, Passion, 2017.

CHAPTER 5

19   "A Beautiful Mind," directed by Ron Howard, starring Russell Crowe, 2001.

20   Go to nami.org

21   So then each one of us will give an account of himself to God. (Romans 14:12 NASB)

CHAPTER 6

22 Heidi Murkoff and Sharon Mazel. *What to Expect When You're Expecting*, *What to Expect the First Year*, and *What to Expect the Second Year*, Workman Publishing Company, varying publication dates.

23 At the time, I read the 1984 printing of the NIV translation.

24 Today, the Timberland Twister is called the Fairly Odd Coaster.

25 These notes were based on a couple books, but I only remember the title of one of them: Ralph Fletcher's *Boy Writers: Reclaiming Their Voices* published in 2006 by Stenhouse Publishers.

26 Galatians 5:22-23

27 "But seek the welfare of the city where I have sent you into exile, and pray to the Lord on its behalf, for in its welfare you will find your welfare." (Jeremiah 29:7 ESV)

28 For I have learned to be content in whatever circumstances I am. (Philippians 4:11b NASB)

CHAPTER 7

29 …The god of this world has blinded the minds of the unbelieving so that they might not see the light of the gospel of the glory of Christ, who is the image of God. (2 Corinthians 4:4 NASB)

30 This is Jesus speaking to Jewish leaders, whom He was chastising for being hypocrites: "You are of your father the devil, and you want to do the desires of your father. He was a murderer from the beginning, and does not stand in the truth because there is no truth in him. Whenever he speaks a lie, he speaks from his own nature, for he is a liar and the father of lies." (John 8:44 NASB)

CHAPTER 8

[31] Some of you may be offended that I, a Christian, drink alcohol. Please note that the bible does not say, "Do not drink" (see Psalm 104:15-16 and Amos 9:14) but instead says, "Do not get drunk" (see Ephesians 5:18 and Proverbs 23:29). However, if drinking causes another to stumble, then don't drink when you are in their company (see Romans 14:21). For example, I do not drink when I am in Uganda because drinking alcohol there is associated with drunkenness and not taking care of your family. Paul said, "To the weak I became weak, that I might win the weak; I have become all things to all men, so that I may by all means save some." (1 Corinthians 9:22 NASB) Read 1 Corinthians 9:19-23 for Paul's more complete description of how he acts like those around him so that he can win some. Also, be careful not to judge what Christians eat or drink (see all of Romans 14 but at least 14:10, 12).

[32] Mayo Clinic. "Endometrial Ablation." mayoclinic.org/tests-procedures/endometrial-ablation/about/pac-20393932 accessed Nov 11, 2018.

[33] And we know that God causes all things to work together for good to those who love God, to those who are called according to His purpose. (Romans 8:28 NASB)

CHAPTER 9

[34] Daniel Henderson. *Transforming Prayer: How Everything Changes When You Seek God's Face*, Bethany House Publishers, 2011.

[35] Stormie Omartian. *Power of a Praying Wife, Power of Praying Parent* and so many more. Harvest House Publishers, varying publication dates.

[36] MomsInPrayer.org

37 "Worship-based prayer seeks the face of God before the hand of God." posted by @DanielHenderson on the National Day of Prayer 2018, also in one or more of Pastor Henderson's books.

38 Albert Hay Malotte. *The Lord's Prayer*. G. Schirmer, Inc., 1935, New York. Print.

39 Thomas Ken. "Praise God from Whom All Blessings Flow." Music attributed to Louis Bourgeois, 1551.

40 jackieevancho.com

41 Dr. Bill Creasy. Logos Bible Study. logosbiblestudy.com

42 Matthew 5:31-32—Look it up on BlueLetterBible.org.
Type Matt 5 in the search box.
Select NASB from the drop-down menu and press search.
Once chapter five loads, click the "Strong's" checkbox.
Scroll down to verses 31 and 32 and click G4202 for unchastity and G3431 for adultery. Notice the definitions of unchastity (G4202) and adultery (G3431) are not the same. Notice that unchastity is the bigger term and that the definition of unchastity includes adultery in addition to other sexual immorality. In this passage, which is part of the Sermon on the Mount, Jesus is saying that the only justification for divorce is one person in the couple has had sex with someone else before or during their marriage.

43 Beth Moore. *A Heart Like His*. Nashville: Lifeway Press, 2002.

44 1 Samuel 13:14, Acts 13:22

45 precept.org

46 Precept Ministries International. *The New Inductive Study Bible NASB*. Harvest House, 2013.

47 Jesus is talking here: "If you then, being evil, know how to give good gifts to your children, how much more will your heavenly Father give the Holy Spirit to those who ask Him?" (Luke 11:13 NASB)

48 But the fruit of the Spirit is love, joy, peace, patience, kindness, goodness, faithfulness, gentleness, self-control; against such things there is no law. (Galatians 5:22-23 NASB)

49 It's called a Jericho prayer based on the story in Joshua 6.

50 Luke 11:13, see above

51 Luke 11:13, see above

52 Galatians 5:22-23

53 Phil Wickham. "Doxology//Amen." *Children of God*, Fair Trade, 2016.

54 To follow Christ's command in Matthew 6:18, I was not telling people that I was fasting, but some people knew anyway. In Matthew 6:17-18, Jesus says: "But you, when you fast, anoint your head and wash your face so that your fasting will not be noticed by men, but by your Father who is in secret; and your Father who sees what is done in secret will reward you." (NASB)

55 Psalm 51:1, 2a, 3; Psalm 139:23-24

56 The peace of God, which surpasses all understanding, will guard your hearts and minds through Christ Jesus. (Philippians 4:7 NKJV)

57 Natalie Grant. "King of the World." *Be One*, Curb Records, Inc., 2015.

58 Matthew, Mark, Luke, and John are full of stories of Jesus healing people.

59 Trust in the LORD with all your heart And do not lean on your own understanding. In all your ways acknowledge Him, And He will make your paths straight. (Proverbs 3:5-6 NASB)

60 My vitality was drained away as with the fever heat of summer. (Psalm 32:4b NASB)

61 Peter is talking here to Simon, a new believer: "Your heart is not right before God. Therefore repent of this wickedness of yours, and pray the Lord that, if possible, the intention of your heart may be forgiven you. For I see that you are in the gall of bitterness and in the bondage of iniquity." (Acts 8:21b-23 NASB) I can relate to Simon's bitterness and bondage.

62 First Chronicles 16:11, 2 Chronicles 7:14, Psalm 24:6, Psalm 105:4, Hosea 5:15

63 But seek first His kingdom and His righteousness, and all these things will be added to you. (Matthew 6:33 NASB)

64 Rejoice in the Lord always; again I will say, rejoice! Let your gentle spirit be known to all men. The Lord is near. Be anxious for nothing, but in everything by prayer and supplication with thanksgiving let your requests be made known to God. And the peace of God, which surpasses all comprehension, will guard your hearts and your minds in Christ Jesus. (Philippians 4:4-7 NASB)

65 Trust in the Lord with all your heart and do not lean on your own understanding. In all your ways acknowledge him, and he will make straight your paths. (Proverbs 3:5-6 ESV)

66 But in your hearts honor Christ the Lord as holy, always being prepared to make a defense to anyone who asks you for a reason for the hope that is in you; yet do it with gentleness and respect. (1 Peter 3:15 ESV)

67 Daniel 3

68 "Do not think that I came to bring peace on the earth; I did not come to bring peace, but a sword." (Matthew 10:34 NASB) "Do you suppose that I came to grant peace on earth? I tell you, no, but rather division." (Luke 12:51 NASB)

69 For a child will be born to us, a son will be given to us; And the government will rest on His shoulders; And His name

will be called Wonderful Counselor, Mighty God, Eternal Father, Prince of Peace. (Isaiah 9:6 NASB)

70   Isaiah 9:6, see above

CHAPTER 10

71   Now the serpent was more crafty than any beast of the field which the Lord God had made. And he said to the woman, "Indeed, has God said, 'You shall not eat from any tree of the garden'?" (Genesis 3:1 NASB)

72   Jesus is talking here: "The thief comes only to steal and kill and destroy; I came that they may have life, and have it abundantly." (John 10:10 NASB)

73   Put on the full armor of God, so that you will be able to stand firm against the schemes of the devil. (Ephesians 6:11 NASB)

74   Ephesians 6:10-20

75   And Mary said, "Behold, I am the servant of the Lord; let it be to me according to your word." And the angel departed from her. (Luke 1:38 ESV)

76   Jesus is talking here: "If you then, being evil, know how to give good gifts to your children, how much more will your heavenly Father give the Holy Spirit to those who ask Him?" (Luke 11:13 NASB)

77   Katharine Wang. Master the Bible Ministries. MastertheBibleMinistries.com

78   In the USA, the rate for aborting babies known to have Down Syndrome is anywhere from 67 to 93% according to a meta-analysis study conducted by Jaime L. Natoli, Deborah L. Ackerman, Suzanne McDermott, and Janice G. Edwards and published with the title of "Prenatal diagnosis of Down syndrome: a systematic review of termination rates

(1995–2011)," March 14, 2012: obgyn.onlinelibrary.wiley.com/doi/full/10.1002/pd.2910 accessed October 2018.

79 Jesus is talking here: "For what will it profit a man if he gains the whole world and forfeits his soul? Or what will a man give in exchange for his soul?" (Matthew 16:26 NASB)

And do not be conformed to this world, but be transformed by the renewing of your mind, so that you may prove what the will of God is, that which is good and acceptable and perfect. (Romans 12:2 NASB)

Do not love the world nor the things in the world. If anyone loves the world, the love of the Father is not in him. For all that is in the world, the lust of the flesh and the lust of the eyes and the boastful pride of life, is not from the Father, but is from the world. The world is passing away, and also its lusts; but the one who does the will of God lives forever. (1 John 2:15-17 NASB)

80 Let me add to this thought by saying that pastors, whether male or female, do need to teach about the sanctity of life so that their congregations know what the bible says. Male pastors, however, need to figure out how to teach this in a way that does not sound patronizing to abortion-minded women. Admittedly, this may be challenging. I recommend that you add a testimony from a post-abortive woman who regrets her abortion. If you don't know of anyone in your congregation, please contact me at facesofabortion.com for a video testimony.

81 JuliesHeartCry.org

82 But I will be writing women's stories soon! Watch for more books in the Faces of Abortion Series, books that include stories from many post-abortive Christian women who want the world to know how much they regret their "choice."

83 Jesus is speaking here: "The thief comes only to steal and kill and destroy; I came that they may have life, and have it abundantly." (John 10:10 NASB)

84 IFGathering.com

85 Jennie Allen. *Anything: The Prayer That Unlocked My God and My Soul*, Thomas Nelson, 2015.

86 In all your ways acknowledge Him,
And He will make your paths straight. (Proverbs 3:6 NASB)

87 Your word is a lamp to my feet
And a light to my path. (Psalm 119:105 NASB)

88 Then He [Jesus] opened their minds to understand the Scriptures. (Luke 24:45 NASB)

89 Trust in the Lord with all your heart
And do not lean on your own understanding.
In all your ways acknowledge Him,
And He will make your paths straight. (Proverbs 3:5-6)
Let every valley be lifted up,
And every mountain and hill be made low;
And let the rough ground become a plain,
And the rugged terrain a broad valley. (Isaiah 40:4 NASB)

90 Hillsong Worship. "What a Beautiful Name." *Let There Be Light*, written by Ben Fielding and Brooke Ligertwood, Hillsong/Sparrow/Capitol, 2016.

91 All Sons & Daughters. "Great Are You, Lord." *Live*, Integrity, 2013.

92 Lincoln Brewster. "There Is Power." *Oxygen*, Integrity, 2014.

93 Here are some old hymns that work well for pure worship:
"All Hail the Power of Jesus' Name"
"All Creatures of Our God and King"
"Praise God from Whom All Blessings Flow"
"His Eye is on the Sparrow"

"Holy Holy Holy"
"I Surrender All"
"It Is Well"
"Jesus Paid It All"
"What a Friend We Have in Jesus"
(Newsboys have an older album of most of these hymns re-done in a contemporary style.)

94 Philippians 4:7

95 Philippians 4:7

96 BahamasGodParentCenter.org

97 Let me credit the term *colonizers* to the "Black Panther" movie (2018). I love that exchange between Shuri (played by Letitia Wright) and Everett K. Ross (played by Martin Freeman) in which she calls him a colonizer.

98 Philippians 4:7

99 Joshua 6

100 Judges 7

101 Your eyes saw my unformed substance;
     in your book were written, every one of them,
     the days that were formed for me,
     when as yet there was none of them. (Psalm 139:16 ESV)

102 Therefore I urge you, brethren, by the mercies of God, to present your bodies a living and holy sacrifice, acceptable to God, which is your spiritual service of worship. (Romans 12:1 NASB)

103 That you abstain from things sacrificed to idols and from blood and from things strangled and from fornication; if you keep yourselves free from such things, you will do well. Farewell. (Acts 15:29 NASB)

104 At this point in their story, their names were Abram and Sarai. See Genesis 16 and 21:1-21.

105 Not many of you should become teachers, my fellow believers, because you know that we who teach will be judged more strictly. (James 3:1 NIV)

106 The brothers immediately sent Paul and Silas away by night to Berea, and when they arrived they went into the Jewish synagogue. Now these Jews were more noble than those in Thessalonica; they received the word with all eagerness, examining the Scriptures daily to see if these things were so. (Acts 17:10-11 ESV)

CHAPTER 11

107 Researchers have identified 15 risk factors that identify post-abortive women at greatest risk of psychological problems. None of those risk factors applied to me. You'll find them online at http://afterabortion.org/1993/identifying-high-risk-abortion-patients-2/ (accessed August 2018). Although none of those risk factors applied to me, I can tell you that my emotions were deadened even more so after the abortion and that I lost my joy at the very moment that my baby died. I just didn't realize all that until I completed the post-abortion healing class offered by my local crisis pregnancy center. The class used the *Surrendering the Secret* curriculum. The *Forgiven and Set Free* curriculum is also good for post-abortion healing, according to my friend Julie Mad-Bondo of Julie's Heart Cry.

108 "Most Studies Show Abortion Linked to Increased Mental Health Problems" http://afterabortion.org/2011/most-studies-show-abortion-linked-to-increased-mental-health-problems/. Accessed August 2018.

109 Dr. Bill Creasy. "Romans." Logos Bible Study at audible.com. See also logosbiblestudy.com.

110 Women are most likely to discuss their decision with the father of the baby according to Care Net's 2016

study, "Study of Women Who Have Had an Abortion & Their Views on Church." http://resources.care-net.org/abortion-and-the-church-research/ accessed August 2018. Doctors are the second most influential, and mothers are third.

111 Then it happened that as Jesus was reclining at the table in the house, behold, many tax collectors and sinners came and were dining with Jesus and His disciples. When the Pharisees saw this, they said to His disciples, "Why is your Teacher eating with the tax collectors and sinners?" But when Jesus heard this, He said, "It is not those who are healthy who need a physician, but those who are sick. But go and learn what this means: 'I DESIRE COMPASSION, AND NOT SACRIFICE' [quoting Hosea 6:6], for I did not come to call the righteous, but sinners." (Matthew 9:10-13 NASB)

112 Matt Mikalatos. *Imaginary Jesus*. Barna, 2010, p. 44.

113 Blueletterbible.org—Type Matt 28 in the search box.
Choose NASB from the drop-down list.
Once Matthew 28 loads, click "Strong's."
Scroll down to verse 19.
Click G1484 to see the original Greek for *nations* and its definition.

114 Guttmacher Institute (which is Planned Parenthood's statistical analysis group, meaning that these stats are from the pro-choice perspective). "Reasons U.S. Women Have Abortions: Quantitative and Qualitative Perspectives." https://www.guttmacher.org/journals/psrh/2005/reasons-us-women-have-abortions-quantitative-and-qualitative-perspectives accessed August 2018.

115 Guttmacher Institute. "Reasons U.S. Women Have Abortions: Quantitative and Qualitative Perspectives." https://www.guttmacher.org/journals/psrh/2005/reasons-us-women-have-abortions-quantitative-and-qualitative-perspectives accessed August 2018.

116 Behold, the Lord's hand is not so short
    That it cannot save;
    Nor is His ear so dull
    That it cannot hear.
    But your iniquities have made a separation between you
    and your God,
    And your sins have hidden His face from you so that He
    does not hear. (Isaiah 59:1-2 NASB)
    Who acts in behalf of the one who waits for Him.
    You meet him who rejoices in doing righteousness,
    Who remembers You in Your ways.
    (Isaiah 64:4b-5a NASB)
    The effective prayer of a righteous man can accomplish
    much. (James 5:16b NASB)

117 Nehemiah and Daniel are two examples of identifying with their people and then repenting. Whereas their people were the Israelites, our people are The Church.

I said, "I beseech You, O Lord God of heaven, the great and awesome God, who preserves the covenant and lovingkindness for those who love Him and keep His commandments, let Your ear now be attentive and Your eyes open to hear the prayer of Your servant which I am praying before You now, day and night, *on behalf of the sons of Israel Your servants*, confessing the sins *of the sons of Israel* which *we* have sinned against You; I and my father's house have sinned." (Nehemiah 1:5-6 NASB, emphasis mine)

I prayed to the Lord my God and confessed and said, "Alas, O Lord, the great and awesome God, who keeps His covenant and lovingkindness for those who love Him and keep His commandments, *we* have sinned, committed iniquity, acted wickedly and rebelled, even turning aside from Your commandments and ordinances." (Daniel 9:4-5 NASB, emphasis mine)

118 You'll find the Old Testament and New Testament verses about sexual immorality at MybodyMyworship.org/bible-verses-on-sexual-immorality.html.

119 John 4:4-42

120 John 8:3-11

121 John 8:11

122 If you need encouragement in your marriage, pray for more of the Holy Spirit for yourself (Luke 11:13). Once you see some change in yourself, pray for more of the Holy Spirit for your spouse. Also, follow Love Harder Marriage Coaching on social media and seek their conferences, books, and events. You can connect at LauraGethers.com.

123 And there are also many other things which Jesus did, which if they were written in detail, I suppose that even the world itself would not contain the books that would be written. (John 21:25 NASB)

124 This is Jesus speaking: "It was said, 'Whoever sends his wife away, let him give her a certificate of divorce' [Deuteronomy 24:1, 3]; but I say to you that everyone who divorces his wife, except for the reason of unchastity, makes her commit adultery; and whoever marries a divorced woman commits adultery." (Matthew 5:31-32 NASB)

125 People fast to:
- humble themselves before the Lord
- loose the bonds of wickedness
- undo the bands of the yoke
- let the oppressed go free
- to break every yoke
- divide your food with the hungry
- to bring the homeless into the house
- to clothe the naked

- and to help your own family when they need help (Isaiah 58:6-7)

126 Therefore I urge you, brethren, by the mercies of God, to present your bodies a living and holy sacrifice, acceptable to God, which is your spiritual service of worship. And do not be conformed to this world, but be transformed by the renewing of your mind, so that you may prove what the will of God is, that which is good and acceptable and perfect. (Romans 12:1-2 NASB)

The word *worship* is the Greek word *latreia*, which means to worship God in a Levitical sense, that is, to worship Him while upholding all the laws, including the sex laws. New Testament believers have not been released from the sex laws:

...but that we write to them that they abstain from things contaminated by idols and from fornication [porneia] and from what is strangled and from blood (Acts 15:20 NASB and repeated in 15:29).

127 Or do you not know that your body is a temple of the Holy Spirit who is in you, whom you have from God, and that you are not your own? (1 Corinthians 6:19 NASB, which has nothing to do with food or muscle tone and everything to do with only having sex within God-honoring marriage, that is, marriage of one man to one woman. Read all of 1 Corinthians 6:12-20 in which God distinguishes between food and sex.)

128 Jesus is talking here: "God is spirit, and those who worship Him must worship in spirit and truth." (John 4:24 NASB) The word *worship* is the Greek word *proskyneō*, which means to revere the Lord.

CHAPTER 12

129 We have troubles all around us, but we are not defeated. We often don't know what to do, but we don't give up. (2 Corinthians 4:8 ERV)

130 Then Jesus said to His disciples, "If anyone wishes to come after Me, he must deny himself, and take up his cross and follow Me. For whoever wishes to save his life will lose it; but whoever loses his life for My sake will find it." (Matthew 16:24-25 NASB) And He [Jesus] was saying to them all, "If anyone wishes to come after Me, he must deny himself, and take up his cross daily and follow Me." (Luke 9:23 NASB)

131 Consider it all joy, my brethren, when you encounter various trials, knowing that the testing of your faith produces endurance. (James 1:2-3)

132 Mark Lowry is awesome! He calls himself a storyteller. Our family calls him a Christian comedian because he's funny! He's also a singer and a song writer. Find him online at MarkLowry.com.

133 Pentatonix. "Mary, Did You Know?" *That's Christmas to Me,* RCA, 2014.

134 Luke 11:13

135 Matthew 6:9-13, Luke 11:2-4

136 Steve Corbett and Brian Fikkert. *When Helping Hurts: How to Alleviate Poverty without Hurting the Poor... and Yourself.* Chicago: Moody Publishers, 2012.

137 Luke 15:11-32

138 For if you forgive others for their transgressions, your heavenly Father will also forgive you. But if you do not forgive others, then your Father will not forgive your transgressions. (Matthew 6:14-15 NASB)

CHAPTER 13

139 Oh, the Lord is good to me and so I thank the Lord for giving me the things I need, the sun and the rain and the apple seed. The Lord is good to me. Amen.

140 And Jesus cried out again with a loud voice, and yielded up His spirit. And behold, the veil of the temple was torn [ripped, schizo] in two from top to bottom; and the earth shook and the rocks were split. (Matthew 27:50-51 NASB)

Behind the second veil there was a tabernacle which is called the Holy of Holies. (Hebrews 9:3 NASB)

141 George Frederic Handel. "Hallelujah." *Messiah,* 1741.

142 On YouTube, search for "The Passover for Christians" on Katharine Wang's Master the Bible Ministries channel.

143 A hot dish is called a casserole or covered dish by non-Minnesotans.

144 And behold, the veil of the temple was torn in two from top to bottom; and the earth shook and the rocks were split . (Matthew 27:51 NASB)

145 After being baptized, Jesus came up immediately from the water; and behold, the heavens were opened, and he saw the Spirit of God descending as a dove and lighting on Him. (Matthew 3:16 NASB)

146 For all of you who want to try it yourself, here's what to do:

1. The ingredients are 3-2-1: 3 egg yolks (preferably organic, cage-free), 2 sticks of butter (the real thing and even better to get organic, grass-fed), and 1 Tablespoon of lemon juice. Get the 3 eggs out early so that they are at room temperature before you start.

2. Separate the eggs and put the 3 egg yolks into the blender. If you forgot to leave the eggs out so that they are at room temperature, first put the eggs in the microwave on a very low setting for 30 seconds or so. The goal is to get the yolks warm without cooking them.

3. Add 1 T of lemon juice.

4. Blend.

5. Melt 2 sticks of butter until they are hot. (I put them into a glass measuring cup and use the microwave.)

6. The blender has a 2-part lid. Remove the center so that you can pour into the blender with the blender on.

7. With the blender going (only egg yolks and lemon juice in there at this point), slowly pour in the hot butter. I don't think it really matters which setting you use on the blender.

8. Turn off the blender and stir with a spatula. The hollandaise will be nice and thick! Pour into your server, using the spatula to scrape the blender. Enjoy!

For more family recipes mentioned in this book, look for *Grandma's Cooking* by Annette DeCourcy and Cheryl Krichbaum from your favorite bookstore!

147 Hard sauce is "hard" because it has alcohol in it, like perhaps rum. But we make ours with almond flavoring, so technically it's not hard. But it *is* very sweet—just butter, powdered sugar, and flavoring.

148 He must increase, but I must decrease. (John 3:30 ESV)

149 For the wages of sin is death, but the free gift of God is eternal life in Christ Jesus our Lord. (Romans 6:23 ESV) Also read Romans 5:15-17.

150 Simon Peter replied, "You are the Christ, the Son of the living God." (Matthew 16:16 ESV)

She said to him, "Yes, Lord; I believe that you are the Christ, the Son of God, who is coming into the world." (John 11:27 ESV)

151 For our struggle is not against flesh and blood, but against the rulers, against the powers, against the world forces of this darkness, against the spiritual forces of wickedness in the heavenly places. Therefore, take up the full armor of God, so that you will be able to resist in the evil day, and having done everything, to stand firm. (Ephesians 6:12-13 NASB)

152 "Cry loudly, do not hold back;
Raise your voice like a trumpet,
And declare to My people their transgression
And to the house of Jacob their sins."
(Isaiah 58:1 NASB)

CHAPTER 14

153 "Do not let your heart be troubled; believe in God, believe also in Me. In My Father's house are many dwelling places; if it were not so, I would have told you; for I go to prepare a place for you. (John 14:1-2 NASB)

154 Jesus is talking here: "...those who were ready went in with him to the wedding feast; and the door was shut." (Matthew 25:10b NASB)
Then he [an angel] said to me [John, the Apostle], "Write, 'Blessed are those who are invited to the marriage supper of the Lamb.'" And he said to me, "These are true words of God." (Revelation 19:9 NASB)

155 I say to you that many will come from east and west, and recline at the table with Abraham, Isaac and Jacob in the kingdom of heaven. (Matthew 8:11 NASB)

156 Beloved, let us love one another, for love is from God; and everyone who loves is born of God and knows God. The one who does not love does not know God, for God is love. (1 John 4:7-8 NASB)

157 Patricia Layton. *Surrendering the Secret: Healing the Heartbreak of Abortion*, Nashville: LifeWay Press, 2008.

158 NASB

159 Matthew 6:12, Luke 11:4a

160 There will no longer be any curse; and the throne of God and of the Lamb will be in it, and His bond-servants will serve Him. (Revelation 22:3 NASB)

161 Therefore, since we have so great a cloud of witnesses surrounding us, let us also lay aside every encumbrance and the sin which so easily entangles us, and let us run with endurance the race that is set before us. (Hebrews 12:1 NASB)

162 "Cry loudly, do not hold back;
Raise your voice like a trumpet,
And declare to My people their transgression
And to the house of Jacob their sins."
(Isaiah 58:1 NASB)

AFTERWORD

163 Then I saw a new heaven and a new earth… And I heard a loud voice from the throne, saying, "He will wipe away every tear from their eyes; and there will no longer be any death; there will no longer be any mourning, or crying, or pain; the first things have passed away." (Revelation 21:1a, 3a, 4 NASB)

164 AbbyJohnson.org, Founder of And Then There Were None (ATTWN), a registered nonprofit organization that exists to help abortion clinic workers leave the abortion industry. abortionworker.org

165 Then I saw a new heaven and a new earth… And I heard a loud voice from the throne, saying, "He will wipe away every tear from their eyes; and there will no longer be any death; there will no longer be any mourning, or crying, or pain; the first things have passed away." (Revelation 21:1a, 3a, 4 NASB)

166 Jesus is speaking here: "Go therefore and make disciples of all nations, baptizing them in the name of the Father and of the Son and of the Holy Spirit, teaching them to observe all that

I have commanded you. And behold, I am with you always, to the end of the age." (Matthew 28:19-20 ESV)

167 So Jesus was saying to those Jews who had believed Him, "If you continue in My word, then you are truly disciples of Mine; and you will know the truth, and the truth will make you free." (John 8:31-32 NASB)

168 Patricia Layton. *Surrendering the Secret: Healing the Heartbreak of Abortion*, Nashville: LifeWay Press, 2008. This is the study that I did.

169 Linda Cochrane. *Forgiven and Set Free: A Post-Abortion Bible Study for Women*, Baker Books, 2015, Grand Rapids, MI. This is the study that my friend Julie Mad-Bondo of Julie's Heart Cry completed.

170 You can search for U.S. pregnancy centers through Care-Net.org. You can search internationally through HeartbeatInternational.org.

171 Linda Cochrane and Kathy Jones. *Healing a Father's Heart: A Post-Abortion Bible Study for Men.* Baker Books, 1996, Grand Rapids, MI.

172 According to the Guttmacher Institute, which is Planned Parenthood's statistical organization (meaning that the results are from the pro-choice movement), 45% of women who had an abortion in 2014 had had at least one abortion previously. Guttmacher Institute. "Which Abortion Patients Have Had a Prior Abortion? Findings from the 2014 U.S. Abortion Patient Survey." https://www.guttmacher.org/article/2017/08/which-abortion-patients-have-had-prior-abortion-findings-2014-us-abortion-patient accessed August 2018.

173 "Cry loudly, do not hold back;
Raise your voice like a trumpet,
And declare to My people their transgression
And to the house of Jacob their sins." (Isaiah 58:1 NASB

174 If your church is looking for support in starting a special needs ministry, look up the Accessibility Summit at AccessibilitySummit.org.

175 Rick Warren. *A Purpose Drive Life: What on Earth Am I Here For?* Zondervan, 2002, Grand Rapids, MI.

176 To learn more, look for "The Law and the Glory #4: The Purpose of Tests" on Katharine Wang's Master the Bible Ministries YouTube channel.

177 Blessed be the God and Father of our Lord Jesus Christ, who according to His great mercy has caused us to be born again to a living hope through the resurrection of Jesus Christ from the dead. (1 Peter 1:3 NASB)

178 Seek first His kingdom and His righteousness. (Matthew 6:33a NASB)

179 Job 3

180 But the anger of Elihu the son of Barachel the Buzite, of the family of Ram burned; against Job his anger burned because he justified himself before God. (Job 32:2 NASB)

181 Job 32-37

182 Job 38-41

183 Jesus is speaking here: "If you then, being evil, know how to give good gifts to your children, how much more will your heavenly Father give the Holy Spirit to those who ask Him?" (Luke 11:13 NASB)

184 I can do all things through Him who strengthens me. (Philippians 4:13 NASB)

185 Luke 11:13

186 Now to Him who is able to do far more abundantly beyond all that we ask or think, according to the power that works within us to Him be the glory in the church and in Christ

Jesus to all generations forever and ever. Amen. (Ephesians 3:20-21 NASB)

ACKNOWLEDGMENTS

[187] Acts 9

FACES OF ABORTION SERIES

ReTested is the first in the Faces of Abortion Series, a pro-life response to the #shoutyourabortion movement. Look for more books that tell stories of post-abortive, Christian women who regret their "choice."

Read these stories to better understand how the abortion-minded think so that you are better equipped for your sanctity of life and sanctity of sex conversations.

facesofabortion.com

ONLINE BIBLE STUDIES
WITH

On your own or as a group, join an online bible study. Cheryl will guide you through biblical study of the sanctity of life, the sanctity of sex, and worshiping through all circumstances.

Find studies at:

MybodyMyworship.org

BRING CHERYL INTO YOUR CHURCH OR ORGANIZATION

Millions of post-abortive women and men are in The Church.

Millions more should be in The Church but aren't—yet.

And unless we teach all that Christ commanded about the sanctity of life and the sanctity of sex in our own local churches, millions more Christians will abort. Let's not let that happen on our watch.

Instead, let's end abortion first in our own churches, then in the communities we serve—both locally and internationally.

Invite Cheryl to encourage and equip your group or congregation to share the love of Christ with the post-abortive and the abortion-minded.

Contact Cheryl:

www.CherylKrichbaum.blog

CPSIA information can be obtained
at www.ICGtesting.com
Printed in the USA
FSHW021044200319
56468FS